Gothic Fiction/ Gothic Form

"I could a tale unfold whose lightest word
Would harrow up thy soul . . ."

George E. Haggerty

THE PENNSYLVANIA STATE UNIVERSITY PRESS
University Park and London

Library of Congress Cataloging-in-Publication Data

Haggerty, George E.
Gothic fiction/Gothic form.

Bibliography: p.
Includes index.
1. Gothic revival (Literature) 2. English fiction—
History and criticism. 3. American fiction—History
and criticism. I. Title
PR830.T3H25   1988   823'.0872   88–12475
ISBN 0-271-00645-5

Gothic Fiction/Gothic Form

For Philip Brett

Contents

Acknowledgments

In writing and rewriting this study, I have had two Regents' Junior Faculty Fellowships and generous support for research and bibliographical assistance. For these I would like to thank the Regents of the University of California and the Committee on Research at the Riverside Campus.

I first read *The Castle of Otranto* as a sophomore in Maurice Geracht's class in "The Eighteenth-Century Novel" at the College of the Holy Cross. It was this inspiring introduction that led me to the graduate seminar that challenged my adolescent interest with professional rigor, as Gothic began to seem a possibility. At Berkeley, Ralph Rader got me started on this project; Frederick Crews nurtured it; and Paul Alpers helped find it a place in the world. I thank them heartily. Ralph Rader deserves special thanks for his encouraging and challenging response to my work from the beginning.

Other people who have encouraged me by reading, by listening, or just by being there include Steven Axelrod, Robert Brina, Laura Brown, Kim Devlin, Carole Fabricant, Jessica Feldman, Lorne Fienberg, Nona Fienberg, John Ganim, David Gewanter, Robert Glavin, Ruth Glavin, Juan Miguel Godoy, Jonathan Goldberg, Stephanie Hammer, Robert Kiely, William Kinnucan, Jean-Pierre Mileur, Davitt Moroney, Stephen Orgel, Donald Ringe, John Seamster, Eve Sedgwick, and Claudia Yukman. I am grateful for all they have done.

Terri Nickel has been the best research assistant anyone could have had. Her own work on Samuel Richardson is an inspiration. I also want to thank Jeff LeBard, Terry Spaise, and Aaron Walden, whose assistance has been invaluable. Roylene Sims typed and retyped the manuscript with energy and enthusiasm. And the people on the staff of the English Department at the University of California, Riverside, have helped me in a thousand ways.

A different version of chapter 1 and a slightly altered version of chapter 3 have appeared in *Nineteenth-Century Fiction* and *Victorian Newsletter*, respectively. I wish to thank the editors of those journals for permission to reprint those essays here. I also wish to thank Philip Winsor, Senior Editor at Pennsylvania State University Press, for his faith in this project and his steadfast support.

I have been especially lucky with this project: My students have responded enthusiastically to "Gothic" ideas; Bill, Pat, and Rick have been more encouraging than an older brother could expect; and my parents have given me their loving support all along. But my greatest debt is expressed in the dedication: Philip once again has seen me through.

Abbreviations

Works frequently cited in the text and notes have been identified by the following abbreviations:

<dl>

AN James, Henry. *The Art of the Novel: Critical Prefaces.* Ed. Richard P. Blackmur. New York: Scribner's, 1934.

CEWNH Hawthorne, Nathaniel. *The Centenary Edition of the Works of Nathaniel Hawthorne.* Ed. William Chavaret et al. 19 vols. to date. Columbus, OH: Ohio State University Press, 1962–

CWEAP Poe, Edgar Allan. *The Complete Works of Edgar Allan Poe.* Ed. James A. Harrison. 17 vols. 1902. New York: AMS, 1965.

HJSS James, Henry. *Henry James: Stories of the Supernatural.* Ed. Leon Edel. New York: Taplinger, 1970.

LMWS Shelley, Mary. *The Letters of Mary Wollstonecraft Shelley.* Ed. Betty T. Bennett. 3 vols. Baltimore: Johns Hopkins University Press, 1980–88.

MSJ Shelley, Mary. *Mary Shelley's Journal.* Ed. Frederick L. Jones. Norman: University of Oklahoma Press, 1947.

NHJ James, Henry. *The Notebooks of Henry James.* Ed. F. O. Matthiessen and Kenneth B. Murdock. 1947. New York: Galaxy, Oxford, 1961.

TSEAP Poe, Edgar Allan. *Collected Works of Edgar Allan Poe.* Ed. Thomas Ollive Mabbott. 3 vols. to date. Cambridge, MA: Harvard University Press, 1969– . Vol. 2: *Tales and Sketches, 1831–42.* Vol. 3: *Tales and Sketches, 1843–49.*

"Turn" James, Henry. *The Turn of the Screw.* 1898. Ed. Robert Kimbrough. New York: Norton, 1966.

</dl>

Introduction:
Gothic Fiction
and Affective Form

"We might as well take as our starting point an observation of Wittgenstein's," Wolfgang Iser tells us, as he attempts to establish the nature of a literary "fact":

> [Wittgenstein] says: "In the proposition a state of affairs is, as it were, put together for the sake of experiment," which fulfills the claim to truth if there are "facts" that correspond to it. For the literary text there can be no such "facts"; instead we have a sequence of schemata, built up by the repertoire and the strategies, which have the function of stimulating the reader himself into establishing the "facts." There can be no doubt that the schemata of the text appear to relate to "facts," but these are not 'given'—they must be discovered or, to be more precise, produced. (*The Act of Reading* 141)

Gothic fiction depends on a similar production of "facts" and needs to be structured formally so as to maximize the possibilities of such production. Iser's theory is built around the notion that "classical norms of interpretation rob the reading experience of a vital dimension in equating meaning with significance" (151).

The purpose of this study is to uncover various ways in which Gothic writers expand the significance of their work through the manipulation of formal effects. Horace Walpole's familiar explanation of the "motives" behind what can reasonably be called the first Gothic novel, *The Castle of Otranto* (1764), suggests that the impulse behind Gothic fiction was an impulse toward formal innovation:

> It was an attempt to blend the two kinds of romance, the ancient and the modern. In the former all was imagination and improb-

ability: in the latter, nature is always intended to be, and sometimes has been, copied with success. Invention has not been
wanting; but the great resources of fancy have been dammed
up, by a strict adherence to common life. (7)

Iser quotes this preface as an example of what he calls Walpole's attempt to "surpass the traditional novel," and he goes on to discuss the
possibility of an "interplay of traditional forms," which engages its audience by manipulating genre and thereby "changing the traditional
expectations of the eighteenth-century reader" (*Implied Reader* 60).

But by attempting simply "to blend . . . the ancient and the modern"
romance and to enrich the nature-bound conventions of the novel
without considering the literary implications of this project, Walpole
set the Gothic novel on a course both self-contradictory and seemingly
self-defeating. Critics have most often understood Walpole's insistence
that "adherence to common life" had been too strict in the novel as an
excuse for the unwieldy and novelistically unprecedented introduction
of the supernatural into a baldly melodramatic tale. But others have
taken Walpole's preface as the formal indication of a serious and sophisticated reaction against the strictures of neoclassicism, similar in
kind to such literary phenomena as the sentimental novel or the poetry
of sensibility.[1] Walpole's novel fits both these descriptions, and I hope
to show how these intentions are interrelated and in what sense they
mark a new fictional enterprise. For Walpole's novel, as awkward and
unsatisfying as it seems, can begin to teach us basic generic distinctions and a new understanding of literary form.[2]

In the first place, what did Walpole have in mind when he asserted
the need for formal liberation in his preface? Robert Kiely reminds us
that "though the conventions of the novel were neither old nor clearly
defined by the middle of the eighteenth century, they appeared to be,
in several respects, uncongenial to the romantic sensibility" (17). Elizabeth Napier carries this an important step further when she describes
two opposed currents in the Gothic novel: "a tendency towards moral
and structural stabilizing characteristic of much previous eighteenth-
century fiction . . . and a contrary inclination towards fragmentation,
instability, and moral ambivalence." "The Gothic novel," she goes on
to say, "remains essentially a genre of imbalance, because its authors
finally neither ascribed convincingly to either extreme nor found a
middle way between them" (5).

I propose in this study to suggest just such a "middle way," a manner
in which Gothicists managed to satisfy the demands of form while at
the same time releasing their expressive "inclination" toward formal

instability and fragmentation. What really takes place is a process of formal insurgency, a rejection of the conventional demands of novel form, first within the gloomy confines of Gothic novel, causing disruption and inconsistency, and later as a liberated and liberating alternative to the conventional novel. Gothic fiction, in other words, plays out a formal drama which is itself Gothic in its implications.

Walpole's notion that "the great resources of fancy [had] been dammed up" in the novel suggests that there was as powerful a formal constriction to answer conventional narrative expectations as there was a personal constriction to follow socially accepted codes of behavior. In the case of Walpole and later Gothicists, however, much more than the superficial organization of the novel was at stake. By introducing into the novel material that emerges so specifically from private fantasy, Walpole brought into focus both the seeming limitations of the novel form as it emerged in the eighteenth century and the terms under which those limitations were to be overcome. In attempting to alter substantially the expressive potential of imaginative fiction, in other words, Walpole faced a disjunction between the novel form and the Gothic material. He dreamt of "an ancient castle" and a "gigantic hand in armour," and so he attempted to give his dream fictional form.[3] But the imagery of a nightmare is at odds with the emerging concept of novelistic realism; verisimilitude will not immediately admit of the magical appearance of superhuman forms; the subjective nature of a dream seems at odds with the objective and social terms of novelistic discourse; the unstructured nature of a dream contradicts the durational and structural demands of the novel; and the terrifying aspect of a nightmare is mediated or may even be rendered ridiculous by the novel's matter-of-fact quality.[4]

Walpole faced all these problems in his attempt to blend the ancient and the modern romance, and in doing so he addressed the literary dilemma confronting every writer of Gothic fiction: What manner of prose narrative most effectively embodies a nightmare vision? The difficulty in answering this question is evident in all Gothic novels—one critic says that they exhibit "an almost continuous display of divisive tension, paradox, and uncertain focus" (Kiely 17)—but evident as well is that spirit of experimentation which was eventually to provide answers to more questions than the first Gothic novelist could even imagine how to ask. Napier insists that the formal failure of Gothic novels explains why "they seldom . . . lead to the profound realizations about human consciousness that some critics have asserted that they do" (7). I share Napier's interest in the question of fictional form, but I must disagree that the Gothic project is a failure. Formal problems abound in Gothic novels, to be sure, but these works achieve a generic revolution that changes the course of the history of fiction. If "Gothic" at first suggests a formal muddle, I hope to show in what sense that muddle is creative, not just formally but imaginatively as well.

In his *Critical and Historical Principles of Literary History*, R. S. Crane asks what explains the "compression" of full-length Gothic novels of the eighteenth century into the shorter and, he claims, more powerful works of the nineteenth (20, 41). The answer to this question lies in the kinds of considerations I have introduced. More specifically, I would suggest that total literary success was not possible for Gothic writers until they understood the nature of fictional expression and recognized the limitations of their concept of the novel, establishing a form more suitable to the full and sustained expression of Gothic concerns. Critics such as Kiely and Napier have described the formal "failures" within the Gothic novel in negative terms, without considering the alternatives to novelistic expression. But once the affective nature of Gothic fiction is established, we can begin to see the positive side to these formal difficulties and to understand why such observations matter and why they have such profound implications for the theory of genre and narrative.

Hans Robert Jauss has suggested the limitations of Formalist theories of literary evolution—"mere opposition or aesthetic variation does not suffice to explain the growth of literature" (33)—but he has also suggested the basis for the kind of formal analysis I am attempting here:

> The pre-orientation of our experience through the creative capability of literature rests not only on its artistic character, which by virtue of a new form helps one to break through the automatism of everyday perception. The new form of art is not only "perceived against the background of other art works and through association with them. . . . " [The Russian Formalist] Victor Shklovsky remains correct only insofar as he turns against the prejudice of classicist aesthetics that defines the beautiful as *harmony of form and content* and accordingly reduces the new form to the secondary function of giving shape to a pregiven content. The new form, however, does not appear just "in order to relieve the old form that already is no longer artistic." It also can make possible a new perception of things by preforming the content of a new experience first brought to light in the form of literature. (41)

Here we have a far more sophisticated expression of Walpole's Gothic intention, for by setting out to release the great resources of fancy, he was looking for a way to liberate the novel from what, in another context, Nina Auerbach calls the "tyranny of the normal" (*Romantic Imprisonment* 20). Walpole's imagery of constrictive form, moreover, suggests his desire to offer a "new perception of things," an ontological as well as an epistemological shift. It is not just that he wanted to view reality in a new way; he wanted to change the concept of reality itself.

In turning from the objective world as represented in the works of contemporary novelists toward a version of reality less obviously empirical, Walpole was participating in that shift of sensibility which animated much of the writing of the period. Further, by interesting himself in primarily affective concerns, he was anticipating the literary implications of this shift. Locke's own insistence that the mind exists to receive impressions that by means of a process of association it actively refashions into complex ideas has been said to have cleared the way for such critics as Addison, Akenside, and Burke to discuss "literature and artistic values as they relate directly to intricate psychological processes in both the artist and the audience."[5] Walpole's novel and those of his Gothic successors were as intimately concerned with such processes as any products of the "Age of Sensibility." In describing works of this period, Northrop Frye says that "where there is a sense of literature as process, pity and fear become states of mind without objects, moods which are common to the work of art and the reader, and which bind them together psychologically instead of separating them aesthetically" (Frye, "Towards Defining an Age of Sensibility" 135). This psychological bond is surely central to Gothic form.

The very terms of Gothic expression, moreover, were anticipated in the work of the aestheticians themselves. Akenside, for instance, in *The Pleasures of Imagination* (1744), describes the process of imaginative thought as follows:

> The child of fancy oft in silence bends
> O'er these mixt treasures of his pregnant breast,
> With conscious pride. From them he oft resolves
> To frame he knows not what excelling things;
> And win he knows not what sublime reward
> Of praise and wonder. By degrees, the mind
> Feels her young nerves dilate: the plastic pow'rs
> Labour for action: blind emotions heave

His bosom; and with loveliest frenzy caught,
From earth to heav'n he rolls his daring eye,
From heav'n to earth. Anon ten thousand shapes,
Like spectres trooping to the wisard's call,
Flit swift before him. From the womb of earth,
From ocean's bed they come: th' eternal heav'ns
Disclose their splendors, and the dark abyss
Pours out her births unknown.
(Bk. 3, 375–90)[6]

It is not necessary to be a student of eighteenth-century aesthetics to notice a relation between Akenside's theory of the imagination and the central concerns of the Gothic novel. Indeed, Akenside's "dark abyss" became one of the most familiar of eighteenth-century land-scapes.[7] His vision of the mind in so profound an act of creativity in-sists on the almost automatic equation of psychological themes and Gothic vocabulary: language itself must reach into uncharted territory in order to express the seemingly supernatural power he hopes to dramatize. When this ability of the imagination to produce what Ak-enside goes on to call "rising phantoms" is literalized, however, as it is in the Gothic novel, its suggestive potential becomes remarkably lim-ited. Once presented objectively, the products of the dark abyss may be as easy (or uneasy) to accommodate as Walpole's lumbering "spectre" that "marched sedately, but dejected, to the end of the gallery, and turned into a chamber on the right hand" (*Otranto* 24). But that is of course not the end of the story. "Sublime reward / Of praise and won-der" may not be a simple matter to achieve, but Gothic novelists labor no less in bringing forth the products of their imaginations as a real challenge to the limits of belief.

The solution to their dilemma is already implicit in Akenside's theory. By focusing on the powers of the imagination, he set the terms whereby aesthetic theory was to expand and flower in the latter half of the eighteenth century. Imagination and the nature of literary creation were central issues for Baillie, Hartley, Burke, and Beattie—all key figures in the shift in critical perspective which was taking place at the time. The terms of their discussion, moreover, helped to establish the nature of literary discourse (see Engell 69–77). In these discussions, objective reality became secondary to subjective responses to it, for in the response both the imagination and private experience exert their unusual power.

Reflecting this transition in aesthetics—the theoretical shift in in-terest from the object to the subject in discussions of the sublime—

John Baillie makes it clear how dramatically the external world has come to assume less importance than the dynamics of psychological response:

> But as a *Consciousness* of her [the soul's] own *Vastness* is what pleases, so nothing raises this Consciousness but a *Vastness* in the *Objects* about which she is employed. For whatever the *Essence* of the *Soul* may be, it is the *Reflections* arising from *Sensations* only which makes [*sic*] her acquainted with Herself, and know her *Faculties*. Vast objects occasion vast Sensations, and vast sensations give the Mind a higher Idea of her own Powers— small scenes (except from Association . . .) have never this Effect; . . . the *Soul* is never filled by them. (6–7)[8]

As slippery as the language of this analysis has come to seem, it offers us the terms whereby we can understand the popularity of Gothic expression. That which gives rise to sensations is the mere occasion for the kind of self-knowledge associationist psychology was beginning to celebrate. The relation of ideas to sensations, Baillie's remarks remind us, was of crucial importance in developing a theory of the mechanics of mental processes themselves. Rather than directly addressing the philosophical question of how the mind transforms the external world into private experience, however, the Gothic novelists attempted to give imaginative worlds external and objective reality. In doing so, they were not simply ignoring the shift in focus to the subjective but were looking for ways of giving private experience external manifestation. This almost naive agenda not only offered corroboration to the leading theories of the age but also pointed up the degree to which those theories were of ultimately limited, if momentarily profound, interest. The general thrust of mid-century theory was to emphasize the activity of mental response in making human experience meaningful in human terms. The Gothic novel helped to demonstrate the impossibility of grafting such a theory onto an eighteenth-century empirical world-view without first providing an entirely new basis for interaction between people and their surroundings as well as between writers and readers; without, that is, seeking a form complementary to their imaginative quest.

The philosopher closest in spirit to the Gothic novelists in this regard was, of course, Edmund Burke. His descriptive terms Beautiful and Sublime themselves manifested an attempt to give objective substance to the private and subjective (see Engell 70–71). Burke insisted that a cataract or an abyss possesses no emotional or psychological significance until the imagination creates such significance as terms like Beautiful and Sublime imply.[9] A "sublime" response to the external world is more than a private experience, according to Burke; it is an experience that can be communicated and shared. That act of communication is the province of language.[10]

In Burke's *Enquiry*, moreover, the primary intellectual concern seems to be to offer scientifically objective terminology and clearly empirical observation as a means of describing intensely private, subjective experience. Burke himself says that he will pursue a study in scientific manner, "however paradoxical it may seem to those, who on a superficial view imagine, that there is so great a diversity of Tastes both in kind and degree, that nothing can be more indeterminate." He says further: "We do and we must suppose, that as the conformation of their organs are nearly, or altogether the same in all men, so the manner of perceiving external objects is in all men the same." And finally, "It must be observed, that [the] power of the imagination is incapable of producing anything absolutely new; it can only vary the disposition of those ideas which it has received from the senses" (6–7, 16).[11]

The nature of the paradox between private experience and public fact is the very subject of Gothic fiction as I have described it. This helps to explain the litany of conventional devices which we recognize and appreciate as intrinsically Gothic.[12] The devices typical of Gothic fiction have not been chosen by accident. They offer the most complex vocabulary for Gothic expression because they have the power to objectify subjective states of feeling: In the novels they were developed as metaphorical vehicles, but their tenors remain inexpressible. They can only be expressed, that is, by each reader in his or her private terms.

Gothic form, then, is affective form. It almost goes without saying that these works are primarily structured so as to elicit particular responses in the reader. Perhaps, however, it is not so obvious that Gothic fiction therefore cannot have specific meaning: indeterminacy is inherent to its nature. That is not to discount the enormously rich studies of the psychological and political implications of these works. Indeed, I cite them throughout this study. But it is central to the nature of Gothic fiction that differing interpretations of the material will seem equally valid.

Consider, for instance, the articles "Gothic Possibilities," by Norman N. Holland and Leona F. Sherman, and "The Gothic Mirror," by Claire Kahane. The first of these articles dramatizes the nature of the psychological interest of Gothic fiction by offering carefully analyzed responses to Gothic effects. For instance:

> Sherman: When I think of a castle, I think of a house of heroic proportions, linked with dynastic histories, wars, and mysteries. I think of kings, queens, knights, and other heroes or villains of folklore who may have lived there. I find, in short, that I associate the castle not only with an idealized past epoch of social history . . . but with my own personal history of fantasies and fears. (282)

We would probably all agree that this is similar to (although certainly more systematic than) the kind of impressionistic criticism that abounds in the work of pioneering Gothic critics, such as Summers, Birkhead, and Varma. Yet in trying to explain why Gothic fiction gives rise to such impressionistic response, Holland and Sherman are interested, as this analysis suggests, in individual images and isolated effects. They are not probing genre in any other way, although they take as their subject the question of generic popularity. Their responses to Gothic imagery are not beside the point, but they do not go far enough to explain generic identity.

Clare Kahane, too, although opposed to Holland and Sherman, seems equally to confuse interpretation and analysis. She examines the "conventional plot" of the Gothic novel but seems primarily interested in specific images:

> What I hope to suggest by my particular focus on dead or displaced mothers is another angle of vision on the Gothic which has been virtually ignored. . . . Indeed, from my perspective the oedipal plot seems more a surface convention than a latent fantasy exerting force, more a framework that houses another mode of confrontation even more disquieting. What I see repeatedly locked into the forbidden center of the Gothic which draws me inward is the spectral presence of a dead-undead mother, archaic and all-encompassing, a ghost signifying the problematics of femininity which the heroine must confront. (335–36)

Kahane's observations are fascinating and her argument is irresistible, but although she speaks of the "forbidden center" here, she gives us no indication of the formal basis of the kind of drawing inward that she describes. Of course, there is nothing inherent in the fictions she discusses to give her interpretation precedence over that of Sherman or Holland. Her reasonable "from my perspective" very quickly becomes interpretive assertion, that, for instance, "the heroine's active exploration of the Gothic house in which she is trapped is also an exploration of her relation to the maternal body that she shares, with all its connotations of power over and vulnerability to forces within and without" (338). What is remarkable about Gothic fiction is that it gives rise to so different and yet so persuasive interpretations.

On the other hand, critics who emphasize the political nature of Gothic, such as Paulson and Punter, are certainly correct in citing the ubiquitous imagery of political oppression in these works. But political readings are also urged with the force of final interpretations, as if any other reading of the material is suspect. Still other critics, myself included, have considered the homosexuality of many of the Gothic novelists as the key to their representation of painful sexual relations.[13] It is not just that Gothic fiction allows such varying interpretations, it encourages them. What is most interesting is how it accomplishes this range of interpretive possibility.

But what does it mean to say that Gothic fiction is structured so as to heighten this multiplicity of interpretive possibilities? Where can we go beyond a variety of intriguing images and a sense of lurid attraction? My answer is to place these images within a larger context. It is, in short, to go to the form of the work. Only by examining the fundamental formal challenge of Gothic fiction and the manner in which it is answered by a variety of Gothic writers can we begin to establish its generic identity and to approach its true nature.

If Walpole did not succeed in establishing a "new form" to accomplish the radical reorientation of readers' perception that he had in mind, at least he set writers on a course that would open up new expressive possibilities. In the pages that follow, I discuss a variety of works by writers ranging historically from Walpole to Henry James. This is not a *history* of Gothic fiction—there are already a number of comprehensive histories—but an analysis of Gothic form. In this study, I discuss a limited number of works in an attempt to demonstrate in close detail how Gothic devices work to transform fictional narrative. The recent vogue of Gothic studies suggests that interest in Gothic concerns is at a high point. If I challenge that interest by refusing to take a primarily thematic approach to this material, I hope to account for a wide variety of thematic analyses at the same time that I question assumptions about the nature of fiction.

My argument is not a description of formal evolution, however. If, in the sixties, Scholes and Kellogg could use a biological model to describe "the nature of narrative," perhaps it is still necessary to assert that later is not necessarily better in an analysis of forms. Walpole and James, the earliest and latest writers I discuss, are worlds apart, and

James is undoubtedly more subtle in his effects. More important at the moment than the question of evaluation, it seems to me, are ways of coming to understand difference and similarity in Gothic works, of perceiving, for instance, why certain Gothic devices "work" and why others do not. I will consider a wide range of responses to a complex literary challenge. Each writer I discuss meets the Gothic challenge in an interesting and instructive manner. None of these works is a "failure," in other words, and together they point us in the direction of true literary sophistication for the Gothic.

This analysis of a variety of Gothic fictions will lead again and again to the same conclusion: Gothic *tales* succeed where Gothic *novels* fail. This is not to give priority to tale over novel, but to suggest in what ways these forms are differently suited to narrative ends. Indeed, novel and tale represent different narrative modes at times working together, and at times conflicting, within a single text. The form I choose to call Gothic tale is a form that resolves the inconsistency and incoherence of many Gothic novels and offers even the best of them a center of focus and a way of achieving their fullest affective power.

Gothic tale: the term *Gothic* has from its first literary appearance implied not just a particular setting but a particular *use* of setting. Although critics have deplored its use to describe any but a limited range of novels that employ a specific set of conventions, it remains helpful in delineating works that have extreme emotional responses as their primary aim. If Napier feels uneasy about the "propriety of employing the term 'Gothic' to describe [nineteenth- and twentieth-century] works" (xiii), Sedgwick suggests, more reasonably, that she would like "to make it easier for the reader of 'respectable' nineteenth-century novels to write 'Gothic' in the margin . . . and to make that notation with a sense of linking specific elements in the passage with specific elements in the constellation of Gothic conventions" (*Coherence of Gothic Convention* 4). Clearly I am in agreement with the second of these positions, and I hope myself to show the degree to which the Gothicism of the works I discuss is not an issue for marginal observation but rather central to their artistic makeup, their form.

"Tale" is an even more slippery term. What besides length, itself by no means a superficial difference—Fowler calls "a specific magnitude" the *sine qua non* of literary kinds (63)—distinguishes the tale from the novel? I think we can begin with a few casual remarks from Frye's *Anatomy of Criticism*: "In novels that we think of as typical, like those of Jane Austen, plot and dialogue are closely linked to the conventions of the comedy of manners. The conventions of *Wuthering Heights* are linked rather with the tale and the ballad." Frye goes on to call *Wuth-*

ering Heights a "romance"—"on the whole better [as a term] than tale, which appears to fit a somewhat shorter form"—and to suggest that this explains why the genre

> often radiates a glow of subjective intensity that the novel lacks, and why a suggestion of allegory is constantly creeping in around its fringes. Certain elements of character are released in the romance which make it naturally a more revolutionary form than the novel. The novelist deals with personality. . . . The romancer deals with individuality, with characters *in vacuo* idealized by revery, and, however conservative he may be, something nihilistic and untamable is likely to keep breaking out of his pages. (*Anatomy* 304–5)

Some of Frye's critical looseness perhaps poses difficulty for us now, but that should not blind us to the very valuable distinctions he is making here. I would like to redeem the term "tale," however, which he so casually dismisses, because the romantic effects he describes are built upon just such a shorter and more intense form. In the case of *Wuthering Heights*, for instance, as I argue in chapter 3, what we think of as its characteristic intensity has its basis in the tale form. More to the point is Frye's suggestion of revolutionary individuality in the talelike form. He says, later, that the "novel tends to be extroverted and personal; its chief interest is in human character as it manifests itself in society. The romance tends to be introverted and personal: it also deals with characters, but in a more subjective way. (Subjective here refers to treatment, not subject-matter.)" (*Anatomy* 308).

In a provocative article, "The Nature of Knowledge in Short Fiction," Charles E. May develops Frye's argument in a useful direction. May expands the notion of the Russian formalist critic B. M. Èjxenbaum, that "the novel and the short story are forms not only different in kind but also inherently at odds." Èjxenbaum distinguishes between the "syncretic" form of the novel and the "fundamental, elementary (which does not mean primitive) form" of the story (Èjxenbaum 4). And May adds that "when we discuss the differences between long fiction and short fiction, we must discuss basic differences in the ontology and epistemology of the two forms" (May 328). "The short story," May adds, "breaks up the familiar life-world of the everyday, defamiliarizes our assumption that reality is simply the conceptual construct we take it to be, and throws into doubt that our propositional and categorical mode of perceiving can be applied to human beings as well as to objects"(333). The compression of short stories, then, leads to "intense focussing for the totality of the narrative experience" for purposes of defamiliarization, which for the Russian formalists is an aesthetic given (335).

These remarks call to mind Walpole's articulation of the need to release the imagination as a way of overcoming the conventional force of the novel. They also offer us terms for a distinction of novel and tale in the nineteenth century. For although the terms *tale* and *short story* are themselves by no means interchangeable, the general description of the potential value of a shorter form seems applicable in either case.[14] As this study proceeds, I hope to make this distinction more vivid, not only by comparing novels and tales but also by describing a variety of Gothic tales and explaining the terms of their particular achievement.

Besides length and the use of setting, narrative technique and the nature of subjectivity in the Gothic tales will be central concerns, as will the nature of character in general in these works, the handling of the supernatural, and the various framing devices that bring us closer to the Gothic experience by distancing us from it. These features are of course aspects of "form," as is the very nature of Gothic language itself; but I intend the term to encompass more than structural detail. Ralph Rader, developing the ideas of such Neo-Aristotelians as R. S. Crane and Sheldon Sacks, argues that literary works have "an inherent structure of meaning and value which is the ground of our response to them" and that a theory of literature would "accordingly have to describe all such works as possessing forms which could present themselves to intuition as self-intelligible and self-justifying, that is, as forms the act of understanding which could be experienced as its own justification." Rader goes on to develop a "grammar of the natural imagination which could spell out the general and particular ways in which works might differ from each other in their self-justifying intelligibility" ("Defoe" 31). It is difficult to share Rader's conviction of an "inherent structure of meaning and value," until we realize that these are not transcendent values, but features of textuality. The "self-justifying intelligibility" of literary works is not necessarily concerned with interpretation, as Rader's discussion of the "pseudo-factual" and "action-model" novel forms makes clear. It is concerned primarily with the manner in which a literary work presents itself to the understanding. If in this sense literary works are self-justifying, a study of form does offer a "grammar of the natural imagination." Gothic works create their own intelligibility in very specific ways. That is my subject here. When I say, therefore, that Gothic form is affective form, I am suggesting that Gothic works only become fully intelligible when we understand the extent of their affective rationale.

All these concerns will become clearer as I proceed. What I want to emphasize here is that affective concerns help to explain the emergence of the Gothic tale as a means of heightening the emotional intelligibility (if I can be allowed to coin such a notion) of Gothic fiction. The Gothic tale, in fact, provides the answer to Walpole's confused desire to unite "two kinds of romance."

But where are these Gothic tales and what do they have to do with Gothic fiction? Well, they are everywhere. They first appear within the Gothic novels, as I shall show, as a way of escaping the demands of novel form. Later, they become the structural basis of novels such as *Melmoth the Wanderer, Frankenstein,* and *Wuthering Heights.* And finally, but not exclusively, they become established in their own right as vehicles of Gothic effect in the short works of Poe, Hawthorne, and Henry James. When Robert Kiely suggests that "for the novelist there was no retreat to the short form, no equivalent of the sonnet or ode" (20), he ignores the kind of generic experimentation that is going on in every Gothic novel. The Gothic tale emerges as the form that can answer the ontological and epistemological, as well as the structural, demands of the Gothicists. From its first hints *within* the Gothic novel as an alternative literary mode offering the Gothicists various expressive advantages to its eerie success in a work such as James's "The Jolly Corner," the Gothic tale offers insight into the nature of generic distinction and literary expression.

> What novels display . . . is not words as such, but the potential of words to create a narrative world which is intelligible or followable but somehow inexhaustible, because it cannot be reduced to a set of schematic principles. The narrative world is at once a universe of possibilities demarcated by the features of a specific mode of presentation—a landscape, setting, or arena within which many (but not any) different things may happen. (Leitch 108–9)

The "universe of possibilities" is even greater in the works I will discuss because it is in the nature of Gothic fiction to extend the lines of demarcation and to insist on a "mode of presentation" that makes almost anything possible. This "mode of presentation" is what I describe as affective form, the form inherent to Gothic fictions.

1

Fact and Fancy in the Gothic Novel

The Castle of Otranto (1764) at times uses its Gothic elements so crudely that their working stands out in sharp relief. The matter of private fantasy comes crashing into the novel after only a couple of paragraphs. When the son of the illicit Prince Manfred fails to appear for his wedding ceremony, "a confused noise of shrieks, horror, and surprise" rises from the courtyard. Manfred goes to investigate:

> The first thing that struck Manfred's eyes was a group of his servants endeavouring to raise something that appeared to him a mountain of sable plumes. He gazed without believing his sight. . . . He beheld his child dashed to pieces, and almost buried under an enormous helmet, an hundred times more large than any casque ever made for human being, and shaded with a proportionable quantity of black feathers. (16–17)

"The horror of the spectacle," the narrator tells us, deprived the prince of speech. "Buried in meditation," we are told, "he touched, he examined the fatal casque" (17). While we may find this description neither horrifying nor affecting, we must note that Walpole establishes the terms of his Gothic vision as both physically gruesome and psychologically alarming. The size of the helmet has potential for the sublime, but by measuring and marking it so specifically, Walpole alienates rather than engages an emotional response. "An hundred times more large" in fact works against the effect Walpole is trying to create. In other words, Walpole seems determined to shock but is unclear about how to do so effectively.

Animated portraits and bleeding statues function similarly in *The*

Castle of Otranto: They obtrude into a world which otherwise we recognize as governed by the same laws as our own. When Manfred's
gloomy ancestor, for instance, steps from his gallery frame and
marches "sedately, but dejected, to the end of the gallery, and turn[s]
into a chamber on the right hand" (24), we may be excused for rolling
our eyes. This much-quoted passage suggests an incongruity of technique and subject that reaches almost to self-parody.

Another way to understand such awkward moments, however, is to
consider that Walpole is attempting to give novelistic substance to his
dreams and to usher fantasy into the realm of the prosaic. The uneasiness of expression that characterizes the attempt reminds us that Walpole's challenge to fictional expression is a real one, beyond the terms
of any simple formula for blending two kinds of romance. On the other
hand, Manfred's fear and ambition, the central focus of the novel, hint
at a more promising area of Gothic exploration, an area in which fantasy and fact can mingle more suggestively. In directing us toward
Manfred's response to Gothic props, as in the paragraph quoted, Walpole was reflecting specific developments in aesthetics and philosophy
that had emerged to challenge the epistemological assumptions of the
age. As I explained in the Introduction, however, an interest in the
dynamics of response is not enough to guarantee an effective "mode
of presentation" that would at once evoke a vivid depiction of response
in the text and create a similar affective impression on the reader.

Walpole says in his preface that he is "desirous of leaving the powers
of fancy at liberty to expatiate through the boundless realms of invention" as a way of "creating more interesting situations" (7). The language of this simple assertion suggests an elaborate notion not just of
imaginative creativity but of affective technique as well. Norman Holland tells us that "all stories . . . have this basic way of meaning: they
transform the unconscious fantasy discoverable through psychoanaly-
sis into the conscious meanings discovered by conventional interpretation" (28). We may not agree with this sweeping and condescending
assertion, but we can see how close to Walpole's own terms such recent
literary theory has become.[1] Walpole's fantasy of "boundless realms of
invention," moreover, suggests a similarly "boundless" range of interpretations, centered on the consciousness of readers and conspiring for
the sake of interest to challenge the powers of creativity. From a deter-
minate world of limited possibilities, Walpole seems to yearn for a
world of indeterminacy and free association.

The primary intellectual enterprise of Walpole's age, as Burke's *Enquiry* seems to suggest, was to offer scientifically objective terminology
and clearly empirical observation as a means of establishing intensely

private, subjective experience. The Gothic novel finds its most fruitful mode of evocation in delineating an imaginative response to the objective world that is grounded in the emotions. In *The Castle of Otranto*, for instance, the young heroine Isabella flees Manfred's sexual advances with all the terror that Manfred's crazed assault warrants:

> The lower part of the castle was hollowed into several intricate cloisters; and it was not easy for one under so much anxiety to find the door that opened into the cavern. An awful silence reigned throughout those subterranean regions, except now and then some blasts of wind that shook the doors she had passed, and which grating on the rusty hinges were re-echoed through that long labyrinth of darkness. Every murmur struck her with new terror;—yet more she dreaded to hear the wrathful voice of Manfred urging his domestics to pursue her. (25)

Walpole here uses techniques which Burke and his contemporaries would have recognized—darkness, confusion, silence, and fear—to construct a simple Gothic scene. If we can look beyond Walpole's rhetorical stiffness, we can see that the scene is constructed so as to identify subjective response and objective sensations: The language of the passage makes them inseparable. The "intricate cloisters," that is, have meaning only in Isabella's psychological response to them, and conversely her psychological state is most fully expressed in the objective terms Walpole has chosen: We understand her terror specifically in terms of the cloisters, the darkness, and the awful silence. If Walpole here strikes an authentic chord whereas he has elsewhere been simplistic and superficial, it is perhaps because the castle itself has more meaning for him than his pale and panting heroine.[2] In other scenes he has presented his Gothic props and then a character's response to them; here props create the response. Walpole does not have to insist on the intensity of Isabella's emotions; he has depicted them by means of his depiction of setting. That intensity is part of what we ourselves create out of the indeterminacy of the situation. Iser says that "an 'overdetermined text,'" that is, the more carefully crafted literary text, "causes the reader to engage in an active process of composition, because it is he who has to structure the meaning potential arising out of the multifarious connections between the semantic levels of the text" (*Act of Reading* 49). Iser's emphasis on semantic levels ignores the nature of a Gothic text, however, in which the semantic possibilities are secondary to an emotional response which precedes meanings and gives rise to them. Walpole has begun to answer the challenge he set

for Gothic fiction by structuring a scene so as to make response primary and meaning subjective.

Ann Radcliffe's heroes and heroines are more fully rendered recep-
tors of Gothic experience, and at times they emerge as actively engaged in creating their own Gothic plights. In her novels, however,
reaction is more remote from experience than *Otranto* has encouraged
us to anticipate. In *The Italian* (1797), for instance, the hero, Vivaldi,
has only to hear of a death in his heroine's household to imagine the
worst:

> An indifferent person would probably have understood the
> words of the monk to allude to Signora Bianchi, whose infirm
> state of health rendered her death, though sudden, not improb-
> able; but to the affrighted fancy of Vivaldi, the dying Ellena only
> appeared. His fears, however probabilities might sanction, or
> the event justify them, were natural to ardent affection; but they
> were accompanied by a presentiment as extraordinary as it was
> horrible;—it occurred to him more than once, that Ellena was
> murdered. He saw her wounded, and bleeding to death; saw her
> ashy countenance, and her wasting eyes, from which the spirit
> of life was fast departing, turned piteously on himself, as if im-
> ploring him to save her from the fate that was dragging her to
> the grave. (41)

Radcliffe's prefatory explanation assures us that Ellena is in no immediate danger, yet the nature of her imagined plight is given vivid
objectification. We are led through a painful and unnecessary death
scene, that is, not only to learn something about Vivaldi's imagination,
but to be brought ourselves into confrontation with a bloody, if fanciful,
corpse. Radcliffe wants to have it both ways: She cautions us against
an overactive imagination while giving our own imaginations more
than enough material to create the horrified response for ourselves.
The reader therefore becomes the victim of Vivaldi's private experience.

In both these scenes, then, a simple event is described so as to maximize affective potential by means of techniques we can call "sublime."
We may find Walpole's technique more sophisticated, but both stand
out as examples of an attempt to put Burke's theories into novelistic
practice. When Robert D. Hume tells us that Gothic writers are attempting "to *involve* the reader in a new way," he hints at the most
obvious yet most profound fact about Gothic fiction: Its primary formal
aim is the emotional and psychological involvement of the reader
(284).[3] Momentary successes such as these, however, are the exception

rather than the rule in the Gothic novel. Even Burke's concept of the sublime offers little assistance in giving an affective intention the structural breadth or depth which the novel form seems to demand. They remain transitory effects which take precedence over formal consistency or coherence. Gothic novels come as a result to seem sensationalistic.[4]

The charge is understandable in works which were struggling even within themselves to find a legitimate fictional means of expanding the nature of literary response. We find ourselves laughing, as we laughed at Walpole's "spectre," again and again in reading Gothic novels. Whether Lewis stops in the middle of a harrowing psychological scene to muse over the mangled justice of the Inquisition or Maturin attempts social commentary in the midst of a supernatural visitation, we experience the sacrifice of Gothic intensity for the sake of anti-Gothic narrative concerns.[5] At times it almost seems as if the novelizing impulse itself works against the affective force of the Gothic experience.

In *Melmoth the Wanderer* (1821), for instance, Maturin's hero retains a certain grandeur in his supernatural guise as long as he remains distant and unknown. His early appearances are accompanied by an eerie sense of the inexplicable and the psychologically alarming. His power is lost, however, when we confront him directly and are forced to listen to the ravings of this "demon of superhuman misanthropy." Melmoth, as the ghostly challenge to all who are near despair, is a figure of affective intensity; Melmoth the satirist is not only less powerful but even threatens to undo the force of his supernatural guise with every flourish of his rhetoric. As he instructs the innocent Immalee in the real horrors of the world, we cannot help but feel alienated from this monster's *saeve indignatio:*

> Another amusement of these people, so ingenious in multiplying the sufferings of their destiny, is what they call law. They pretend to find in this a security for their persons and their properties—with how much justice, their own felicitous experience must inform them! . . . So pleadings go on, and years are wasted, and property consumed, and hearts broken,—and law triumphs. One of its most admirable triumphs is in that ingenuity by which it contrives to convert a difficulty into an impossibility, and punish a man for not doing what it has rendered impracticable for him to do. (306)

It is not that what Melmoth says is ineffective or uninteresting. Its power as satire is considerable. But his assertions depend largely on abstraction and on a structure of language which directs the reader away from an emotional and toward an intellectual response. This passage is satiric in the sense that it employs language in a manner opposed to that use of language I have cited in scenes of Gothic intensity. In insisting on the referential function of language, or to use Roman Jakobson's terms, the metonymical function, which directs the reader to social contextualization and denotation, as opposed to the Gothic use of language, which we have seen in signal instances to be primarily metaphorical and indeterminate, Maturin is sacrificing the Gothic intensity of his work in favor of an agenda even more extreme than that which Jakobson assigns to the realistic novel.[6] Melmoth's ravings are more than justified in satiric terms, but the several such chapters which form the core of this novel dispel its Gothic force by employing a very different affective technique from that which I have suggested will render the private experience accessible and powerful. The results can only be deflating.

The obvious disjunction between form and intention, which Jakobson's terms help explain, should not blind us, however, to the attempt of these writers to meet the challenge of their new fictive endeavor. Gothic fiction requires a balance between the metaphorical richness of the moment of Gothic intensity and the demands of space, time, character, and setting, which were essential to the novel form. In other words, the great challenge to the Gothic writer was the paradox between the subjective world of dreamlike private experience and the public objective world of the novel.

The demands which objectivity impose are everywhere apparent in the Gothic novel. Sedgwick says, for example, that in Gothic fiction "it is the position of the self to be massively blocked off from something to which it ought normally to have access."[7] Such blockage suggests a discomfort with form, an inability to realize potential. This represents one way in which the novelists dramatize the problem I have been discussing. Others are familiar: space is always threatening and never comfortable in the Gothic novel; castles loom with superhuman capacity for entrapment; cloisters induce claustrophobia; rooms become too small; vistas too grand. The space of the novel becomes a source of haunting in itself: Story lines are ruptured, fragmented, suppressed, misplaced, even forgotten.[8] Time, too, either ticks with threatening deliberation or flies with destructive rapidity: The durational demands of the novel are challenged, parodied, avoided, but rarely met. Characters are grotesque, monstrous, even sentimental, but rarely convincing. Setting swells with nightmarish presence or recedes into sublime distance, but it is rarely handled with the subtlety or sophistication that novel readers take for granted. But we are beginning to see, as Walpole's Preface suggests, that more than literary disability is at issue here. It seems rather that Gothic discomfort with the conventional demands of the novel is of theoretical as well as psychological interest.[9]

The formal problem is therefore similar in every Gothic novel: Gothic intentions are repeatedly undermined by an insistence on a kind of development of character or setting or plot, which leaves the subjective world answerable to the demands of external reality. Public and private exist as part of a dualistic system that writers and readers both ultimately use to reaffirm their sense of the nature of civilized life. Gothic fiction, however, has as its most basic premise the need to resolve such duality. A century of experimentation demonstrates various attempts to accomplish this resolution and achieve the degree of profundity we associate with literary masterpieces. Successes are various. Within the Gothic novel itself, however, there are very definite signs of how ultimately subjective and objective worlds can be made formally complementary.

The first provisional solutions to this concern with public and private reality are the long periods of suspension created by such novelists as Reeve and Radcliffe; during such periods readers are allowed to entertain the notion of supernatural presences to their horror until such time as the novelist chooses to expose her devices as mere tricks of the imagination. In a novel such as *The Old English Baron* (1778), this technique is pointless because the book never seriously attempts to challenge the terms of genteel, moralistic novelizing. In Radcliffe's work, on the other hand, the challenge to the reader's assumptions is too profound to be dismissed with a simple explanation. For Coleridge, "curiosity is raised oftener than it is gratified," and for Virginia Woolf, the attempt at gratification leaves us no recourse but to laugh.[10]

Suspense is a simple plot device, the formal basis of many a realistic novel; in Radcliffe's hands, however, suspense begins to assume metaphorical significance. When in *The Mysteries of Udolpho* (1794) Emily St. Aubert faints dead away after looking behind a curtain, we are invited to create the horror of the spectacle for ourselves. Radcliffe insists for several hundred pages that we do so, and our ultimate laughter and derision at her unveiling of a waxen image may just be an attempt to excuse ourselves for the real discomfort we had allowed ourselves to create at Radcliffe's suggestion. If critics such as Sedgwick and Kahane are not laughing at such scenes, it is not because as critics they lack irony.[11] Instead, they are acknowledging the uneasiness inherent in Radcliffe's suspensions. What both these critics react to in Radcliffe is that sense that the author taps a range of responses that mere realistic explanation will not satisfy.

The specific nature of the psychological bond here—whether of anxiety or desire—is less important than the structure that makes that bond possible. Kahane says that Emily's "misapprehension is itself a constitutive metaphor of the novel's secret" and that "the novel allows me first to enjoy and then to repress the sexual and aggressive center of Udolpho" (339–40). Without subscribing to the specific terms of Kahane's private response, we can still see in what way she is describing a technique that is common to Gothic: The reader is drawn into participation with fictional events in a way that other fictional forms do not encourage. Our desire to see behind the curtain, that is, becomes more powerful than our fear for Emily. Our own apprehensions and misapprehensions become the subject here.

Radcliffe's insistence on "explanation," what Kahane suggestively calls her repression of threatening desire, is a measure of her refusal to take the formal implications of her material seriously. She insists on a kind of "novelistic" resolution that dispels the ghosts and returns us to the real world. Our impulse to laugh at her attempt to regularize this material suggests that this kind of resolution may be formally antagonistic to its affective nature.

On the other hand, Radcliffe's technique offers a potential for a kind of formal resolution that other writers use more deftly and with more devastating effect. Dread need not be rationally explicable, Radcliffe's superficial explanations suggest, but as members of civilized society let us say that it is. In any case, she is testing the possibility of ontological confusion and deciding that the implications of her Gothic fantasy are too harrowing to be followed to their logical conclusions. If she "represses" threatening desire, she also succumbs to the fear of a world beyond the power of explanation.

The fullness of Radcliffe's Gothic achievement emerges more vividly in other respects than in her manipulation of the supernatural. As I have already suggested, character and plot are carefully considered and reasonably executed in her novels, but neither in a way that significantly contributes to the development of Gothic technique. Of far more moment is her manipulation of setting and, in particular, her technique of picturesque description.

Radcliffe's specific contribution to the depiction of landscape can easily be recognized by examining a classic instance from *The Mysteries of Udolpho:*

> On the other side of the valley, immediately opposite to the spot where the travellers rested, a rocky pass opened toward Gascony. Here no sign of cultivation appeared. The rocks of granite, that screened the glen, rose abruptly from their base, and

stretched their barren points to the clouds, unvaried with woods, and uncheered even by a hunter's cabin. Sometimes, indeed, a gigantic larch threw its long shade over the precipice, and here and there a cliff reared on its brow a monumental cross, to tell the traveller the fate of him who had ventured thither before. This spot seemed the very haunt of banditti; and Emily, as she looked down upon it, almost expected to see them stealing out from some hollow cave to look for their prey. Soon after an object not less terrific struck her,—a gibbet standing on a point of rock near the entrance of the pass, and immediately over one of the crosses she had before observed. These were hieroglyphics that told a plain and dreadful story. (54)

This kind of descriptive language is by its very nature metonymic in function: Radcliffe is creating a context that is as objective as the term *picturesque* implies. The scene is painted with care because Radcliffe wants us to see it and to understand it with her. The understanding, however, is more complicated than it might at first seem. This is a sublime setting, one that is meant to inspire a mood of awe. The adjectives are selected to establish mood rather than to describe in any specific way—they depict the scene less than they create a response to it: rocky, barren, gigantic, long, monumental, hollow, terrific, plain, and dreadful. The nouns function similarly, naming specific objects at the same time that they direct attention away from the objects to the mood: pass, rocks, points, clouds, woods, cabin, larch, shade, precipice, cliff, cross, traveller, fate, spot, haunt, banditti, cave, prey, object, gibbet, point, rock, pass, crosses, hieroglyphics, story. What vocabulary could more clearly point to an affective rather than a descriptive intention? The language is gauged much more for effect than for meaning.

To insist that we understand the scene in this way, moreover, Radcliffe places Emily at its center, not to observe it but to respond to it. In creating a meaning that exploits the terrifying possibilities of the few simple details of the scene (she "almost expected to see [banditti] stealing out from some hollow cave to look for their prey"), Emily teaches us how to read it. Radcliffe does not need to delineate Emily's response. Indeed, any further denotation would defeat Radcliffe's purpose, for she wants her readers to create Emily's horrors for themselves. Radcliffe sees that the field for resolving the dilemma between public form and private meaning in the Gothic novel lies in the consciousness of the reader. She still has not solved the problem of breadth or depth, but she has suggested a manner of absolving the novel of its purely representative function while not sacrificing its intimate relation to the world we know. Other writers carry this technique further than Radcliffe was able to do—her social concerns were ultimately too pressing to be expressed through indirection—but her depiction of response is subtle and sophisticated.

Lewis is signally more bold in his manipulation of Gothic effects: He introduces the supernatural, for instance, baldly and without apology into his fictive world. Much of *The Monk* (1795) therefore becomes merely marvelous, not at all concerned with making Gothic effects convincing.[12] His instinct toward sensationalism, on the other hand, bespeaks an unwillingness to settle for the refined effects of Radcliffe and a blatant desire to shock his readers. Effect in fact becomes the primary rationale in Lewis's fiction. He has often been quoted as replying to the challenge to his illogical use of black Africans in a play as follows: "I thought it would give a pleasing variety . . . if I made my servants black; and could I have produced the same effect by making my heroine blue, blue I should have made her" (quoted in Peck 75).

To accomplish this *effect* in *The Monk*, Lewis presents the reader a continuous series of physically gruesome or emotionally repugnant scenes. A distraught lady is brutally suffocated by her confessor; a Mother Superior is torn to pieces by a hysterical mob; an incarcerated girl clings to the corpse of her putrefying infant; and so on. Lewis sets the limits of horror in the Gothic novel and is rarely exceeded in luridness even by his most avid imitators. By so concentrating on the horrid and disgusting, Lewis attempts to offer a new rationale for fictive expression and to challenge the limits of realism. In a scene such as the second of the three I mention above, Lewis uses language in an objective and descriptive way, but the terms of that description, as in Radcliffe's portrayal of the countryside, accomplish more than what their simple descriptive function at first suggests:

> They tore her one from another, and each new tormentor was more savage than the former. They stifled with howls and execrations her shrill cries for mercy, and dragged her through the streets, spurning her, trampling her, and treating her with every species of cruelty which hate or vindictive fury could invent. At length a flint, aimed by some well-directing hand, struck her full upon the temple. She sank upon the ground bathed in blood, and in a few minutes terminated her miserable existence. Yet though she no longer felt their insults, the rioters still exercised their impotent rage upon her lifeless body. They beat it, trod upon it, and ill-used it, till it became no more than a mass of flesh, unsightly, shapeless, and disgusting. (344)

Unlike Radcliffe, who directed her readers to the sublime elements of the scene before them, Lewis focuses on the merely physical. At the same time, however, he equates the gruesome physical actions with a series of abstractions (cruelty, hate, vindictive fury, impotent rage) that define his concerns more theoretically than Radcliffe's gibbets and banditti do hers. Lewis's expressive excesses, on the other hand, insist on the objective reality of this scene in a way which Radcliffe's sublime descriptions do not. In other words, Lewis has heightened the metaphorical significance of language here by making it more vividly objective. Without the filter of a responding consciousness, there is no other way to assure affective success. If we are disgusted, Lewis has succeeded.

Lewis adapts this technique as well in scenes in which he is experimenting with the supernatural. In "The Narrative of the Bleeding Nun," for instance, he uses a simple ghost story to lend supernatural eeriness to the story of Raymond and Agnes, a pair of thwarted lovers whose separation is central to the plot of the novel. Raymond himself relates this tale, telling of his attempt to elope with Agnes against her parents' will: The couple plan to disguise Agnes as the Bleeding Nun—reputed to walk the halls of her castle home at the stroke of one on a certain night of the year—using this preposterous superstition to their advantage. As the clock strikes the appointed hour, therefore, Raymond makes off with his supposed sweetheart, only to find that he has absconded with the Bleeding Nun herself. Raymond is suitably upset at his situation, but his immediate horror is eclipsed by that which follows during his recovery from the first shock. He tries to sleep off the ghostly vision:

> That repose I wooed in vain. The agitation of my bosom chased away sleep. Restless in my mind, in spite of the fatigue of my body, I continued to toss about from side to side, till the clock in a neighbouring steeple struck "one." As I listened to the mournful hollow sound, and heard it die away in the wind, I felt a sudden chillness spread itself over my body. I shuddered without knowing wherefore; cold dews poured down my forehead, and my hair stood bristling with alarm. Suddenly I heard slow and heavy steps ascending the stair-case. By an involuntary movement I started up in my bed, and drew back the curtain. A single rushlight, which glimmered upon the hearth, shed a faint gleam through the apartment, which was hung with tapestry. The door was thrown open with violence. A figure entered, and drew near my bed with solemn measured steps. With trembling

apprehension I examined this midnight visitor. God Almighty! it was the bleeding nun! (169–70).

There is much that fails here: The ghost pops up like a cardboard image in a chamber of horrors; dramatic preparation remains hopelessly thin; the scene itself feels remote and unconvincing. But notice how Lewis holds his prose in check so that the "measured steps" of the ghost are echoed in the rhythm of the lines describing her approach. More significantly still, we see Lewis deriving intensity from a delineation of Raymond's response. "I listened . . . I felt . . . I shuddered . . . I heard . . . I started . . .": The account attempts to dramatize private experience. The "I" here becomes more than mere perceiving subject; it in fact challenges subjectivity by sacrificing the personal to the horror of the ghostly vision. "Raymond," that is, becomes less a character than a barometer of emotional pressure in the tale. But as such, it is his emotional response that stands for all emotion—that of the reader as well—in the tale. Inside and outside are confused, as that horror becomes an end in itself. "I"—the linguistic sign of subjectivity—proves finally a mere reflector of the imagination of the reader, and the reader must respond by assuming the interiority of the horrified narrator.

The awkwardness of this rote litany is at least mediated by its rationale. The language of the passage moves in two directions at once. We understand that Raymond tells us what he believes he has seen, and we use this information to explain to ourselves something about the nature of private experience. Language is not only offering us the context and substance of a ghostly vision, it is telling us how such a vision is possible. The personal intensity is supplied by the reader.

Throughout this tale, Lewis uses Raymond to express horrors that could not objectively engage his readers. Insofar as the experience is contained in a personal tale, we remain free from the absolute empirical checks that function in novel reading. The filter of Raymond's consciousness gives the Bleeding Nun a context in which we can begin to accept her. Because the tale is told from Raymond's perspective, the external "reality" of the novel is not necessarily jeopardized by what he relates. "By showing within the frame of the novel itself the generation, the production of the supernatural, its imposition on characters who have professed incredulity, and its congruence to the natural world rightly conceived," Peter Brooks tells us, "Lewis has fictionally 'proved' the terms of the rest of his novel, and prepared us for the continuation of the tale to be played out amidst forces which are both beyond man's control . . . and yet inhabiting within man, as they inhabit within nature" (256). That is, the tale provides an epistemological basis for the introduction of the supernatural and shifts the ontological center of gravity in the work toward the fantastic realm to which Walpole aspired. In discussing the formal feature of internal narratives, J. Hillis Miller has remarked that "the palpably fictive or subjective quality of the interpolated story tends to affirm the historical reality of the first level of the narration." Miller goes on to suggest that the reader may "come to feel like the first participant in an echoing series of representations within representations, each equally real and equally imaginary" (30).

Of all the Gothic novelists, Maturin seems to have had the clearest sense of the formal issues involved in Gothic expression and of the possibilities of the formal experimentation that Miller describes. *Melmoth* consists of a series of tales loosely bound together by means of various interlocking devices and a general frame. The central unifying feature of the work is the title character himself, who reappears in every tale as a lost soul searching for others as desperate as he.

One of the most interesting tales in Maturin's work is Alonzo de Monçada's own history, "The Tale of the Spaniard." It tells of a childhood shrouded in mystery, of familial rejection, of enforced monastic life resulting in violent struggles with authority, with conscience, and what seem to be forces of the underworld. It then turns to incarceration at the hands of the officers of the Inquisition, the paramount horrors encountered in those precincts, and finally, near-tragic escape. At one point in this series of events Monçada is trapped in a tunnel beneath a monastery he is trying to flee:

> Our wanderings in the passage seemed to be endless. My companion [a fellow prisoner] turned to right, to left,—advanced, retreated, paused,—(the pause was dreadful)!—Then advanced again, tried another direction, where the passage was so low that I was obliged to crawl on my hands and knees to follow him, and even in this posture my head struck against the ragged roof. When we had proceeded for a considerable time, (at least so it appeared to me, for minutes are hours in the *noctuary* of terror,—terror has no *diary*), this passage became so narrow and so low, that I could proceed no farther, and wondered how my companion could have advanced beyond me. I called to him, but received no answer; and, in the darkness of the passage, or rather hole, it was impossible to see ten inches before me. I had the lamp, too, to watch, which I had held with a careful trembling hand, but which began to burn dim in the condensed and

narrow atmosphere. A gush of terror rose in my throat. Sur-
rounded as I was by damps and dews, my whole body felt in a
fever. I called again, but no voice answered. In situations of
peril, the imagination is unhappily fertile, and I could not help
recollecting and *applying* a story I had once read of some trav-
ellers who attempted to explore the vaults of the Egyptian pyr-
amids. One of them, who was advancing, as I was, on his hands
and knees, stuck in the passage, and, whether from terror, or
from the natural consequences of his situation, swelled so that
it was impossible for him to retreat, advance, or allow a passage
for his companions. The party were on their return, and finding
their passage stopped by this irremovable obstruction, their
lights trembling on the verge of extinction, and their guide terrified beyond the power of direction or advice, proposed, in the
selfishness to which the feeling of vital danger reduces all, to
cut off the limbs of the wretched being who obstructed their
passage. He heard this proposal, and, contracting himself with
agony at the sound, was reduced, by that strong muscular
spasm, to his usual dimensions, dragged out, and afforded room
for the party to advance. He was suffocated, however, in the
effort, and left behind a corse. All this detail, that takes many
words to tell, rushed on my soul in a moment;—on my soul?—
no, on my body. I was all physical feeling,—all intense corporeal
agony, and God only knows, and man can only feel, how that
agony can absorb and annihilate all other feelings within us,—
how we could, in such a moment, feed on a parent, to gnaw out
our passage into life and liberty, as sufferers in a wreck have
been known to gnaw their own flesh, for the support of that
existence which the unnatural morsel was diminishing at every
agonizing bite. (192–93)

In this set piece the range of Maturin's technique emerges: the terror
of the experience is vivid and almost palpable; as hysteria increases,
the physical confinement intensifies; mental despair is reflected in a
fantasy of dismemberment. Maturin makes these details vivid so that
the reader can more fully understand what is happening to Monçada
psychologically. Further, Maturin makes clear that all this is happening
to Monçada, in that the entire passage is his attempt to express the
horror of the moment. The narrative perspective ("so it appeared to
me") helps to distinguish this experience from the ordinary and
heighten the license that the artist thereby achieves ("minutes are
hours in the *noctuary* of terror"). Maturin insists that in addition to

the direct presentation of the terror, there is personal reflection on it so that we can understand, and even feel, its power. Lest we think him above the downright gruesomeness of Lewis, however, Maturin here seems to allow himself to be carried away by potentially horrifying images. But the seemingly gratuitous story of impassable passages, threatened dismemberment, and death ultimately serves to expand our understanding of the terror Monçada feels: The terror cannot directly be delineated as powerfully as this story enables Maturin indirectly to suggest. We do not stop to wonder whether or not such imaginings are appropriate to the situation, because the horror of the image of the dismembered body creates for us an expression of Monçada's fears that we can understand objectively. Objective detail, that is, heightens our sense of the subjective reality.

The last phase of this passage suggests yet another important feature of Maturin's technique. "All this detail . . . rushed on my soul in a moment;—on my soul?—no, on my body. I was all physical feeling." Physicality itself becomes a source of Gothic power. Imaginative fancy is supplanted by physical fact. Monçada's description *embodies* the Gothic horror to give it a presence that in the imagination it lacks. We are led thereby into direct confrontation with the human dimensions of horror, while remaining free to imagine the details of their psychological effect for ourselves. We participate in the act of creation and determine for ourselves the nature of our own haunting. Iser claims that the text does not disappear "into the private world of its individual readers," and disagrees strongly with the "emotive theory" of psychoanalytic critics.[13] But in the process of "assembl[ing] the world of the text," in Iser's terms, Maturin assures that he casts a net wide enough to touch a vast range of private responses. We do not need to "analogize" to be affected here. The "I" of the narration collapses into a generalized vision of the horror of privacy. The generalizing comments of the last sentence underline Maturin's need to pin his effects to a larger scheme. He wants us fully to understand in our own terms that "agony can absorb and annihilate all other feelings within us."

Maturin leaves us with an image totally removed from the present scene—the self-cannibalism of sufferers in a shipwreck—to provide an analogy of the desperation his character feels. By shifting from fiction to horrifyingly recognizable fact, this image taps a range of responses otherwise unavailable to him. In that transition, Maturin attempts to evince the real dimensions of the terror he has created. If it seems to modern readers merely sensationalistic, we can at least admire the attempt to center subjective terror in the objective. Maturin is attempting to expand the limits of novelistic expression by means of a consistent affective technique that engages "circumstantial realism" to its own ends.

With Alonzo de Monçada's history, Maturin insists, moreover, on the narrow focus of a tale. As in Lewis's tale, the point of view is subjective and personal. Private experience establishes the terms of the presentation, and we are therefore liberated to a degree from the conventional narrative gauge of what is possible. Extreme states of feeling, no less than extreme patterns of imagery, fail to disrupt the surface continuity of the work because the tale (where "minutes are hours") is not subject to the structural or temporal demands of the novel form and remains freer to express the extraordinary. For Sedgwick, Maturin's narrative procedure "represents the broadest structural application of the otherwise verbal or thematic convention of the unspeakable" (*Coherence of Gothic Convention* 20). The form of the novel, that is, reinforces the theme of ontological crisis in the work and challenges the assumptions of the reader about the nature of reality. For it is not the unspeakablity that matters here so much as the suspension of meaning, which breaks down the reader's skepticism about the unknown. At the same time, language functions differently from the manner in which it functions in a novel. It is not simply that we can interpret Monçada's words metaphorically; they insist on including a metaphorical dimension within the metonymical function of narrative expression. The story that Monçada imagines carries him deeper into the abyss in which he is plunged.

Charles E. May argues that the tale form is particularly suited to the kind of ontological confusion to which Maturin's intense subjectivity seems purposefully to lead. "The short story," he says, "attempts to be authentic to the immaterial reality of the inner world of the self in its relation to eternal rather than temporal reality" (in contrast to the novel) and that the short story insistently tends toward the mythic and spiritual (328–29). The intense physicality of Maturin's tale may seem an odd candidate for mythic power, but such flights of Gothic fancy break down the confines of everyday experience and release, in Walpole's terms, the "great resources" of visionary privacy. May makes an analogy between this fictional state of affairs and Martin Buber's concept of "I-Thou" mystical experience, which can intrude into a comfortable everyday world: "In this chronicle of solid benefits the moments of the *Thou* appear as strange lyric and dramatic episodes, seductive and magical, but tearing us away to dangerous extremes, loosening the well-tried context, leaving more questions than satisfaction behind them, shattering security—in short, uncanny moments we can well dispense with" (Buber 34; quoted in May 333). In dealing with Gothic fiction, of course, the terms of this analogy are apt. For a psychological visionary like Maturin, such a description of the effect of interpolated tales on his fictional world is in itself uncanny.

In the "Tale of the Spaniard," Melmoth finally appears to the hero, Alonzo de Monçada, at the climax of a long series of brutal circumstances, which culminate in the physical and mental torment wrought by the Inquisition. Monçada is tempted, as countless Gothic heroes are, to offer his soul as the price of escaping the hideous tribunal; and, like them, he has a mysterious visitor in his prison chamber. But rather than terrifying him, this visitor only offers him tales of ages past—past, indeed, what anyone alive at that time could be expected to have experienced. Monçada suspects nothing, but there is a kind of dramatic irony at work for the reader: We know that this character is Melmoth the Wanderer and that his single purpose is to procure Monçada's soul. We question only whether he will succeed.

Within the tale, however, this question is never answered directly; indeed, the tale lacks an ending. Perhaps it remains unresolved because Maturin knew enough to resist both the deflating resolutions of Radcliffe and the fantastic denouements of Lewis. The Inquisition scenes burst into a general conflagration at the prison, which interrupts Monçada's own drama and transforms his private nightmare into a public spectacle of destruction that very quickly becomes a scene of communal horror; but our experience of that horror is still Monçada's own:

> The flames at last began to descend into the court. Then commenced a scene of horror indescribable. The wretches who had been doomed to the flames, imagined their hour was come. Idiots from long confinement, and submissive as the holy office could require, they became delirious as they saw the flames approaching, and shrieked audibly, "Spare me—spare me—put me to as little torture as you can. . . . " At this moment, while standing amid the groupe of prisoners, my eyes were struck by an extraordinary spectacle. Perhaps it is amid the moments of despair, that imagination has most power, and they who have suffered, can best describe and feel. In the burning light, the steeple of the Dominican church was as visible as at noonday. . . . The night was intensely dark, but so strong was the light of the conflagration, that I could see the spire blazing, from the reflected lustre, like a meteor. The hands of the clock were as visible as if a torch was held before them; and this calm and silent progress of time, amid the tumultous confusion of mid-

night horrors,—this scene of the physical and mental world in an agony of fruitless and incessant motion, might have suggested a profound and singular image, had not my whole attention been riveted to a human figure placed on a pinnacle of the spire, and surveying the scene in perfect tranquillity. (241–42)

After Monçada has undergone intense physical and spiritual torment, fused in the near-madness that his incarceration causes, this display of wholesale torment comes almost as a relief. In a sense, the scene is a public testament of what he has already suffered privately. These flames represent a living hell, the most apt metaphor for his condition, a condition, we are here forced to realize, that all his fellow prisoners share. Monçada speaks of his own despair because Maturin wants us to feel the meaning of the word in this vision. "Amid the moments of despair . . . they who have suffered, can best describe and feel": Monçada's physical suffering shapes the narrative and determines its significance. If the Inquisition represents the most excruciating psychological and physical ordeal any human being could undergo, this scene expresses that ordeal in terms which recreate it vividly for the reader.

In this tale, the conventional restraints of experience are ignored, yet we are carried along. We appreciate the subjectivity of what Monçada relates and are willing, because he deals with what we can intuitively understand, to grant a certain degree of unreality as a means of expanding the ability of language to express the inexpressible. "The Tale of the Spaniard" reaches its climax in a totally subjective vision. The objective reality of Melmoth becomes more vivid because of his role in Monçada's private nightmare. The nightmare vision itself has attained a degree of objective power.

The key to this subjectivity lies in its ability to confuse our sense of what is "real." Such confusion is at the heart of the tale form: In the tale's momentary suspension from the world of the novel, we are left without the reassurance of what we think of as "natural" limits. The ontological basis of the experience of fiction has shifted, and "realism" has given way to "fantasy" as a way of interpreting experience itself. We are not offended by this shift, because the tale allows us to understand it within Monçada's own subjectivity and to give it whatever "meaning" we find most powerful. Charles E. May suggests that "the short story is closer to the nature of reality as we experience it in those moments . . . when we sense the inadequacy of our categories of conceptual reality." He goes on to explain that the reality the short story presents us with is the reality of those sub-universes of the supernatural and the fable which exist within the so-called "real" world of sense perception and conceptual abstraction. It presents moments in which we become aware of anxiety, loneliness, dread, concern, and thus find the safe, secure and systematic life we usually lead disrupted and momentarily destroyed. (337–38)[14]

In the terms of my discussion here we accept this subversion of novelistic reality because the private vision of the tale strikes a responsive chord in the reader and reaches beyond "realism."

Walpole attested to the limitations of the novel because he felt the need to subvert our naturalistic expectations. Maturin accomplishes this, as Lewis attempted to, by attending to subjective horror so closely that it starts to attain a kind of objective force of its own. The tale thus offers an alternative to the conventions Walpole decried and acts as a necessary reminder that Gothic experience and the novel form were not automatically compatible. Once novelistic techniques were shaped to the affective intentions of Gothic writers, however, a new range of expressive possibilities emerged. It is almost as if in liberating Maturin from the strictures of the novel, the tale releases him from the confines of objective reality as well. This release is of crucial importance to Gothic fiction. For only when Gothic writers have a clear sense of the formal properties most suited to their affective intention as separate from the conventions of the early novel, can they achieve the range of expressivity they seek yet free themselves from the label of sensationalism. Formal coherence becomes the only way to achieve Walpole's Gothic dream.

What Lewis and Maturin have begun to demonstrate, therefore, is a means of overcoming the dichotomy that Walpole first recognized as inevitable in Gothic fiction. Objective and subjective states blend in the depths of a perceiving consciousness in tales such as theirs, and as a result, the limits of the real are extended and detail of a kind that is inadmissible in an objective narrative readily finds a place. We might even be tempted to say that in these novels, subjective reality begins to assume objective force: The terms of what is real have shifted to include subjective fantasy. Perception, in other words, weakens the division of inside and outside, subjective and objective experience, by making the external world an internal experience at the same time that it insists on its obvious externality. The result is harrowing, to be sure, but it is also potentially liberating, as we shall see.[15]

Just as for Burke, the sublime takes a person out of herself as a way of expanding who she is, so Gothic experience leads characters through all those hidden recesses and over those abysses as a means of expanding the terms of human experience for themselves and for the reader.[16] Napier claims that "the uneasy shuttling between structures did not produce, as it would later, for example, for Wordsworth and Coleridge, those sublime moments of discontinuity in which a 'higher' meaning is sensed or achieved. This is why the denomination of Gothic as romantic in Weiskel's sense of the word is misleading" (5–6). I would argue, however, that the moments of subjective intensity that I have described offer their own powerful sublimity, if not achieving "'higher' meaning," at least shaking our complacent belief in the limits of fictional expression. Napier insists on the "systematic failure" of Gothic novelists to "lead to the profound realizations about human consciousness that some critics have asserted that they do" (7). It seems to me, on the contrary, that in achieving such profound realizations about the nature of fiction, and therefore about the nature of human consciousness, the Gothic novelists have earned the right to be taken more seriously.

The Gothic novel is a liberating phenomenon, which expands the range of possibilities for novelistic expression. The first Gothic writers were not as interested in developing a coherent conception of literary expression that acknowledged these discoveries as they were in using them to break down existing limits to expression—the dam, as Walpole expressed it, behind which "the great resources of fancy" had gathered. Gothic novelists structured their works so as to heighten the range of affective possibilities, and in doing so set Gothic on a course that leads directly to less qualified successes.

If perception offers the means whereby Gothic writers overcome the seeming contradiction of their craft, the formal realization of the dynamics of perception finally determines the stature of individual works of Gothic fiction. Walpole's rudimentary attempt to introduce us into his dreamlike world offers the basic vocabulary of Gothic expression, to be sure, and the basic technique for giving that vocabulary a special power. Walpole's Gothic experiment fails to be fully convincing, nevertheless, in part because he remained uncertain as to how to achieve his formal ends. Later Gothic novelists seem to offer a set of structural principles and a mode of discourse that begin to suggest the manner in which perception can become the formal basis of a fictional experience. As Gothic fiction flourishes in the nineteenth century, Walpole's desire for formal innovation is fully realized in works that do not labor under the marginality that the qualifying adjective "Gothic" has assured.

The works by Shelley, Brontë, Poe, Hawthorne, and James that I discuss in this regard achieve their mastery of Gothic material by means of the form I have called the Gothic tale. The tale, in the hands of these writers, becomes more than a form capable of answering Walpole's dream; it becomes a structure of belief and understanding that defies the tenets of realistic novelizing. If the tale avoids certain expressive limitations of the novel, it does not, as we shall see, totally abjure the tenets of novelistic technique. The tale is primarily subjective, and yet it gives objective reality to the matter it relates. Supernatural events become increasingly natural in the world of the Gothic tale. It emerges as the form that allows private experience to be suspended between novelistic fact and romantic fantasy, between daylight and moonlight, with the result that a new power of literary expression is realized.

2

Frankenstein
and the Unnameable

For years after Mary Shelley first sent her "hideous progeny" into the world, she watched its fortunes with a parent's concern. When her novel proved the basis of a successful play, she was fascinated. In a letter to Leigh Hunt, she expresses that fascination in terms of particular interest:

> Frankenstein had prodigious success as a drama & was about to be repeated for the 23rd night at the English opera house. The play bill amused me extremely, for in the list of dramatis personae came,———by Mr T. Cooke: this nameless mode of naming the un[n]ameable is rather good. (*LMWS* 1:378)

By so emphasizing the unnameability of her—of Victor Frankenstein's—creation, Shelley defies those critics who have so neatly and precisely found names to describe the novel's central horror. That does not stop me from adding my own names to the list, nor does it limit the power that readers have traditionally found in this exploration of the boundaries of experience. Shelley has so constructed her novel as to make the horror available to each reader in his or her own terms. She accomplishes this not by means of coy and euphemistic language but by careful observation and precise description. She leads us into a world beyond our own, both seducing us with the familiarity and alarming us with the hideousness of what she finds there.[1]

Unlike other early Gothicists, Shelley achieves such eerie popularity with *Frankenstein* because she is able to devise a form that can embody her affective intentions. Other Gothic novelists struggle with the exigencies of novelistic form, whereas Shelley liberates Gothicism from the demands of realism, subverts the nature of novelistic authority, and

releases the power inherent in her tale.[2] How she does that is my subject here. "The experience of reading," Jauss has suggested, "can liberate one from adaptations, prejudices, and predicaments of a lived
praxis in that it compels one to a new perception of things," and it
"anticipates unrealized possibility, broadens the limited space of social
behavior for new desires, claims, and goals, and thereby opens paths
of future experience" (41). *Frankenstein* accomplishes all of this by
challenging the limits of narrative form.

Shelley was certainly aware of the problems inherent to Gothic fiction and of the conflict between Gothic and realistic modes. As the
Journal indicates, she assiduously read both Radcliffe and Lewis
shortly before composing *Frankenstein* (*The Monk* and *The Italian* in
1814; *Tales of Wonder* and *The Mysteries of Udolpho* in 1815), as well
as Godwin's *Caleb Williams* (1816), Brockden Brown's *Wieland* (1815)
and *Arthur Mervyn* (1817), Maturin's *Bertram* (1816), and a vast array
of other novels from Richardson and Fielding to Edgeworth and Scott.
Lewis in fact visited the Shelleys at Montalégre in August 1816. Percy
Shelley says that they "talk of Ghosts" and that Lewis "tells us many
mysteries of his trade." Percy goes on to wonder whether the "persons
who profess to discredit these visitations really discredit them, or, if
they do in the daylight, are not admonished by the approach of loneliness and midnight to think more respectably of the world of shadows"
(*MSJ* 57). Mary Shelley clearly did have respect for the world of shadows, and while it is true that it took her lover's encouragement to get
her to expand her idea for a ghost story into a novel, she claims full
responsibility for the uncanny vision that has become central to our
modern mythology: *Frankenstein*.

She does so publicly in the Introduction to the revised 1831 edition
of the novel, which functions like a Gothic tale itself, a "crystalline . . .
record," as James calls "The Turn of the Screw," "of so many intense
anomolies and obscurities" (*AN* 173). Far from ending speculation as
to the nature of the work, Shelley's Introduction heightens the affective
possibilities of the text by dramatizing the harrowing precincts of her
own subjectivity. Percy had spoken in their journal of the "approach of
loneliness and midnight," and that is what she recreates for us here.

"I shall . . . give," Shelley tells us, "a general answer to the question,
so very frequently asked me—'How I, then a young girl, came to think
of, and to dilate upon, so very hideous an idea?'"(5). Surely these remarks are meant to be provocative and almost sensational. Shelley reminds us, in this innocent-seeming sentence, of her sex, her youth, the
shock of her authorship, and the titillating nature of her tale. This self-
indictment is neither ingenuous nor defensive; instead it is her own

Gothic technique. For by so introducing her account, she insists that we apprehend the novel in personal terms and that we focus on these very private details of authorship. Explanatory Gothic prefaces are common—I have considered Walpole's similar self-dramatization—but none so deftly works to force the reader to ask the questions that the author wants so mockingly to answer. She engages our interest in a personal tale, just as, throughout the novel, characters engage one another in longer but similarly structured confessional passages.[3] This "life story," largely fabricated, is addressed to the reader to gain a sympathetic response. "Hear my tale," the nameless creature says to Frankenstein; and here the author says the same to us.

The Introduction is therefore the first of the series of frames that, according to Newman, signals "the presence of some enigma" within the novel (144). Shelley tantalizes us with the possibility of an inner truth, and critics traditionally respond by naming that truth and giving it explanatory power. But the closer we approach the truth of this novel, the more subtly it recedes into unnameability. The novel itself, in other words, is structured so as to encourage interpretation at the same time that it eludes it. Here Shelley relates her own case history—a relatively happy childhood, a desire to be creative, solitude and reflection, the illicit excitement of knowledge (in her case of Gothic fiction and galvanism), confrontation with the unknown—and challenges us to interpret it in relation to her tale.

Kristeva suggests that the kind of psychological horror she describes in Proust or Céline arises from the opposition between I and Other, between Inside and Outside. She says further that "owing to the ambiguous opposition I/Other, Inside/Outside—an opposition that is vigorous but pervious, violent but uncertain—there are contents, 'normally' unconscious in neurotics, that become explicit if not conscious in 'borderline' patients' speeches and behavior" (7). Shelley heightens such "contents" as a way of making her Gothic novel successful.

This technique becomes clearer as Shelley describes her own moment of imaginative intensity:

> Night waned upon this talk, and even the witching hour had gone by, before we retired to rest. When I placed my head on my pillow, I did not sleep, nor could I be said to think. My imagination, unbidden, possessed and guided me, gifting the successive images that arose in my mind with a vividness far beyond the usual bounds of reverie. I saw—with shut eyes, but acute mental vision,—I saw the pale student of unhallowed arts kneeling beside the thing he had put together. I saw the hideous

phantasm of a man stretched out, and then, on the working of some powerful engine, show signs of life, and stir with an uneasy, half vital motion. Frightful must it be; for supremely frightful would be the effect of any human endeavour to mock the stupendous mechanism of the Creator of the world. . . . [The artist] sleeps; but he is awakened; he opens his eyes; behold the horrid thing stands at his bedside, opening his curtains, and looking on him with yellow, watery, but speculative eyes.

I opened mine in terror. The idea so possessed my mind, that a thrill of fear ran through me, and I wished to exchange the ghastly image of my fancy for the realities around. (9)

I have quoted this passage at length because its effect is cumulative. It is not enough to say that this passage is *like* a passage from a Gothic novel—like, for instance, an intense moment of private confrontation on the part of one of the internal narrators of Lewis or Maturin—for this is itself a Gothic passage, which transforms the material of idle speculation into the powerful and persuasive haunting of Mary Shelley. The author has, moreover, given us terms for interpreting the Gothic novel as a version of her own subjective horror and for understanding subjectivity as a Gothic confrontation. Under the control of her imagination, she becomes passive and increasingly appalled at the content of her own vision. "I saw" becomes the formula here, and throughout the novel, for attesting to the substance of privacy and giving it public reality, that is, making "inside" "outside" and confusing the distinction between subject and object, metaphor and metonymy. Shelley is "possessed," afraid: She sees a monster and understands its private implications. It is at the creator's bed; it is at her bed. It stares with watery, speculative eyes; she opens hers and stares into the darkness. This monster and this creator, she seems to be emphasizing, are her own. Her own abject midnight solitude has placed her in the middle of the Gothic novel she has herself written.[4]

By inviting us to share in this vision, she places us there as well. For who is there to listen to this tale, who is there to be seduced by its horror, but the reader? We are led first into easy familiarity, the tone of the opening is almost conspiratorial, then into the author's private experience, then her bedchamber, her very bed, and then into her dreams. We are meant to understand the horror of this vision and to share with her, as spectator, to be sure, but also as friend. Why else this informal tone, this disarming address? The novelist is alone with her vision, and she tempts us to make it our own.

It is no accident that critics have taken *Frankenstein* so personally: The author seems intent on personalizing the Gothic experience. She plays up the circumstance—her lover, their important friends, the romantic setting, the haunting itself, Percy's encouragement—not just because they are central to the nature of her creativity, but also because such details lend an air of authenticity to the report and place her at the center of an intriguing tale. She uses a metaphor of motherhood to clinch this self-dramatization, not primarily on account of the horror that such a relationship implies, but because this sexualizes the experience and places her at the crux of the intimate act of creativity.[5] She thereby transforms her complicated feelings about motherhood and female oppression into her most effective source of Gothic power. She focuses the interest of the text in her own private experience, and that is where critics have been wandering ever since:

> And now, once again, I bid my hideous progeny go forth and prosper. I have an affection for it, for it was the offspring of happy days, when death and grief were but words, which found no true echo in my heart. Its several pages speak of many a walk, many a drive, many a conversation, when I was not alone; and my companion was one who, in this world, I shall never see more. But this is for myself; my readers have nothing to do with these associations. (10)

Ah, but we do! What could Shelley have done to have encouraged more intense fascination with her private life? We crave more knowledge, and her rhetorical suggestion is that we shall know more if we read into these "several pages," where the truth resides. She encourages her readers to search for this truth in the tale and in her own experience—perhaps she would even find the degree to which *she* has been analyzed in the *Frankenstein* literature gratifying. For that is what she seems to invite here. In a sense, she offers herself as a substitute for the truth that she knows we shall not find in the novel. But she also knows that fiction can only reveal the private reality of the reader her- or himself. She makes this impassioned plea for her "progeny" and commits this veiled act of self-exposure as a way of leading us into the search for our own unnameable horror. Shelley has created a picturesque life to attract and a private haunting to appall us, engaging us in a dialogue that the novel can only intensify, for it is a dialogue with ourselves.

In discussing dialogue in narrative, Sternberg suggests that a text that contains both speakers and listeners "doubles the imaging itself by splitting a single communicative act into message sent ('said') and message received ('heard')" (300). The implications for any fictional text are interesting, but for *Frankenstein*, in which hearers and listeners themselves double and redouble—at one point we are listening to Shelley telling the story of Walton telling the story of Victor telling the story of the creature telling the story of hearing the story of the De Lacey family—they are staggering. If, as Sternberg tells us, "hearing entails doubling" (301), *Frankenstein* geometrically multiplies the possibilities of meaning. That process is begun in the Introduction, between author and reader. We listen to the author's rendition of her private experience and then create a version of that experience to suit ourselves. This is where the narrative of seduction begins.[6]

Those who disapproved of the novel when it appeared did so in terms that suggest a fear of narrative violation. The following criticism, for instance, appeared in *The Quarterly Review* (January 1818):

> Our taste and our judgment alike revolt at this kind of writing, and the greater the ability with which it may be executed the worse it is—it inculcates no lesson of conduct, manners or morality; it cannot mend, and will not even amuse its readers, unless their taste have been deploreably vitiated. (quoted in Spark 140)

The reviewer seems to understand the technique of the work very well, and although he is wrong to think that there is no lesson in *Frankenstein*, his fear of its effect is fully justified. The danger, for this reviewer, is the fictional nature of the "narrative content"; he seems to expect a neatly packaged "moral" and to equate meaning in fiction with an explanation that can serve a useful public function. This rage for explanation, for searching out the hidden meaning, is not limited to the early critics of *Frankenstein*. New modes of interpretation are in some ways no better. As Sontag says, "The old style of interpretation was insistent, but respectful; it erected another meaning on top of the literal one. The modern style of interpretation excavates, and as it excavates, destroys; it digs 'behind' the text, to find a sub-text which is the true one" (6).

Whether or not Shelley was affected by such early reviews, her 1831 Introduction plays down the question of meaning or "moral," except in her Radcliffean mention of the "human endeavour to mock the stupendous mechanism of the Creator of the world," and emphasizes instead the atmosphere of the night in question, the intensity of her private experience, and its importance as a source of recollection for her.

In doing so, she teaches us to read *Frankenstein* in an intensely subjective and personal way.[7]

It has been argued that within *Frankenstein*, narrative "serves both as a way of seducing a listener, and as a means of displacing and sublimating desire that cannot be satisfied directly" (Newman 143–44). This is the nature of Gothic narrative in general, not just *within* a work like *Frankenstein*, but between work and reader as well. Newman says that "once a narrative has been uttered, it exists as a verbal structure with its own integrity, and can, like myth, think itself in the minds of men (and women). Being infinitely repeatable in new contexts, it has achieved autonomy; it now functions as a text" (147). But each time this narrative is repeated, it invites a new participation, and that participation becomes complicity, because in the natural doubling process, the reader becomes the ultimate alter ego on whom the burden of interpretive responsibility finally falls. By engaging her readers in such a procedure, Shelley seems to insure that on some level they will believe what she says. They have to: They are already involved. In this sense, *Frankenstein* is "like myth."

A tale is not a myth, of course, but Shelley seems to understand how one could be. The textual implications of mythmaking could not have been far from the author's consciousness while she was working on *Frankenstein*. As she herself described, she was ensconced in a cosy hideaway with two of the greatest poets of her generation. Both were involved in mythmaking projects of their own. Percy Shelley of course took such matters very seriously. In his poetry, the narrator often creates a "thou" as a way of transforming self-consciousness into an outer-directed consciousness that can challenge and expand the limits of privacy.[8]

Mary Shelley attempts to transform the nature of Gothic narrative by turning the lyric, mythmaking voice of her husband into a narrative structure that uses an "I-Thou" configuration to "think itself in the minds of men (and women)." It is worth recalling Buber's description of a situation in which moments of "I-Thou" intensity obtrude into the everyday world of "I-It": "strange lyric and dramatic episodes, seductive and magical, but tearing us away to dangerous extremes, loosening the well-tried context, leaving more questions than satisfaction behind them, shattering security."[9] Buber seems to have in mind profound and unsettling literary effects as the basis of his idea of myth, and just such a confusion of the personal and the literary is what Shelley describes in her Introduction. In addition to quoting this passage from Buber in attempting to describe the effect of the form of the short story, May discusses Deikman's analysis of experience and draws the following conclusions: a "bias for the active, everyday encounter with the external world and our consequent scorn for the receptive mode of a more mystic, taking-in quality reflects our bias for the I-It world of the everyday and the novel that embodies it rather than for the I-Thou world of the uncanny moment" (334). The latter he associates with the form I call the tale. May associates this mode of thought with Cassirer's "mythical" thinking: "instead of extensive distribution, intensive compression. This focusing of all forces on a single point is the prerequisite for all mythical thinking and mythical formulation" (Cassirer, *Language and Myth* 33; quoted in May 334–35). This "mythical thinking" may be recognized as Romantic, but note how similar *Frankenstein* is to the kind of uncanny intensity that is described here. Consider, moreover, the degree to which Shelley's self-presentation centers on the kind of receptivity to the uncanny moment that May outlines.

If Shelley makes the assertion of mythicality and challenges us to accept it, she also uses the rationale of the tale form to evoke the mythic possibilities of her subject. The situation in *Frankenstein*, however, is not as transcendent as my use of Buber's theological perspective makes it sound. It seems to me that Kristeva describes the narrative situation here, and in other Gothic works, with singular elegance:

> For, when narrated identity is unbearable, when the boundary between subject and object is shaken, and when even the limit between inside and outside becomes uncertain, the narrative is what is challenged first. If it continues nevertheless, its makeup changes; its linearity is shattered, it proceeds by flashes, enigmas, short cuts, incompletion, tangles, and cuts. At a later stage, the unbearable identity of the narrator and of the surroundings that are supposed to sustain him can no longer be *narrated* but *cries out* or is *descried* with maximal stylistic intensity (language of violence, of obscenity, or of a rhetoric that relates the text to poetry). The narrative yields to a *crying-out theme* that, when it tends to coincide with the incandescent states of a boundary-subjectivity that I have called abjection, is the crying-out theme of suffering-horror. (141)

What better way to explain the endless fragmentation of Gothic texts and the constant focus on boundaries between inside and outside in a novel such as *Frankenstein*? The "flashes, enigmas, short cuts, incompletion, tangles, and cuts" that we experience in Gothic works are the direct result of this breakdown of the distinction between subject and object. The "I-Thou" technique of *Frankenstein* is another way of reacting to this breakdown, in Shelley's case an attempt to transform it from private suffering-horror, private abjection, by means of a poetic transformation of enigma into belief.

> Did I request thee, Maker, from my clay
> To mould Me man? Did I solicit thee
> From darkness to promote me?—

This epigraph to *Frankenstein,* from *Paradise Lost* (10:743–45), takes us straight to the heart of the matter. Besides opening a whole range of allegorical possibilities here, which include most centrally God's relation to Adam, "I-Thou" is established as a basic mode of discourse, while the aggression and pathos of this plea remind the reader of both the nature of abjection and the horror of self-contempt. Within the novel, this theme is continually repeated, directly or indirectly. This need to address the Creator, to create a bond with the Other, is an attempt to mythologize the misery of one's own solitude. If Adam is to be the archetype of this need to confront the Other, to bring into relation with himself the Other as "Thou," Shelley begins a similarly mythologizing experience in her Introduction and thereby expands the expressive possibilities of her narrative. Shelley uses the "I-Thou" form of the talelike personal revelation as a way of liberating her material from the confines of realistic novel-ism, on the one hand, and sensational Gothicism on the other. The result is a work that breaks down distinctions between subjective and objective experience and that reverberates with the interpretive possibilities of mythopoesis.

The novel itself opens with the one word with which all the various potentialities of *Frankenstein* are finally realized, "you":

> You will rejoice to hear that no disaster has accompanied the commencement of an enterprise which you have regarded with such evil forebodings. I arrived here yesterday; and my first task is to assure my dear sister of my welfare, and increasing confidence in the success of my undertaking. (15)

This letter is addressed *To Mrs. Saville, England,* but in fact the narrative begins with a resounding and aggressive use of the second-person pronoun; and nowhere in the first paragraph, which I have quoted in its entirety, is there any suggestion that the writer is speaking to anyone but ourselves. His sister is mentioned in an odd third-person construction that falls short of direct address, and we find ourselves, as it were, accused of the "evil forebodings" that we may in fact already feel. If we do not already feel them, surely this opening is meant to encourage us to. The novel, then, begins with a note of reassurance and a hint of danger, calming yet titillating as it seduces us into narrative complicity. "Mrs. Saville," it seems to me, is a necessary fiction, which Shelley uses as a means of engaging us more directly in her Gothic tale.

Veeder makes much of Margaret Saville, "because gender qualifies for judgment in *Frankenstein*" (82), and goes so far as ingeniously to suggest that "Margaret as the embodiment of Mary [Shelley]'s values cannot empathize with Promethean drives" and that she symbolizes "that native community which is the union of male with female and the ideal of Agape" (83). Should such themes be at work in *Frankenstein*, and Veeder's case is convincing, the reader can certainly not be aware of them at the opening of the novel. Indeed, it seems to me that it is our own relation to the speaker that is on the line here:

> I am already far north of London; and as I walk in the streets of Petersburgh, I feel a cold northern breeze play upon my cheeks, which braces my nerves, and fills me with delight. Do you understand this feeling? (15)

Rarely is fiction so direct in its determination to engage the reader in the sensations of the speaker. Again the first-person narrative is an account of personal response ("Inspirited by this wind of promise, my day dreams become more fervent and vivid" [15]), as well as imaginative fantasy ("I try in vain to be persuaded that the pole is the scene of frost and desolation; it ever presents itself to my imagination as the region of beauty and delight" [15]). As Walton moves from the physical to the emotional and the imaginative, we are invited to participate, and for all that we might say about these aspirations in retrospect, surely this direct mode of confrontation with the speaker is meant to capture our own imaginations. Walton's quest becomes our own quest here, as his subjective report is doubled in our response to it.[10] By challenging us to assent to Walton's precarious schemes, by tapping our own desire for purpose and meaning, to say nothing about excitement, Shelley ensures our own involvement in the development of her tale and our private horror at its reverberations.

"Do I not deserve to accomplish some great purpose?" Walton asks his sister. And in an ejaculation that is riddled with self-doubt, he exposes the embarrassing truth that this question is not rhetorical: "Oh, that some encouraging voice would answer in the affirmative" (17). This need for affirmation very quickly becomes focused in a single desire: "You may deem me romantic, my dear sister, but I bitterly feel the want of a friend" (19).

Veeder considers the homosexual overtones of such assertions but decides that "for Robert [Walton], Victor [Frankenstein], and Percy [Shelley], the primary significance of the male bond is narcissistic. . . . Male love is thus one stage closer to the self-embrace which is the true goal of Prometheans and the chief reason . . . for Frankenstein's creation of the monster" (88).[11] But if Walton has been desperate for an understanding friend "who could sympathise" (19), he finds one in Veeder and in other readers and critics who have found him engaging enough to attempt to explain his function here (see Veeder, especially 81–89). And, more importantly, he finds that friend in each and every reader who answers his plea for affirmation with silent assent. For even if we distance ourselves from Walton with critical mockery, we listen to his tale and think about his predicament. The narcissism that he displays in his plea for understanding is, however biographically interesting for the author, another attempt to engage our interest and support for this adventure. Walton promises in return a report from the Coleridgean "land of mist and snow" (21); what more enticement do we need?

Walton, moreover, establishes his qualifications for such an enterprise: "A belief in the marvellous, intertwined in all my projects, . . . hurries me out of the common pathways of men, even to the wild sea and unvisited regions I am about to explore" (21–22). The power of Walton's *belief* not only qualifies him singularly for the encounter he is about to undergo; but also it reminds us where we are and what is expected of us. Belief is in fact what Walton's letters are all about, and the language of belief animates his reports and teaches us how to enter this world of the unknown.

By participating in Walton's quest, we are prepared for the central focus of the novel; and by attending to his use of language here, we learn something about the epistemology of horror in *Frankenstein*. Walton's syntactical pomposity, his hyperbole, vivid description, imaginative figuration, rhetorical questioning, ejaculation, exclamation—all these modes of expression suggest the "flashes, enigmas, short cuts, incompletion, tangles, and cuts" that Kristeva describes as the "crying-out" narrative theme of the horror of abjection (141).

Frankenstein answers Walton's desire for a friend. "For my own part," Walton says, "I begin to love him as a brother; and his constant and deep grief fills me with sympathy and compassion" (27). There is much that is suggestive about this immediate sympathy between Walton and Frankenstein, but to emphasize the mere fact of homosexuality would be to miss its larger significance. For Walton must become a passive receptacle for Frankenstein's grief, more a symbolic sexual object than a literal one. In doing so, he fulfills his own responsive role and establishes an "I-Thou" receptivity that answers his belief with a mystifying and transforming, that is, with a mythic, experience.

Walton's presentation of Frankenstein's own narration recalls the moment of vision that Shelley recounted in her Introduction:

> Even now, as I commence my task, his full-toned voice swells in my ears; his lustrous eyes dwell on me with all their melancholy sweetness; I see his thin hand raised in animation, while the lineaments of his face are irradiated by the soul within. Strange and harrowing must be his story. (31)

Walton's evocative style is his way of recreating this moment for his sister, and for us. But the terms are so clearly sexualized that they would be confusing if we did not understand that Walton's enthralled receptivity is the only possible response to Frankenstein's commanding authority. This is not sexuality in a merely physical sense, however; it is rather the sexuality of narrative, the intercourse of fictional belief. Walton must be fully receptive to the "strange and harrowing" story that Frankenstein has to tell; he has to subject his own subjectivity to the power of this Other in an "I-Thou" act of union, which allows him to transcend the limits of his own personality. Critics dismiss Walton as a pale version of Frankenstein, but who else could elicit this tale from the embittered creator and who else could teach us so precisely how to read it?

Walton's receptivity is rooted in his ability to accept what is strange and wonderful, his belief in the marvelous. Frankenstein has prepared Walton by challenging this ability:"Were we among the tamer scenes of nature, I might fear to encounter your unbelief, perhaps your ridicule; but many things will appear possible in these wild and mysterious regions, which would provoke the laughter of those unacquainted with the ever-varied powers of nature" (30). Surely our own receptivity, our own power of belief is being challenged here as well.

This "frame," then, introduces us into the world of *Frankenstein* and makes its ontological assumptions accessible to us. Newman speaks of "framing's double logic, the tendency of the frame simultaneously to establish boundaries and to announce, even to invite, their violation" (154). Walton seems to offer his own passivity as a way of breaking down the boundaries between subject and object and suffusing them with the glow of imaginative transfiguration. Just as Shelley was receptive to her midnight vision and we have been receptive to the authority of that very personal tale, Walton opens up the possibility of Gothic fiction by agreeing to listen.[12]

If "the short story breaks up the familiar life-world of the everyday, defamiliarizes our assumption that reality is simply the conceptual construct we take it to be" (May 333)—if it dramatizes through such defamiliarization and doubt the state of mind that Kristeva calls abjection—then surely such a technique is at work in the opening pages of *Frankenstein.* Walton's letter begins to confuse our sense of inside and outside here, as the image of sexual receptivity graphically suggests, and to employ a language that can answer that new sense of reality, alive to the possibility of the subject/object collapse. Shelley accomplishes this by means of her own special version of "I-Thou," in which belief works to undermine all our assumptions about reality and perception.

Frankenstein's tale begins with a description of his happy but obsessive youth:

> It was the secrets of heaven and earth that I desired to learn; and whether it was the outward substance of things, or the inner spirit of nature and the mysterious soul of man that occupied me, still my enquiries were directed to the metaphysical, or, in its highest sense, the physical secrets of the world. (37)

In his "fervent longing to penetrate the secrets of nature"(39), Frankenstein attempts to break down the rigid borders of selfhood and to convert the subject/object dichotomy of his world into a visionary "I-Thou." In speaking of the subject/object division as formative, Kristeva asks, "How can one prevent its misfires from leading either to the secret confinement of archaic narcissism, or to the indifferent scattering of objects that are experienced as false" (46). Clearly Victor Frankenstein is in danger of that first confinement, trapped in a subject/object paralysis that renders him remote from experience and unable to defy the conventional limits of privacy. This "secret confinement" suggests a narrative limitation as well, for as long as subject and object are opposed, Gothic fiction remains remote and unsatisfying.

Frankenstein the novel, however, dissolves this subject/object barrier, and in doing so, defies the conventional limits of the novel form and opens a new range of narrative possibilities. For Horace Walpole, "the great resources of fancy" had been "dammed up" by the forces of the conventional. Mary Shelley here shows how to break down those barriers and release the expressive potential of Gothic fiction. Unlike Walpole, whose dream remains remote and unrealized, Shelley has managed to create a tale to harrow up our souls.

Frankenstein's moment of discovery helps to demonstrate how subtly she accomplishes this:

> Now I was led to examine the cause and progress of this decay, and forced to spend days and nights in vaults and charnel-houses. My attention was fixed upon every object the most insupportable to the delicacy of the human feelings. I saw how the fine form of man was degraded and wasted; I beheld the corruption of death succeed to the blooming cheek of life; I saw how the worm inherited the wonders of the eye and brain. I paused, examining and analysing all the minutiae of causation, as exemplified in the change from life to death, and death to life, until from the midst of this darkness a sudden light broke in upon me—a light so brilliant and wondrous, yet so simple, that while I became dizzy with the immensity of the prospect which it illustrated, I was surprised, that among so many men of genius who had directed their enquiries towards the same science, that I alone should be reserved to discover so astonishing a secret.
>
> Remember, I am not recording the vision of a madman. . . . I succeeded in discovering the cause of generation and life; nay, more, I became myself capable of bestowing animation upon lifeless matter. (51–52)

Knowledge for Frankenstein is that "elsewhere as tempting as it is condemned" (Kristeva 1), a "journey, during the night, the end of which keeps receding" (8), and this eerie description embodies the culmination as well as the corruption of his quest. Because we are on this journey with Frankenstein, we attend to his process of discovery very carefully. It is as dazzling as it is horrifying, but exhilaration is at every stage undercut by the narrative procedure. Frankenstein's obsession with the boundary between life and death, his minute analysis of the sources of his abjection, suggests a hatred of nature—his own nature as well as Nature—and an inability to bring his knowledge into relation with himself.

This passage is often compared to that famous moment of narcissistic poeticizing in Percy Shelley's "Alastor." But the tone of the poet's confession in "Alastor" is strikingly different from that in *Frankenstein*:

> Mother of this unfathomable world!
> Favour my solemn song, for I have loved

Thee ever, and thee only: I have watched
Thy shadow, and the darkness of thy steps,
And my heart ever gazes on the depth
Of thy deep mysteries. I have made my bed
In charnels and on coffins, where black death
Keeps record of the trophies won from thee,
Hoping to still these obstinate questionings
Of thee and thine, by forcing some lone ghost
Thy messenger, to render up the tale
Of what we are. (lines 18–29)

In this passage, we see the basis of the mythopoesis with which Shelley will be able to break through the boundaries of his narcissism. The poet addresses Nature directly, transforming personification into a personal encounter. As Bloom says in his discussion of "To Night," Shelley is "not personifying the phenomenon of night; that is, he is not animating what is *for him* not animate" (*Shelley's Mythmaking* 6). The "I-Thou" configuration creates the means of meeting the challenge of abjection and confronting the unknown. Even if the poet does not succeed, his act of love toward Nature promises him the possibility of future success. Scientific knowledge is secondary to personal knowledge, and the poet remains in mystery but outside himself.

Victor Frankenstein's investigations are more ghoulish and more successful, but they have nothing to do with poetry. (Indeed, he will have been responsible for the death of poetry, in the figure of Clerval, before his quest is completed.) Oddly passive in his pursuits—"led to examine" and "forced to spend"—his language suggests more a private compulsion than a personal receptivity. Because his interest is scientific rather than poetic, his relation to the world could be called "I-It." His sense of the subject/object split is rigid and isolating. Rather than seducing Nature, as the poet does, Frankenstein uses the material of his compulsive investigation to "[pursue] nature to her hiding-places" (54) and to violate her privacy. It is not an act of love; it is rape. In "examining and analysing all the minutiae of causation," Frankenstein achieves knowledge but he sacrifices the "delicacy of the human feelings" and becomes inhuman in his discovery.

If we attend to Frankenstein, it seems to me, we feel slightly polluted by this violation of the bounds of nature. It is unsettling. Oddly, in the moment of the most brilliant illumination, Frankenstein questions his unique position and the nature of his triumph. He even reminds us of the possibility of madness, as if we would question the bold direct assertion with which the passage ends. The lightning flash of illumination bursts into this thunderous assertion of power. We understand this struggle to overcome the boundaries of isolation, and we understand what it means to see our desires turn to corruption. Therefore we can believe in Frankenstein and even make the terms of his horror our own.

Kristeva uncannily describes the time when the abject is a "magnetized pole of covetousness." But, she says, "The clean and proper (in the sense of incorporated and incorporable) becomes filthy, the sought-after turns into the banished, fascination into shame. Then, forgotten time crops up suddenly and condenses into a flash of lightning an operation that, if it were thought out, would involve bringing together the two opposite terms but, on account of that flash, is discharged like thunder. The time of abjection," she says, "is double: a time of oblivion and thunder, of veiled infinity and the moment when revelation bursts forth" (8–9). Frankenstein's knowledge is fatal to his happiness—he never emerges from the abjection into which he now sinks—an abyss separating him from the world and condemning him to the isolation of his knowledge.

After Frankenstein has confronted his own hideous creation and fled from its frightening stare, he has a dream that complements Mary Shelley's original Gothic dream:

> I slept, indeed, but I was disturbed by the wildest dreams. I thought I saw Elizabeth, in the bloom of health, walking in the street of Ingolstadt. Delighted and surprised, I embraced her; but as I imprinted the first kiss on her lips, they became livid with the hue of death; her features appeared to change, and I thought that I held the corpse of my dead mother in my arms; a shroud enveloped her form, and I saw the grave-worms crawling in the folds of the flannel. I started from my sleep with horror. (58)

This dream has been much discussed, and I see no reason to rehearse its harrowing psychological implications. It is worth noting, however, how typically Gothic are these images of incestuous matricide and how deftly Shelley has introduced a putrefying corpse into her narrative.[13] Without the squeamishness of Radcliffe or the sensationalism of Lewis (whose scene of incestuous matricide in *The Monk* is one of the most intense moments of Gothic confrontation in his text), Shelley has depicted Victor Frankenstein embracing the corrupted corpse of his dead mother. Before we look into Shelley's own family experience, we must remember what she was reading (she had just finished *The Monk*) and what readers she was appealing to. The fact that so many critics have spent so much energy in arguing over the meaning of this scene suggests how fully successful she has been. It works, moreover, because we believe in Victor Frankenstein, and our belief liberates our literary preconceptions and inherent formal snobbery, compelling us to a "new perception of things" (Jauss 41).

The passage continues:

> I started from my sleep with horror; a cold dew covered my forehead, my teeth chattered, and every limb became convulsed.

The opening rendition of private horror is not so different from Raymond's sleepless horror at the Bleeding Nun in *The Monk*,[14] but as the passage proceeds, it becomes different enough to convince many critics that they are not reading a Gothic work at all. It ceases to follow the rationale of horror and begins to assume a quality of haunting rare in other Gothic novels:

> . . . when, by the dim and yellow light of the moon, as it forced its way through the window shutters, I beheld the wretch—the miserable monster whom I had created. He held up the curtain of the bed; and his eyes, if eyes they may be called, were fixed on me. His jaws opened, and he muttered some inarticulate sounds, while a grin wrinkled his cheeks. He might have spoken, but I did not hear; one hand was stretched out, seemingly to detain me, but I escaped, and rushed down stairs. I took refuge in the courtyard belonging to the house which I inhabited; where I remained during the rest of the night, walking up and down in the greatest agitation, listening attentively, catching and fearing each sound as if it were to announce the approach of the demoniacal corpse to which I had so miserably given life. (58)

Moonlight is used here to create a world between light and darkness and to suffuse the scene with its unsettling glare. Just as the animated corpse seems a figure of death-in-life, so the moonlight is a light that suggests darkness—later it becomes metaphorically associated with the creature. Here, it "force[s] its way through the window shutters," as a way of suggesting that Frankenstein cannot shut out the light of the knowledge he has discovered; nor can he himself hide from the pursuit of his creation, who here peeps into the bed in which he has sought refuge. A waking dream? The detail of observation—the eyes, the grin, the hand—all suggest the grotesque reality of this vision and convince us that Frankenstein has really seen what he describes. More importantly, the emphasis is on response rather than observation. The personal pronoun "I" is the real center of attention, and the creature exists as an object, to be observed, to be feared, and to be rejected. This final portrayal of anxiety suggests that this haunting reaches beyond Gothic convention into the precincts of private horror. If we recognize a special quality to this anxiety, it resides perhaps in the last phrase: "the demoniacal corpse to which I had so miserably given life." This phrase dramatizes the horror directly, for "I" stands between the corpse and life and becomes the focus of what is growing desolation.

The corpse represents "fundamental pollution" in our culture, Kristeva says, a "body without soul," that the Bible emphasizes is to be "excluded from God's *territory*" (109). Frankenstein defies that taboo, but does so at the expense of his own subjectivity, which becomes polluted with the misery he himself creates. The object of his quest becomes an aspect of his subjectivity, and he is lost:

> I passed the night wretchedly. Sometimes my pulse beat so quickly and hardly, that I felt the palpitation of every artery; at others, I nearly sank to the ground through languor and extreme weakness. Mingled with this horror, I felt the bitterness of disappointment; dreams that had been my food . . . were now become a hell to me. (58–59)

Frankenstein's private hell, with which the passage closes, is as realistic a haunting as we find in the Gothic novel. He attends to the physical dimensions of his horror, but the bitterness he describes results from the knowledge that it is the power of his own imagination that has been the measure of his undoing.

Shelley achieves novelistic success on her own terms because she has kept her haunting within the subjective focus and has emphasized less the delineation of the "monster" and more the terms of subjective response. Just when we might ourselves become focused on the creature, she insists on dealing with the response of the creator. Therefore the creation itself takes on a psychological dimension that gives the fantasy an otherwise inaccessible legitimacy. We suspend the empirical checks that we employ in novel reading, because Shelley has structured events here with the rationale of a tale. All that matters is that the horror itself is convincing; and, as it is depicted here, it could hardly be more so. Shelley has successfully transformed the novel form to achieve her Gothic ends. If there is an "ontological gap" between the everyday world of the novel and the world of the tale, Shelley has brought the novel form across that gap and transformed it in her mythic narrative.[15]

Frankenstein constantly reminds us of the possibility that he is mad; again and again he repeats the unbelievability of his tale. Yet no one suggests that the monster is just a private fantasy. We read instead that the creature is an alter ego, not that he does not exist, but that he exists in order to be interpreted. Interpretation, however, already concedes belief. Frankenstein seems to think that no one will give credence to his tale; that anyone whom he approached would consider his tale the raving of a madman. Yet critics are constantly busy explaining in just what ways the creature is "real," for Shelley has conceived her tale so that we are incapable of dismissing it as madness.[16]

We do not doubt the existence of this creature from beyond the grave, because he makes so much sense. On the other hand, we never stop asking what Shelley means by creating him. He becomes so readily the material of psychoanalytic readings that imaginatively Shelley must have already understood the private implications of the work of her Gothic contemporaries, for only those confusions and inconsistencies that hamper the effectiveness of the Gothic novel are here avoided. *Frankenstein* baffles critics not because it is incoherent but because its coherence so ingeniously undermines our perspective. We are seduced, and abandoned.

Of course not all critics interpret *Frankenstein* psychologically. Those who do not, however, only expand the possible interpretations that Shelley's tale encourages. Surely there is every reason to think that Victor Frankenstein's haunting suggests the ruthlessness of patriarchy (Hodges), that Shelley felt that her interest in political despotism makes the novel a "feminist critique of her age" (Scott 193), and that a key concern here is the limitations of the "utilitarian vision of an engineered society" (Spivak 256). But this is the nature of the tale that Shelley has conceived. Its "meaning" is not determined by anything in the narrative, although various interpretations are possible. If most have been psychosexual, that says more about the nature of interpretation than about the meaning of *Frankenstein*. As Iser says, "Textual repertoires and strategies simply offer a frame within which the reader must construct for himself the aesthetic object. Textual structures and structured acts of comprehension are therefore the two poles in the act of communication, whose success will depend on the degree in which the text establishes itself as a correlative in the reader's consciousness" (*Act of Reading* 107).

The center of the novel, the inner layer of narrative, is of course the creature's own story. Victor Frankenstein calls his creature "my own spirit let loose from the grave" (77), but this is hardly how we apprehend the creature as he tells his tale. His narrative ability rivals that of his maker. He speaks with an "eloquence" that is remarked several times by Frankenstein, as a warning as to where the real power in this work lies.[17]

Frankenstein meets his creature in the shadow of Mont Blanc, that image of natural power which for Percy Shelley suggests "the secret Strength of things / Which governs thought" ("Mont Blanc," lines 139–40). For Frankenstein, "These sublime and magnificent scenes afforded me the greatest consolation that I was capable of receiving" (96). Clouds cover the peaks, but he determines to "penetrate their misty veil, and seek them in their cloudy retreats" (96). Such language recalls his earlier frantic pursuit of nature. But the nature that he has so rudely forced now knows him too well, and it answers in the voice of the shadowy creature himself. "I am thy creature;" he exclaims, "I ought to be thy Adam; but I am rather the fallen angel, whom thou drivest from joy. . . . Hear my tale" (100–101). The disarming intimacy of his address, which gives the "I-Thou" configuration direct expression, suggests that the creature knows the degree to which his own subjectivity is dependent on that of this Other, his creator. But he has from the first been receptive to the fact of that Otherness in a way that Frankenstein has not. His response is natural, as are his demands. These are truly acts of "self-consciousness" in Bakhtin's terms (287), and they suggest the mystical otherness implicit in the Gothic: Buber suggests that anyone who "takes his stand in relation shares in a reality, that is, in a being that neither merely belongs to him nor merely lies outside him" (Buber 63; see Bloom, *Shelley's Mythmaking* 6). Frankenstein's creature understands that his only hope resides in this man who reviles him. His tale, therefore, represents this hope. It is a tale told to gain "compassion," but it is also told to challenge ("Listen to me; and then, if you can, and if you will, destroy the work of your hands") and to threaten ("On you it rests, whether I quit forever the neighbourhood of man, and lead a harmless life, or become the scourge of your fellow-creatures, and the author of your own speedy ruin" [101]). It has a clear enough moral to satisfy the critical strictures of the editor of *The Quarterly Review*. But placed in the center of Shelley's Gothic structure, it becomes the central version of abjection, isolation, and horror. Its simplicity makes it threatening and profound.

When Frankenstein's creature inhabits his hovel and peers into the domestic secrets of the De Lacey family, he is only mimicking the modus vivendi of his creator. Instead of the secrets of Nature, however, he learns the secrets of human nature: His education is the converse of that of Frankenstein. He speaks of old De Lacey's "benevolent smiles" (110) and the children's "trait of kindness" (111) before he can even understand their speech. And when he does begin to "unravel the mystery of their reference" (112), among the "most familiar objects of discourse" are "the words, *fire, milk, bread,* and *wood,*" the cottagers' names, and their relations: "The girl was called *sister,* or *Agatha;* and the youth *Felix, brother,* or *son*" and "the old man had only one [name], which was *father*" (112). Heat, sustenance, and familial relations: These are what this creature first learns. This is the elemental world which in contrast to Frankenstein's mad pursuits seems to form the center of the novel: kindly, warm, and protected. The creature participates in this world vicariously and grows with its sorrows and its joys. The creature's growing self-awareness, however, represents at the same time a growing knowledge of his own monstrousness: "I had never yet seen a being resembling me, or who claimed any intercourse with me. What was I? The question again recurred, to be answered only with groans." (121).

Gilbert and Gubar suggest that "the monster's narrative is a philosophical meditation on what it means to be born without a 'soul' or a history, as well as an exploration of what it feels like to be . . . a thing, an other, a creature of the second sex" (235). I agree that "the drastic shift in point of view that the nameless monster's monologue represents probably constitutes *Frankenstein*'s most striking technical *tour de force*" (235), and I see no reason to resist their argument that the horror here is the horror of sexual difference. But if patriarchy fails in this novel, the terms of its failure suggest a human failing and not just a sexual one.

In his brief reading course in Western Civilization, the creature pursues *Paradise Lost,* Plutarch's *Lives,* and Goethe's *The Sorrows of Young Werther.* He is introduced to public and private virtue beyond his personal experiences in the hut, and tries to use his reading to learn about himself, to place himself in history and human experience. But this creature comes to understand that he has no relation other than that with his creator. This bond will not admit the consolation of family or the contextualizing breadth of the human community. It is as private and subjective as the Gothic experience itself. The creature, for all his receptivity, becomes as isolated, as abject, as his creator, destined to work out his identity in relation to him and to transform the meaning of solitude.

The creature learns that his unnameability deprives him of the role he seeks within the family. De Lacey, in the moment of crisis, asks the one question that the creature has not learned to answer: "'Great God!' exclaimed the old man, 'who are you?'" (135). Critics have suggested that this De Lacey family represents a lost and lamented ideal in the novel and that Shelley is using it to criticize the isolationist heroics of her poet-husband.[18] The creature's peremptory rejection by the kindly and benevolent De Laceys gains him our sympathies because the family carelessly rejects what it cannot name. This scene of rejection is violent and unyielding: "Felix darted forward, and with supernatural force tore me from his father . . . dashed me to the ground, and struck me violently with a stick" (135). Whether sentimental fiction or patriarchal society are at fault here, the scene is brutal and damaging.

Even this "happy" family, then, is in the end ruthless and self-protective. Its members reject what they do not understand, in this case a nameless and hideous creature who has emerged from the world of shadows to provide them with needed firewood and to clear their paths of snow. They take such aid for granted and reject its source. This act of rejection suggests the true limits of the domestic ideal, of the family itself, and even of the ontology of the everyday world. Far from holding up this familial circle as an ideal, Shelley seems to be exposing its own monstrosity.

What the creature comes to understand, then, both through his reading and his own private experience is the meaning in human terms of his difference: rejection and isolation, abjection and horror. Just as the domestic narrative is a closed form that cannot admit the "resources of fancy," so this happy family cannot admit the forces of darkness that give it life. Simple happiness comes to be seen as a limited and niggardly quality, because domestic tranquillity depends on a narrow conception of experience and a limited vision. The narrative in which such happiness is transcribed is ruthless in what it excludes and restrictive in what it offers. The family questions and rejects the possibility of transformation that the creature offers, just as the editor of *The Quarterly Review* refuses to acknowledge the transformation of fiction that this novel represents.[19]

The real haunting therefore seems to reside in the seeming domestic receptivity of what is in fact a closed domestic unit. The monster's plea for love and understanding contrasts vividly with the family's false promise of solace and peace. "Happy" Felix is transported by fury; Agatha faints; Safie flees: The family dissolves into a horrifyingly disfigured version of itself and then disappears.

When the creature sets fire to this scene of his innocence and hope, he is dissolving the bonds he never could have had. This ritual burning seems much like a ghoulish rite of passage:

> As the night advanced, a fierce wind arose from the woods, and quickly dispersed the clouds that had loitered in the heavens: the blast tore along like a mighty avalanche, and produced a kind of insanity in my spirits, that burst all bounds of reason and reflection. I lighted the dry branch of a tree, and danced with fury around the devoted cottage, my eyes still fixed on the western horizon, the edge of which the moon nearly touched. A part of its orb was at length hid, and I waved my brand; it sunk, and, with a loud scream, I fired the straw, and heath, and bushes, which I had collected. The wind fanned the fire, and the cottage was quickly enveloped by the flames, which clung to it, and licked it with their forked and destroying tongues. (138–39)

This is too elaborate a description for the point to be mere rage and destruction. It is the creature's first destructive act, an act of self-realization that is carried out in a frenzy that we now understand. The creature here reverts to the elemental power from which he has sprung. The "insanity in [his] spirits, that burst all bounds of reason and reflection" is a natural power: This is who he is. The moonlit madness and the scream comprise a moment of Gothic intensity that has rarely been remarked.[20] The "forked and destroying tongues" of fire suggest that this destructive urge has sprung from the conversational duplicity of the De Lacey family. Their honeyed words are here revealed in all their destructive power. This rage has also sprung from the kind of self-betrayal that the creature's attraction to the form of domesticity represents. This is a moment of transfiguration for the creature himself and for the terms of the narrative. It is a moment of personal liberation that suggests as well an explosion of the limits of narrative convention. Now the creature can say that he stands with "the world before me" (139): He has given up all worldly attachments in favor of his own will. The narrative can now assume the form of his own unconventional power.

The scene works because Shelley has suspended disbelief in such a way that we hear these ravings as if we were listening to the power of nature itself. This is the unnameable center of the novel, not the domestic tranquillity of the De Laceys, but this chilling scream of self-recognition on the part of Frankenstein's wretched creation. All the potential horror of the tale is brought out directly in this revolutionary scene. The sentimentality fades away at this moment of self-confrontation, and the horrifying truth of private experience shatters conventionality with a new Gothic power. Critics have said that the monster tells a sentimental tale, but what really happens is that he listens to one, and it almost destroys him. Instead of fitting into a happy family community, this creature gives in to the elemental madness that is his real power. This is the real hero of *Frankenstein*—a natural force that transforms the circumscribed terms of narration into the open and limitless potential of self-realization. Narrative reaches into the unnameable and redefines the terms of fictional experience.

Once he has accepted the truth of his nature, Frankenstein's creature becomes indestructible and increasingly vindictive. The power of nature is not a tame or friendly power after all. But his destructiveness is not arbitrary:

> Unfeeling, heartless creator! You had endowed me with perceptions and passions, and then cast me abroad an object for the scorn and horror of mankind. But on you only had I any claim for pity and redress, and from you I determined to seek that justice which I vainly attempted to gain from any other being that wore the human form. (139)

An "unfeeling, heartless creator" has "cast [the creature] abroad [as] an object." This is what Frankenstein's act of creation embodied—a ruthless possession of nature that refused to recognize any subjectivity but his own. He still sees his creation as an object and refuses to give it value. It is a cruel God that not only turns his back on his creation but also fails to acknowledge the terms of his existence. Frankenstein attempted to negate the creation by ignoring it and hoping it would go away. That is, instead of confronting the fact of intersubjectivity that his act of creation implied, he ran from it in horror, and now the object has returned to destroy him.

Frankenstein feels that to grant the creature subjective presence would be to accept his own final isolation and despair. That he cannot do. He clings to the solace of family and affection until all those closest to him have been slaughtered by his own creation. He becomes obsessed with an everyday world that the creature has blasted and cursed. The violence of the creature's vision of experience teaches Frankenstein finally what it means to be human. It teaches, that is, the horror implicit in life and the terror of all that lies beyond human understanding, translating a private Gothic experience into publicly horrifying terms. It is Frankenstein's own version of a mystical experience.

The murders that ensue are a sign that violence has been released into the world. It is Frankenstein's violence, in that he created it, but it is also a natural violence that is beyond his power. Veeder suggests that the order of the deaths suggests a "scale of increasing intimacy" (153), and that the creature's ultimate goal is the destruction of the father. Because Victor himself is so quick to feel guilt about these deaths, the intention of the creature is often ignored. He is not driven by the will of Frankenstein; rather, he bases his action on his own emotion. He kills William out of a spirit of "eternal revenge" (142) and frames Justine out of frustration and fear: "The murder I have committed because I am forever robbed of all that she could give me, she shall atone" (144). These murders of a child and a servant/ward—two members of the family group isolated from the father (Veeder 152)— suggest an attack on the family itself. In their very distance from the father, these characters represent the protective quality of family and its generosity, those qualities of domestic narrative that the creature has already so vividly exposed as false. Justine's death has the further virtue, from this thematic perspective, of proving the falsity of law, of human judgment, and of the family unit itself. (Alphonse never believes her story.) Unlike Lewis or Maturin who so often introduce social concerns in contradiction to their Gothic obsessions, Shelley makes these social observations central to the Gothic experience she describes: Basic human inhumanity finally determines the Gothic nature of these killings. Indeed, once the creature has placed the incriminating (familial) evidence on Justine, the judicial and religious systems work perfectly: Justine is even forced to confess. No horror the "monster" perpetrates is any worse than this.

Furthermore, Frankenstein's familial relations, his attempt to recover happiness, make him vulnerable to the creature's attacks. To the degree to which he attempts to please his family and his friend, he brings destruction to them and pain to himself. The last deaths, those of Elizabeth and his father, are only his own fault in the sense that he tries to cling to some ideal of domestic happiness. His knowledge and power have placed him beyond the family, and by attempting to return he brings only the pathos of his own destructive self-contempt. These deaths are tormenting in themselves, but for Frankenstein, guilty reflection makes them even more harrowing. His own sense of responsibility and helplessness is what makes his suffering so great and his isolation so complete. "No one was near me who soothed me with the gentle voice of love" (178), Frankenstein says after Clerval's murder. But this adult isolation is a lesson that experience should long before have taught him. His very brand of heroism and genius of course can mean nothing but isolation and death.

The creature mocks all Frankenstein's attempts at grief and especially his attempts to harness nature to his own power:

> "By the sacred earth on which I kneel, by the shades that wander near me, by the deep and eternal grief that I feel, I swear; and by thee, O Night, and the spirits that preside over thee, to pursue the daemon, who caused this misery, until he or I shall perish in mortal conflict. . . . "
>
> I was answered through the stillness of the night by a loud and fiendish laugh. (202)

The creature can laugh because Frankenstein attempts to employ myth-making language without really feeling its power. It is too late for him to commune with forces outside himself. His one mastery of that power he refuses to recognize, as the creature knows and his mockery here suggests. That does not mean that Shelley herself mocks any poetic exuberance of this kind. These powerful expressions of belief are only meaningless when used hypocritically. Elsewhere she has shown how uncannily meaningful they can be.

The final chase is a further mockery of the "mortal conflict" that Frankenstein predicts. Frankenstein is kept on the trail of his prey, no longer affecting any role other than that of a proud and contemptuous hunter. But of course he is really the hunted: He only survives through the creature's kindness and his contempt. Frankenstein's obsession has now taken full possession of him, and his horror is played out in this parody of his earlier investigations. Indeed, the form of the novel is repeated in this final chase, the hero in mad pursuit of an elusive communion with the unknown, when in fact a tormenting intimacy is already in place, to his utter frustration. This pursuit is doomed, and Frankenstein is at last left to his isolation, "drifting on a scattered piece of ice" (208). The frame closes—we are brought back to the beginning of the novel—as Frankenstein dwindles, weakens, and finally dies. There is no success for Frankenstein: He remains trapped in the delusions of his own subjectivity.

We are in danger of feeling isolation and despair ourselves at the novel's close—none of the lightning flash of creativity here, just an abject and pathetic end. In the final few pages, however, the central narrative and the frame are inverted, as Walton and the creature stand face to face. "Blasted as thou wert," the creature says to the corpse of Frankenstein, "my agony was still superior to thine" (223). This odd reversal of the creation scene suggests that Frankenstein and his creature have at last achieved the consummation of their death-in-life/life-in-death existence. There remains only the creature's own funeral pyre, a self-assertive/self-destructive gesture signifying the power of what he is. Wailing in grief at his loss and addressing the withered corpse, the creature achieves an oddly heroic stature, more admirable, really, than Frankenstein has ever been. The creature speaks in human terms, but the power of his final suffering is surely superhuman, titanic. (Perhaps it is the creature who is Promethean—brutally tormented for his attempt at doing good.) His suffering earns him the right to be considered human at last, but even Walton realizes that he is more than this. "I shall ascend my funeral pile triumphantly, and exult in the agony of the torturing flames," the creature finally cries. "My ashes will be swept into the sea by the winds" (223). Thus he realizes his mythic power in nature, which has been reflected in the grandeur of his goodness and his villainy.

The novel ends with Walton's very careful report of his confrontation, a new level of challenge and belief. Walton turns back from his quest in part because he realizes what mysteries lie beyond his experience. *Frankenstein* has evoked that same sense of mystery for the reader, challenging each of us with our own fears of the unknown. As we watch the creature lose himself in "darkness and distance" at the novel's close, we realize that Shelley has brought a creature from her "world of shadows" to haunt us in our own. Her "hideous progeny" challenges our complacency and forces us to question our assumptions about the nature of experience. She has emphasized the personal nature of this tale to carry us into an uncanny world, strange and defamiliarizing. The enigma that is central, the enigma of the creature himself, challenges our sense of the limits of narrative—our own as well as those of novelistic convention. The author has recounted in subjective and persuasive terms the nature of her own dream, and out of that she has created a monster both pathetic and frightening. She has worked out a narrative form that keeps us from rejecting the fantasy, and we are trapped in our response, both to create the horror for ourselves and to come to terms with it. From the first moment, we are subject to the workings of her imagination. We are ourselves "seduced" by narrative here, and we are left reeling with the "unnameable" power of the tale.

3

Gothic Narrative in *Wuthering Heights*

Emily Brontë's remarkable novel has often been placed within the Gothic tradition in fiction, and it is indeed from within that tradition that this harrowing tale of a solitary gypsy youth who first liberates and then nearly destroys a pair of Yorkshire families finds its conventional vocabulary and its range of images.[1] But Brontë was not merely attempting to resuscitate the graying features of a dying form. For like no other writer of her age, Emily Brontë in *Wuthering Heights* looks to the roots of Gothic fiction, uncovers the most deeply embedded formal problems, and works to establish a solution both powerful and persuasive.

As I have argued, the problems so widely noted in the Gothic novel are the result of a basic contradiction between novelistic structure and affective intention.[2] Brontë was not only aware of such formal inconsistency in the Gothic novel, she seems to have structured her novel both to mirror these tensions and to demonstrate the formal means of their resolution.[3] Even more effectively than *Frankenstein*, *Wuthering Heights* directly confronts the formal dilemma facing every Gothic novelist and works out with literary exactitude the means of resolving the conflict between Gothic intention and novel form.

Brontë does this in the first place by writing instead of a conventional novel an extended tale, as critics have in some sense noted. Frye, for instance, suggests that "in novels that we think of as typical, like those of Jane Austen, plot and dialogue are closely linked to the conventions of the comedy of manners. The conventions of *Wuthering Heights* are linked rather with the tale and the ballad." Although he goes on to call *Wuthering Heights* a "romance"—"on the whole better than tale, which appears to fit a somewhat shorter form"—Frye gets at the quality of *Wuthering Heights* when he suggests that such a work "radiates a glow of subjective intensity that the novel lacks" and represents what is "naturally a more revolutionary form than the novel," a form that can be distinguished by the fact that "something nihilistic and untamable is likely to keep breaking out of [its] pages" (304–5).

To distinguish novel and tale in this case is to note important differences between Brontë's novel and those of her contemporaries, differences that seem to me only to be clouded by the use of the term "romance." Brontë seems so interested in exploring the nature of fictional narrative and so clearly attentive to every feature of fictional exposition in *Wuthering Heights* that to see it as a "romantic" novel is neither to do justice to its formal inventiveness nor to begin to explain the sources of its peculiar power.

Such an argument helps to explain, first, the odd structure of *Wuthering Heights*. Critics have described the frame structure of the novel carefully and have argued its function in the affective structure of the work.[4] Brontë's decision to employ internal narrators who tell their own accounts of the action that transpires is in itself a Gothic gesture. These private accounts have talelike force in that they attempt to explore the subjective and the personal and to give coherent expression to much that is incoherent and beyond understanding as well as interpretation. Unlike the internal narrators in such novels as *The Monk* or *Melmoth* or even *Frankenstein,* however, Brontë's narrators are barely moved by the otherworldly threats that beset them. They are not Gothic heroes themselves, that is, paralyzed with terror and gasping with disgust. Instead, Lockwood and Nelly Dean are created out of the formal stuff of novels. As a result, they indirectly place the novelistic version of experience against something more remote and more powerful. In so creating them, Brontë challenges novelistic form with Gothic meaning as it had never before been challenged. Lockwood, it could be said, attempts to "novelize" the events he witnesses and indeed to force a novelistic resolution on the action; but his very failure to be convincing in this regard is the measure of the limitation of not only his response but also the version of literary representation for which he stands.[5] Lockwood's inadequacy, in other words, is not merely temperamental: It represents the failure of a certain kind of novelistic imagination that his failure both exposes and censures. Nelly, too, attempts to mold her material into a readily accessible novelistic form, and again her failure becomes itself a metaphor for the limits of interpretation.[6] By their presence, Lockwood and Nelly both distort the story by producing "truth" in their own likenesses and restrict its meaning by rejecting what they do not understand. Brontë in other words uses these novelistic characters to display the limits of the novel's own expressive power.

Lockwood's pathetic attempt to come to terms with the largely "second generation" household at Wuthering Heights has been richly remarked.[7] His structures of response, like those of other Gothic heroes before him, render him incapable of interpreting his experience correctly. In addition to mistaking a heap of dead rabbits for a family of kittens and assuming a marital relation between Heathcliff and the second Cathy, Lockwood demonstrates a general anxiety in the face of what he does not understand and an urge for meaning, which results in endless misconstruction. This anxiety is of course vividly represented in his attempt to "read" the various inscriptions that he discovers around his bed, and in his brutal reaction to the pleading Catherine Linton of his dream, whose wrist he rubs to and fro on the broken window pane "till the blood ran down and soaked the bed-clothes" (30). The repressed fear and aggression suggested by this dream begin to represent the kind of disfiguration of the tale that socializing, civilizing, contextualizing, novelizing versions of it perpetrate.[8] In other words, Lockwood is the first critic of *Wuthering Heights*, and as such he literally attempts to cut it to shreds.

The implications for the interpretation of Gothic fiction are unmistakable. Lockwood misinterprets because he overinterprets: He cannot resist the urge to contain the experience he encounters within the simplest and most mundane explanations, and those which of course say more about him than about the world he is encountering.[9] As with many critical responses to Gothic texts, Lockwood's urge is to simplify and explain away anything that mystifies him, and if it continues to worry him, to destroy it. It is not just that Lockwood is confused at the Heights, he is linguistically incapable of even the most basic understanding.

Challenged by Heathcliff to explain his midnight raving, Lockwood finds himself unwittingly incapable of using language in a way which Heathcliff can understand:

> "The truth is, sir, I passed the first part of the night in—" here, I stopped afresh—I was about to say "perusing those old volumes;" then it would have revealed my knowledge of their written, as well as their printed contents; so, correcting myself, I went on—"in spelling over the name scratched on that window-ledge. A monotonous occupation, calculated to set me asleep, like counting, or—"
>
> "What *can* you mean by talking in this way to *me!*" thundered

Heathcliff with savage vehemence. "How—how *dare* you, under
my roof—God! he's mad to speak so!" And he struck his forehead with rage. (32)

Lockwood begins this explanation of the immediate cause of his
dream by calling upon "truth." But of course truth is just what his
polite conversation is structured to evade. Lockwood's repression of the
truth and his mode of self-editing suggest at once the effeteness of
"literary" language as well as its duplicity. This language reveals more
than it hides, however, because its blithe urbanity is a measure of its
inability to contain the essential reality it has not even begun to understand. Heathcliff's reaction emphasizes both what Lockwood has said
and how he has said it. He accuses Lockwood of madness because he
seems so oblivious to the power behind his words. Lockwood feels indeed that he can control language as he chooses and here use it to lead
him through a difficult moment. To him Heathcliff's reaction clearly
seems as akin to madness as his own prattling does to Heathcliff.

Communication between these two characters therefore seems impossible, and critics have explained this circumstance variously.[10] But
what has been called an "epistemological disjunction between listeners and speakers" (Macovski 367), has profound implications on the
nature of narrative as well as the nature of the narrators. Jakobson's
distinction between what he calls "two aspects of language" is useful
in describing this disruption more specifically. For Jakobson, "the development of a discourse may . . . take place along two different semantic lines: one topic may lead to another either through their similarity or through their contiguity. The *metaphoric* way would be the
most appropriate term for the first case and the *metonymic* way for the
second, since they find their most condensed expression in metaphor
and metonym respectively. In aphasia one or the other of these two
processes is blocked. . . . "[11] In this case it seems that Lockwood suf-
fers what Jakobson would call a "similarity disorder," while Heathcliff
seems the victim of the converse "contiguity disorder." Lockwood, in
other words, sees little beyond the immediate contextualizing syntax
of his words, and he moves haphazardly through contiguous associations. Heathcliff, on the other hand, sees nothing but meanings here;
he reads profound significance into everything Lockwood carelessly
says. Lockwood is all structure and Heathcliff all content, as it were,
and it would take more than a midnight chat to bring them into real
communication. Their anger is indeed nothing more than the frustration they experience at seeming to speak the same language while
being constitutionally unable to understand each other.

I have described a similar tension in every Gothic novel, which results in a kind of literary aphasia, if you will, rendering literary expression both unsatisfying and self-defeating. In a sense, the very metonymical nature of the novel, inherently concerned with the contextualization of experience and the socialization of the private, formally contradicts the metaphorical demands of the Gothic, which began with a dream and developed by means of fantasy situations and characters, at times carefully developed and at times blandly automatic, but rarely fully integrated into the demands of the novel's content and scope. Here Brontë confronts these two linguistic, epistemlogical, formal modes—the modes I have been calling novel and tale— and suggests the problems that arise from subjecting one form of expression to the inevitable misinterpretation of the other. She suggests, furthermore, as we shall see, a means of resolving this seemingly insuperable dilemma.

To describe Lockwood, then, as an "unreliable narrator" is to distort his central function here. His ruthless distortions of the "truth" are part of his breeding. They emerge simply from what it means to be a member of society, a civilized human being. His interpretations therefore may be unreliable, but they are intrinsic to the nature of Brontë's enterprise. His superficiality offers us, as readers, a measure of what "civilization" cannot comprehend. Without Lockwood, Heathcliff would be beyond our powers of sympathy as well. Lockwood teaches us how not to understand Heathcliff, and by doing so he throws us into sympathy with and concern for the Gothic protagonist. In addition, Brontë uses him to teach us about reading, not just what Heathcliff is but how he is: That is really the question the novel seeks to answer.

Nelly Dean has also been accused of misinterpretation and manipulation.[12] She is without question unsympathetic to her "friends" Heathcliff and Catherine and does indeed act counter to their mutual understanding and even physical survival. Yet Nelly is not therefore to be censured as better or worse than her heroic companions. It is merely a question of difference, a difference that further measures for us the distance between her simple well-meaningness and the complexity and intense subjectivity of Heathcliff and Catherine. Nelly too represents the ruthless limitations of novelistic contextualization and interpretation, and her at times detrimental inadequacies are but those limitations dramatized. Indeed, she is not emphasized as a speaker, nor Lockwood as a listener, except when the clash of her ontological makeup with that of the Gothic characters is most apparent. And this clash is the clash between novel and tale.

Nelly gives Lockwood, for instance, this description of events at the Grange after Catherine's hysterical scene upon Linton's dismissal of Heathcliff:

> While Miss Linton moped about the park and garden, always silent, and almost always in tears; and her brother shut himself up among books that he never opened—wearying, I guessed, with a continual vague expectation that Catherine, repenting her conduct, would come of her own accord to ask pardon, and seek a reconciliation—and while *she* fasted pertinaciously, under the idea, probably, that at every meal, Edgar was ready to choke for her absence, and pride alone held him from running to cast himself at her feet, I went about my household duties, convinced that the Grange had but one sensible soul in its walls, and that lodged in my body.
>
> I wasted no condolences on Miss, nor any expostulations on my mistress, nor did I pay attention to the sighs of my master. . . .
>
> I determined they should come about as they pleased for me; and though it was a tiresomely slow process, I began to rejoice at length in a faint dawn of its progress, as I thought at first.
>
> Mrs. Linton, on the third day, unbarred her door; and having finished the water in her pitcher and decanter, desired a renewed supply, and a basin of gruel, for she believed she was dying. That I set down as a speech meant for Edgar's ears; I believed no such thing, so I kept it to myself, and brought her some tea and dry toast. (103)

To catalogue Nelly's reported behavior here is less interesting than to consider the language in which it is expressed. The first paragraph is but a single sentence, the subject of which, in the final clause, is "I." This is not merely to say that Nelly is an egoist and that she interprets experience primarily in relation to herself, but more importantly to demonstrate that her language itself is incapable of finding any other center but that "I." This is not a story about Nelly Dean, but she tells it nevertheless from the only perspective she knows—her own. She translates experience into the limits of her "I-It" vision and therefore indicts her own lack of imagination to the degree that she criticizes the extravagance of those around her.[13] Nelly's impatience and even seeming cruelty in scenes such as this comprise more than a comment on the recalcitrance of servants. Nelly can express no more than she understands—a world of contiguity, cause and effect, action and reaction, "I-It": "[W]earying, I guessed," "under the idea, probably," "I went about . . . convinced," "I wasted no condolences," "I determined," "she believed she was dying . . . I believed no such thing." Nelly continually asserts her assumptions and beliefs because without them the experience of this household would seem arbitrary and meaningless. She treats everything representationally because, like Lockwood, she has no other linguistic terms with which to treat them: Nelly Dean is all presence; the absence of metaphor has no meaning for her.

The central characters in the novel, on the other hand, if Heathcliff and Catherine can be called such, understand experience metaphorically and exist in an "I-Thou" relation, which transforms their reality into something uncanny and beyond the terms of everyday experience and normal interpretation.[14] Uncanny is precisely what Buber calls such intensity of experience, represented by "strange lyric and dramatic episodes . . . loosening the well-tried context" (34)—just such episodes as *Wuthering Heights* abounds in.[15]

Like their Gothic predecessors, Catherine and Heathcliff inhabit a world which for them is so charged with meaning that it is almost unbearable. They both speak a language that moves among these meanings with only the slightest concern for contiguous syntactical structure. They express themselves in ways that only baffle us, constantly protesting the limits of their own beings and challenging what we think of as personal identity, as when Catherine says of Heathcliff, "He's more myself than I am" (72) and "I *am* Heathcliff" (74). Macovski suggests that the status of such assertions is "perhaps the most perplexing critical dilemma surrounding *Wuthering Heights*" (379), but do not readers understand these statements instinctively, without resorting to critical expostulation? Such attempts to break through the limits of language in *Wuthering Heights* are central to its affective technique; they comprise the intensity of "I-Thou" identification that transforms the world we know into an uncanny, strange, magical world in which such statements have expressive power. It is impossible to translate them into critical prose, yet we understand them.

In Catherine's final "madness," for instance, her mind wanders among what Nelly calls "associations," in a realm of fantasy.[16] As she pulls feathers from a torn pillow, she murmurs:

> That's a turkey's . . . and this is a wild-duck's; and this is a pigeon's. Ah, they put pigeons' feathers in the pillows—no wonder I couldn't die! Let me take care to throw it on the floor when I lie down. And here is a moor-cock's; and this—I should know it among a thousand—it's a lapwing's. Bonny bird; wheeling over our heads in the middle of the moor. It wanted to get to its nest, for the clouds touched the swells, and it felt rain coming. This feather was picked up from the heath, the bird was not shot; we saw its nest in the winter, full of little skeletons. Heath-

cliff set a trap over it, and the old ones dare not come. I made him promise he'd never shoot a lapwing after that, and he didn't. Yes, here are more! Did he shoot my lapwings, Nelly? Are they red, any of them? Let me look. (105)

Catherine gives way completely to the metaphorical mode (goes mad, that is) when it is clear that social acceptance of her feelings for Heathcliff—their contextualization—is impossible. Syntactic coherence gives way to noncontiguous assertions of meaning and associations of significance. The specific terms of the speech, although they have been interestingly discussed, are no less engaging than the significance of the language itself here in the novel's structure.[17] For placed against Nelly's prim and even destructive morality or Lockwood's civilization, this madness suggests a liberated world of wind and light and energy, a world, in other words, of love. Catherine's speech is heartrendingly pathetic, to be sure, but its very pathos is the measure of our own inability to share in Catherine's vision. "You're wandering," Nelly Dean imaginatively suggests. "I'm not wandering: you're mistaken," Catherine answers (105). Nelly is mistaken, and we are as well, insofar as we attempt to force Catherine into our own restrictive linguistic structures for meaning. Meanings, for Catherine, reside in a heap of feathers, in a lapwing, in a cloud. She sees Heathcliff in them all because he is part of her "I-Thou" relation with nature. He therefore understands her; he speaks her language.

Meaning for Catherine, then, is private. The fears that we might uncover in this passage are less important for themselves than for the fact that they defy even the last word in psychoanalytic interpretation, such as that proposed by Homans (16–18). The mood is one of abject horror, pain, deprivation, and death. The nest "full of little skeletons" domesticates the Gothic nightmare, in a sense, but it also opens a harrowing realm of private desolation that moves us more than the clinking of a dozen trapdoors. Macovski suggests that what is important about such speeches in *Wuthering Heights* is their confessional aspect: "Narrative address itself constitutes a sign of interpretive engagement, despite the fact that many of the novel's secrets remain opaque"; "a confessional impulse can be realized a truth only in the presence of a listener who both assimilates and attempts to interpret it" (371).[18] In other words, what is important here is not what Catherine means but that she engages in a dialogue with Nelly. I would take this argument one step further to suggest that the relation with Nelly is not so important as the relation with the reader, for Nelly's misinterpretations only encourage us to try to interpret correctly. Our inability to do so, moreover, is what constitutes the Gothic effect. For Gothic literature conventionally defies interpretation as it encourages us to search for explanations. Here there is more than enough material for precise analysis, but any interpretation falls short of encompassing the subjective vision that Brontë has created for us. As in the gloomy abysses of the Gothic novel, meaning here recedes and only baffling metaphor remains. We are caught, as Miller says, in an uncanny moment: The "act of interpretation always leaves something over, something just at the edge of the circle of theoretical vision which that vision does not encompass. . . . The text is overrich. It always slips away from any attempt to explain it fully" (94).[19] We are trapped between metaphorical language that we cannot explain and metonymical interpretations that we cannot accept. Brontë has created a new kind of haunting that realizes the nature of the most unsettling moments in Gothic fiction and gives them a new rationale. This occurs at moments in the Gothic novel, as we have seen, but here Brontë is not content with asserting the power of the Gothic; indeed she seems to want to contrast Gothic inaccessibility with another, more transparent mode of discourse, embodied in the second generation.

Heathcliff's own program of revenge after Catherine's death is an attempt to overturn the established order of things and to assert the primacy of his private vision. Like a Gothic hero, he tries to disrupt the contiguity of experience and make his own subjectivity (and horror) a threatening power. His "I-Thou" experience is momentarily threatened, and he takes it out on those around him. This behavior, too, is a kind of madness, but while Catherine's madness is self-destructive, Heathcliff's is self-assertive. As such, it pits the world of private meanings against the world of public ones, brings the linguistic axes of metaphor and metonym into confrontation, and challenges the threatening power of the tale with the reasonable realism of the novel. If there is to be resolution, Brontë is surely concerned not with which side wins but with how the two can be brought into meaningful relation.

> Catherine Earnshaw, may you not rest, as long as I am living! You said I killed you—haunt me, then! The murdered *do* haunt their murderers, I believe. I know that ghosts *have* wandered on earth. Be with me always—take any form—drive me mad! only *do* not leave me in this abyss, where I cannot find you! Oh, God! it is unutterable! I *cannot* live without my life! I *cannot* live without my soul! (139)

Heathcliff is in his own way both as pathetic and inaccessible as Catherine. If throughout the second half of the novel, as this quotation suggests, he inhabits a world of ghosts—a world tormenting him, as it were, with too much meaning—he tries in that sense to give his private haunting public form and becomes, to the public eye, mad. His frustrated attempts to gain control of the Earnshaw and Linton families bespeak the impossibility of translating that madness directly into social action. More than a Gothic villain, he becomes like the Gothic novelist him- or herself in attempting to introduce private subjective meaning into an objective public world without first finding the formal means to accomplish such a union. It is true that Heathcliff is speaking in language that we can understand, and that his loss is made very real in the novel. But Heathcliff's frustration reaches beyond the powers of explanation just where it becomes most articulate. In order to come from the tale into the novel, as it were, he must sacrifice his "soul." In other words, the magical power of his "I-Thou" relation is lost, and he cries out in anger and inflicts pain on those around him. Heathcliff's tale would become a rather tawdry novel of estates and wills, if we did not understand his mad acquisitiveness as an expression of his private abjection.

In the action of the second half of *Wuthering Heights,* Brontë attends directly to those concerns and not only demonstrates the nature of the resolution to her own story but also works out new terms for effective Gothicism in the novel. From one point of view, the story of the second generation is the outline of Heathcliff's frustrated revenge and ultimate death. From another, it is the story of young Catherine's discovery of Heathcliff's world, her forced marriage to his son Linton, her confrontation with death, and her ultimate toleration for and then love of Hareton Earnshaw. Only by understanding these in relation to one another can we establish the precise nature of Brontë's achievement.[20]

Both Linton and Hareton are sons of Heathcliff, the former physically and the latter spiritually (see Eigner 96–99). As his sons, they come to represent both the two sides of Heathcliff's own personality and their relation to the worlds the novel depicts. For Bersani, "The claustrophobic inbreeding in the novel is paralleled by psychological repetitions which also draw the characters into a single family" (199). That kind of repetition is what we experience here. Linton is the pathetic outward sign of Heathcliff's attempt to control the world of contiguity in the novel. He is the implement of Heathcliff's revenge, and in that role his simpering weakness provides a manifestation of the impotence of Heathcliff's plan. As Linton becomes more clearly a tool of his father's revenge, he becomes less a person with whom we can sympathize, an almost allegorical figure of peevishness and perverted self-vindication. Indeed, this is what Heathcliff himself must seem to those who only know him from without. Ironically Linton's death complements his weakness as representative of the ultimate failure that Heathcliff must experience in his attempt at this kind of resolution. It leaves Heathcliff with everything, but nothing.

If Linton comes to represent Heathcliff's impotent program of revenge, his attempt to assert private meaning in the public world, Hareton clearly represents the side of Heathcliff that the novel seems so to celebrate: "Well, Hareton's aspect was the ghost of my immortal love," Heathcliff says, "of my wild endeavours to hold my right, my degradation, my pride, my happiness, and my anguish—" (255). Hareton, for Heathcliff, belongs to that metaphorical world of madness and private meaning, the world of the Gothic tale. At the same time, it is important that Hareton is not really Heathcliff's son, because that would include Heathcliff in the kind of worldly success that had failed at Linton's death. As a spiritual son, however, Hareton offers the terms whereby Heathcliff's private vision can be made public reality, limited and awkward at first, but finally approaching something like resolution.

Hareton's love is perhaps the most capacious of anyone's in the novel. It does not insist on complete possession nor is it absolutely exclusive. We can see this most clearly in the scene in which Cathy forces a confrontation between herself and Heathcliff as objects of Hareton's love. Because he loves them both, he does everything within his power to avoid the confrontation while attempting to offend neither of them. When the confrontation does occur, "Hareton attempted to release [Cathy's] locks, entreating [Heathcliff] not to hurt her that once" (253). Hareton's actions suggest that violence between the generations is not necessary. When Heathcliff drops his hand from her head—whether as a result of Hareton's entreaties or of Catherine's looks—he has begun to recognize how unrealistic his stance has become in relation to his own desires. In seeing their love, he is reminded of his own, and in his own words, "it partly contributes to render me regardless how he and his cousin go on together. I can give them no attention, any more" (255). Our ability to see Hareton partly as a manifestation of what was best about Heathcliff makes the union between Hareton and Cathy much more than the domestic resolution that Nelly and Joseph would make it. Instead, it dramatizes the psychological regeneration that reaches fruition for both generations in Heathcliff's death.[21]

By focusing our attention on the second generation as a reflection and reinterpretation of the first, Brontë accomplishes both thematic and formal resolution. Much has been said about resolution and reintegration in *Wuthering Heights*. Burgan, for instance, sees the ending as "designed ... to answer the problems posed by beginning," both dramatically and psychologically (404); Armstrong suggests that the second half of the novel suppresses Romantic concerns in a Victorian resolution (253–54). These are new versions of the classic interpretations of the meaning of the second generation, one that sees the second generation as the fulfillment of the first and one that sees it as its perversion.[22] I would go further than either of these critics to suggest that Brontë's Gothic devices animate the novelistic material of the second half of the work, primarily through the role of Heathcliff, and transform this novel into something unlike any other novel we have. That is, the tale mode, the intense subjectivity of those early Gothic moments, which in the Gothic novel defied extension and contextualization, here expands to embrace the second generation in *Wuthering Heights* as well as the first, and to liberate the final scenes of the novel from the Victorianism that they seem to threaten. Romance and realism exist in ambiguous relation here, and Brontë thereby challenges our conventional distinctions between modes of novelizing. She does even more: The tale here releases the novel from the limits of its own vision and creates a form that can answer the demands of both novel and tale. Brontë does not make Nelly Dean and Lockwood triumph in *Wuthering Heights,* however much their homely domesticity and urbane gentility may lead us to think so. She insists instead that we look beyond the world of metonymic language, if not into a world of metaphor, at least into a realm where private vision can be given public meaning after all.

The process of "reunion" with Catherine, of course, begins for Heathcliff almost immediately after her death, but Brontë has constructed the action so that we do not experience his torment except in the excessive revenge to which it drives him. The result is to force us to feel the most discomfort at the very moments when Heathcliff feels the greatest distance from Catherine. That we only recognize this in retrospect is Brontë's method of preventing us from scrutinizing too carefully the terms of her otherworldly resolution. If we were to see Heathcliff roaming the moors night after night, the meaning Brontë places on these excursions would become banal. There is also the possibility that we should not remain at all sympathetic to his suffering in the midst of his savagery. For this reason, Brontë makes Nelly narrate most of the denouement of the story after Heathcliff has died. Finally, lest an overexplicitness dispel the impact she seeks, Brontë allows Nelly to describe, but rarely to interpret, Heathcliff's actions just before his demise. This momentary refusal to contextualize places Heathcliff just beyond the metonymical scope of language into a realm we can only approach by analogy:

I peeped in. Mr. Heathcliff was there—laid on his back. His eyes met mine so keen and fierce, I started; and then he seemed to smile.

I could not think him dead, but his face and throat were washed with rain; the bedclothes dripped, and he was perfectly still. The lattice, flapping to and fro, had grazed one hand that rested on the sill; no blood trickled from the broken skin, and when I put my fingers to it, I could doubt no more—he was dead and stark!

I hasped the window; I combed his black long hair from his forehead; I tried to close his eyes—to extinguish, if possible, that frightful, life-like gaze of exultation, before anyone else beheld it. They would not shut; they seemed to sneer at my attempts, and his parted lips and sharp, white teeth sneered too! (264)

Nelly herself is like a Gothic narrator here, inviting us to listen to her personal experiences in the potentially terrifying moments of confrontation with Heathcliff's corpse. The stages of her apprehension are dramatized in affective terms: Personal impressions are carefully delineated, as are the features of the form before her. We are directed first to Heathcliff's face, then his body, then his lacerated flesh. We look more closely at Heathcliff now than at any time in the narrative, and we confront his corpse as closely as we confront any in the Gothic tradition. But in this final look, just as in all his inexplicable looks over Nelly's shoulder throughout the last section of the novel, we see even more than Brontë allows Nelly to articulate, and, as in other Gothic fictions, we see it precisely because of what she does not—cannot—say. The setting and the pose, which we are asked, as it were, to contemplate and provide "meaning" for on our own, strongly suggest that Heathcliff is reaching out to his beloved Catherine at last. The rain is a cleansing, soothing image when compared to the blood Lockwood produced in similar circumstances. Heathcliff's sneer forbids us to share his final vision, but this refusal to articulate his private reality places him at last beyond the contextualizing force of the novel itself, in a realm that in its ultimate inexplicability is fully Gothic. The tale's uncanny power here obtrudes into the narrative and changes its terms.[23] We witness the transformation of the novel into an unsettling and defamiliarizing form, one that has used the rationale of the tale to challenge its conventional boundaries.[24] This transformation is the essence of the Gothic nature of *Wuthering Heights* and helps to explain why its resolution is so unsettling and so profound.

Those critics who resist Brontë's attempt to resolve the relationship between Catherine and Heathcliff in a transcendent realm ignore the peculiar nature of the action the author has constructed.[25] As a resolution of the public world of the novel, the mere death of Heathcliff and the succession of the second generation is sufficient. Yet the work insists on a reading that accomplishes more than this structural completion. Brontë pays careful attention to a kind of growing supernatural awareness on Heathcliff's part, our interest in which naturally supersedes our concern with a happy ending for the young lovers. "I have a single wish," Heathcliff says, "and my whole being and faculties are yearning to attain it. They have yearned towards it so long, and so unwaveringly, that I'm convinced it *will* be reached—and *soon*—because it has devoured my existence. I am swallowed in the anticipation of its fulfillment" (256). The power of metaphor here is to release Heathcliff from the confines of his separation at the same time that it makes him less likely to continue in this world. But it also releases him subtly from our empirical checks in novel reading, and makes it less likely that we will resist the otherworldly suggestions that Brontë scatters throughout the second half of the novel. Heathcliff is consumed within his own anticipation just as his language, and Gothic (metaphorical) language in general in the novel, becomes self-absorbed and ultimately self-reflexive. There is no public role for Heathcliff and Catherine, except within our response; in our imaginations we create that role, for that is the realm in which Brontë finally tries to place them. As a physical union, if united at all, they are united in the grave. As an imaginative union, on the other hand, they reach beyond the grave and animate the novel with a spirit of otherworldliness both harrowing and convincing.[26]

Cathy and Hareton have been called substitutes for Heathcliff and Catherine, and surely Brontë means us to understand their final happiness in those terms. But as Nancy Armstrong suggests, Hareton is a much domesticated version of Heathcliff, pale in comparison to his predecessor, and certainly not as challenging to the family structure of the novel (Armstrong 254). But that domestication is an aspect of the formal resolution itself. It is not simply perverse to note that Heathcliff is responsible for this union and that it is his own spirit that gives it life. Cathy takes it upon herself to tame this spirit, as it were, a project most readily accomplished by teaching Hareton to read and write. As he struggles to form words to her specifications, she offers him kisses as a reward. Throughout this period, Cathy learns as well that Hareton's immense private world of love can be shared and realized publicly after all. When she first attempts this, of course, she risks the force of Heathcliff's wrath and his insistence that her love will make Hareton a beggar. But after his death, Lockwood grumbles that *"they* are afraid of nothing" (265).

At the close of the novel, Cathy and Hareton are set to marry and move into the Grange. They seem poised to realize private happiness in a public form. The emphasis on literacy here suggests that the resolution is centered in a rehabilitation of language, not merely a domestication of wild spirits in limiting syntax (and happy home), but also the expansion of the possibilities of meaning through a new energy and a new expressive power. This is just the kind of "blend" Horace Walpole was asking for. This is not merely a tidy Victorian ending, therefore, but a Romantic rethinking of the terms of Victorian closure.

Cathy and Hareton do offer a resolution, then, that combines metaphor and metonymy in a reintegration of linguistic modes. They are neither haunted by private meanings nor trapped within public ones. The image of their indoor/outdoor existence at the Heights, with windows open to the sun and the fire blazing within, suggests this union of public and private, and its prospect for a bright future.

This potentially smug conclusion is nevertheless given substance by the gloom of the churchyard graves of Heathcliff and Catherine. What happiness there is at the Heights, we feel, finds its source, if perversely, in the power now buried at the Kirk. Cathy and Hareton have not overthrown the threats to order that Heathcliff and Catherine represent, but they have used that power to find the terms of success for their own paler love. Our response to this young couple would be less sympathetic surely without a sense of that darker union in the grave. Indeed, their story would mean little without the context of the other pair of lovers, so much grander and so much less successful than they. Nor would the dead lovers be as moving as they are without this reflection of worldly happiness. Victorian novel and romantic tale are combined at the close, in other words, in a promising fulfillment of the original impetus, so apparent in the Gothic novel, to find the appropriate form for Gothic fiction. This is not the death of the Gothic, but really its second birth. Brontë teaches us how Gothic conventions can be transformed into novelistic ones and how the novel can be liberated to include Gothic effects without collapsing.

It is not a weak compromise, therefore, that Brontë offers the Gothic dilemma. She has depicted instead a world in which literary forms can collide without destroying a work but giving it life. The story, at its close, remains open to all the possibilities of interpretation; the public has been contained within the private, and the private within the public. In *Wuthering Heights,* Brontë has liberated language from the rigid dichotomies of the Gothic novel and found instead an idiom capable of animating the social form with the private fantasy. At the end of the novel, we do not question whether Cathy and Hareton will be happy or whether Catherine and Heathcliff will realize their union. Instead we experience a resolution, both of the tale itself and of the formal confusion that has beset Gothic fiction from the outset. Those competing modes of fictional expression—Walpole's "ancient and modern romance"—are here blended so as to open, rather than close, the Gothic possibilities of the text:

> I lingered round them [the graves], under that benign sky; watched the moths fluttering among the heath and hare-bells; listened to the soft wind breathing through the grass; and wondered how any one could ever imagine unquiet slumbers for the sleepers in that quiet earth. (266)

Lockwood's final speech reminds us of how much there is to comprehend at the end of *Wuthering Heights* and how much lies beyond comprehension. For like Lockwood, we can only look and wonder. That is the measure of Brontë's achievement here.

4

Poe's Gothic Gloom

Edgar Allan Poe was the first American to write truly sophisticated Gothic fiction. Much has been written about Charles Brockden Brown and Washington Irving as Gothicists, and recently the immense popularity of minor American Gothic writers has been fully documented and discussed.[1] That Poe emerges from such a distinguished background is less interesting for what it says about the state of American letters than for its implications in a discussion of Gothic form. Poe was not only the first American to excel in the Gothic mode, he was the first writer in either England or America to formulate a thorough and convincing theory of the Gothic and to create a complementary collection of tales both to support and develop his critical theory.[2]

Poe began his Gothic enterprise in a mood of mockery and contempt. His first tales, the proposed "Tales of the Folio Club," were meant, at least in part, as a parody of the sensational excesses of the Gothic novel. In these "Tales," a group of benighted club members were to trade stories of the bizarre and mysterious. Typical of these tales is Poe's first published story, "Metzengerstein." In the scheme of the "Tales of the Folio Club," according to E. H. Davidson, "Metzengerstein" would probably have been assigned to "Mr. Horribile Dictû, with white eyelashes, who had graduated at Gottingen" (Davidson 499; *TSEAP* 2:205).[3] The tale itself is a lurid play on the notion of "metempsychosis," which challenges the self-indulgent use of horror in Gothic fiction and ridicules the very nature of the form; at the same time, however, it offers the prospect of real Gothic achievement.

"Horror and fatality have been stalking abroad in all ages": The opening sentence of the tale immediately suggests an ironic perspective at work (*TSEAP* 2:18). G. R. Thompson observes that "when the tale is read carefully, the many seeming lapses in taste and precise control of point of view and style can in fact be seen to form a unified pattern of satiric irony" (53).[4] Poe could not be content, however, to allow all this irony to be single-edged. His opening sentence announces "horror and fatality" so simply that we can hardly take them seriously. Yet Poe does take them very seriously indeed. The subtle personification implied by "stalking" suggests that the very concepts themselves will be under scrutiny here. More than merely ironic, they signal Poe's very serious fascination with the mechanism of Gothic expression.

Here, for instance, is a passage in which Poe employs Gothic effects at the same time as he mocks them. He is describing the hero of the tale:

> Upon the succession of a proprietor so young, with a character so well known, to a fortune so unparalleled, little speculation was afloat in regard to his probable course of conduct. And, indeed, for the space of three days, the behaviour of the heir out-heroded Herod, and fairly surpassed the expectations of his most enthusiastic admirers. Shameful debaucheries—flagrant treacheries—unheard-of atrocities—gave his trembling vassals quickly to understand that no servile submission on their part— no punctilios of conscience on his own—were thenceforward to prove any security against the remorseless fangs of a petty Caligula. (*TSEAP* 2:21)

Poe's ironic intention is unmistakable here: The gentle mockery in the so amply satisfied "expectations" plays against the implicit parody of Gothic excess. Stock phrases such as "out-heroded Herod" and "the remorseless fangs of a petty Caligula" would be perfectly within Gothic conventions of evasive and euphemistic statement, were it not that they come within a few lines of one another and are connected by so obvious a list of the shameful, flagrant, and unheard-of. But such vague overstatement, which is so often an embarrassment in the Gothic novel, here works to Poe's advantage. By forcing his readers to fill in the horrid details for themselves, he makes them become vulnerable to more subtle effects which are to follow.

More importantly, however, Poe's technique carries us beyond the parodic into the realm of a newly self-conscious Gothicism. The parody is meant not to distance us from Gothic effects but to make us even more susceptible to them. Poe begins to show just how such "limitations" as Gothic overstatement or euphemistic description can actually work for rather than against the Gothicist. In this passage, Poe has simply shown that he is willing not only to out-herod Herod but to out-lewis Lewis.

Throughout "Metzengerstein," Poe similarly undercuts the techniques of previous Gothic fiction while demonstrating how those techniques can be transformed in the service of a more effective Gothicism. Every description involves this double-edged procedure. The Baron, for instance, sits in a "vast and desolate upper apartment of the family palace of Metzengerstein" and contemplates "the rich although faded tapestry hangings which swung gloomily upon the walls." Poe's ensuing description abounds in satiric jibes at heroism, at family tradition, and, more typically, at Gothic imprecision ("the shadowy and majestic forms") while it carefully creates an atmosphere of the violent ("muscular war-coursers plunging over the carcasses of fallen foes") and the bizarre ("the mazes of an unreal dance to the strains of imaginary melody" [TSEAP 2:21–22]). Certain critics feel that the satiric intention delimits the meaning of such tales (see, for instance, Thompson 63–65); but much more important to Poe's future accomplishment is his ability to use the most standard Gothic descriptive set piece to begin to develop a new expressive focus for the tale.

The terms of Poe's interest become clearer still as the description centers on the grotesque image of a figure no less inherently terrifying than an "enormous, and unnaturally colored horse," surely gauged to undercut the Gothic tradition of animated portraits. As the passage proceeds, the animal deftly imitates its Gothic forebears by altering its position, to the extreme horror and astonishment of Metzengerstein:

> The neck of the animal, before arched, as if in compassion, over the prostrate body of its lord, was now extended, at full length, in the direction of the Baron. The eyes, before invisible, now wore an energetic and human expression, while they gleamed with a fiery and unusual red; and the distended lips of the apparently enraged horse left in full view his sepulchral and disgusting teeth. (*TSEAP* 2:22–23)

This horse very clearly rears its head in two very different directions: If we have any sense of the frequency with which ancestors step out of portraits in Gothic novels, we have no choice but to acknowledge Poe's immense pleasure in satirizing the genre. In that spirit, the "distended lips" and the "sepulchral and disgusting teeth" again serve mercilessly to caricature the naïveté of the Gothic tradition. The scene, in these terms, comes very near to being an outright comic rendition of "serious" Gothic concerns.

At the same time, the description "works" in a way that its countless models do not. For all that is ridiculous about the horse, there is in addition something unsettling about it. The combined critical laughter over this scene is understandable, but when the joke is over, critics fail to note Poe's use of a technique upon which his later successes are conceived.[5] For although the image of the horse is humorously grotesque, the isolated features of eyes, lips, and teeth ultimately undermine their own comic force. They are disturbing in their isolation and nightmarish in their depiction. Poe has selected and presented objective details that become menacing in their very objectivity, while pretending that his attitude toward them is merely ironic.[6]

When Metzengerstein is carried to his destruction on a similarly fierce and disturbing beast, we are reminded of the worst excesses of the Gothic novel:

> The career of the horseman was indisputably, on his own part, uncontrollable. The agony of his countenance, the convulsive struggle of his frame, gave evidence of superhuman exertion; but no sound, save a solitary shriek, escaped from his lacerated lips, which were bitten through and through in the intensity of terror. One instant, and the clattering of hoofs resounded sharply and shrilly above the roaring of the flames and the shrieking of the winds—another, and, clearing at a single plunge the gate-way and the moat, the steed bounded far up the tottering staircases of the palace, and, with its rider, disappeared amid the whirlwind of chaotic fire. (*TSEAP* 2:29)

Narrative perspective is only vaguely defined here, and the description is little more than perfunctory. Poe is measuring the limits of one kind of Gothic expression, that which attempts to capture emotional feeling in literary discourse. By focusing on a single detail, however, he demonstrates how those limitations can begin to be overcome. Terror is depicted in the "lacerated lips, which were bitten through and through": Poe isolates an objective detail in place of lurid psychological exploration, thereby equating the physical and the psychological as deftly as any of his predecessors. The singleness of the image, however, stands out not just as an attempt to tap the techniques of a Lewis or a Maturin, but to illustrate something more basic about the nature of literary effect.

"Metzengerstein" occupies a unique place in Gothic fiction. It looks back to what are the severest limitations of earlier Gothic while at the same time suggesting the terms under which such defects become in

Poe's hands unmistakable virtues. Poe's impressionistic concern and his ability to create a powerful emotional context even while engaging in parody lead him to a set of formal dicta that complement his artistic intention.[7] Here he is already able to isolate just those effects needed to create a particular impression and to avoid the unwieldiness which at times seems inherent to the Gothic novel. In this tale, setting, character, and action remain under the control of the author and function as he intends them. His parody of Gothic fiction emerges from such intimate familiarity that he could not but appropriate what was most promising and employ it for his own ends.

Poe greatly celebrates the tale as a literary form because it allows a writer the freedom to manipulate his audience so closely. Very early in his career he places the tale high in his literary hierarchy, second in grandeur only to the short poem.[8] Whether or not this opinion can be attributed to Poe's own inability to compose successful longer works matters little to us here. For in defending this stance he proposes a theory of fiction that helps to explain why tales, indeed why his tales, become the most appropriate Gothic medium.

As Robert D. Jacobs points out, Poe derived the doctrine of "single effect" from various eighteenth-century aestheticians, but in so doing he transformed it into something unmistakably his own (162–63). Jacobs says that by the unity of effect, Poe "was demanding an interdependence among the various elements of form which would enable the objective structural unity . . . to be the vehicle of a subjective unity of impression" (163). He illustrates this point by quoting from a review of Dickens's *Pawnbroker's Shop*, in which Poe demonstrates unity of effect through an analogy with painting, where, in his words, "We remember the personages of the sketch not at all as independent existences, but as essentials of the one subject we have witnessed" (*CWEAP* 9:48). Jacobs usefully reflects that in narrative regarded as a picture, a spatial rather than a temporal concept, dramatic effect is lost. Poe seeks an emphasis on neither character nor action but on atmosphere (Jacobs 164). If we modify this notion to suggest that both character and action are developed for their "atmospheric" potential in his tales, we shall be close to understanding the basis of Poe's technique.

Poe is the first Gothicist to recognize the degree to which the focus of setting or character could be limited without rendering a work superficial or unconvincing. He uses his concept of single effect to give the simplest material an intensity almost unknown to earlier Gothic fiction. Or, more precisely, Poe's technique begins to suggest the manner in which the momentary flashes of real power in the Gothic novel could come to inform and sustain entire works. The tale is most suited to this endeavor for reasons beyond the obvious one of length, although it would be unwise to underestimate the importance of restricted scope in consolidating Gothic intensity. Formalist critics see length as anything but a superficial concern.[9] Equally important, however, is the tale's traditionally subjective focus, its tendency to suspend "novelistic" concerns with objective reality in favor of a more diffuse and ultimately internal perspective.[10]

A tale, then, resists the breadth of focus and the almost automatic social interest of the novel in favor of intensely personal concerns. "The novel exists to reaffirm the world of 'everyday' reality," May says. "The short story exists to 'defamiliarize' the everyday" (329). Surely it is Poe's influence on the American short story that gives rise to such generalizations. If the result of this diminution at first seems a reduction of expressive potential, it remains only to examine examples of truly accomplished Gothic tales to see how little of what we consider novelistic grandeur is lost. In any case, we can already see how Poe avoids the formal confusion that seems inherent to the Gothic novel.[11] By negating novelistic expectation of breadth and realistic concern Poe is able to bring the formal nature of his work more directly in line with his affective ends and extend the limits of Gothic expression into the very emotional reality of his readers.

"The Pit and the Pendulum" demonstrates Poe's technique in miniature and offers an interesting point of comparison with Gothic novels. This tale, one of Poe's most popular, recreates the subject and technique of countless scenes of inquisitorial horror in the works of Lewis, Maturin, and their imitators. Yet in contracting his tale into just a few pages, he seems to be setting forth a list of the ways in which physical torture can be given narrative form. Lewis's subjective litany from "The Narrative of the Bleeding Nun" ("I listened . . . I heard . . . I shuddered . . . I felt . . . I started" [*The Monk* 169–70]) here becomes the rationale of an entire tale. Poe never describes the central—indeed the only—character beyond the scene in question, nor is the setting itself any more than a series of briefly glimpsed but intensely felt instruments of torture.

Yet Poe's emphasis does not reside in the merely physical:

> So far, I had not opened my eyes. I felt that I lay upon my back, unbound. I reached out my hand, and it fell heavily upon something damp and hard. There I suffered it to remain for many minutes, while I strove to imagine where and *what* I could be. I longed, yet dared not to employ my vision. I dreaded the first glance at objects around me. It was not that I feared to look

upon things horrible, but that I grew aghast lest there should be *nothing* to see. At length, with a wild desperation at heart, I quickly unclosed my eyes. My worst thoughts, then, were confirmed. The blackness of eternal night encompassed me. I struggled for breath. The intensity of the darkness seemed to oppress and stifle me. The atmosphere was intolerably close. I still lay quietly, and made effort to exercise my reason. I brought to mind the inquisitorial proceedings, and attempted from that point to deduce my real condition. The sentence had passed; and it appeared to me that a very long interval of time had since elapsed. Yet not for a moment did I suppose myself actually dead. . . . —but where and in that state was I? (*TSEAP* 2:684)

Admittedly, in the course of the tale Poe resorts to physical excesses as gruesome as any in the Gothic novel. But here we can detect the psychological groundwork for the tale, which indeed becomes the basis of Gothic effect. The mental and physical exist in odd relation as the result of incarceration and torture, and the narrator, remote from his own body and its processes, puzzles over his own state of existence.[12] Such ontological confusion becomes Poe's most powerful source of Gothic effect.

Later events in the tale, especially the descending pendulum and fiery wall, transform the narrator into an almost purely physical being. At this moment, however, his mental processes remain foremost. "I longed . . . I dreaded . . . I feared . . . I brought to mind" are far different expressions of experience from those just quoted from *The Monk.* Yet these processes are what the narrator substitutes for physical experience. He does not "look," that is, he "long[s], but dare[s] not to employ [his] vision." The Inquisition, Poe seems to be saying, has turned such a simple act as seeing into a complex structure of dread. The relation between the mental and the physical is no longer clear. That is why the tale can present so brutal a series of threatening devices yet remain primarily emotionally affective. The narrator survives; he is not even harmed. Yet we recognize his torment as real. The confusion of mental and physical states has made that even more vivid for the reader. The objective instruments of torture only have meaning in their subjective interpretation. The narrator asks what state he is in, but as the tale proceeds it becomes clear that he is in a state of abjection from which he only releases the reader in the final clause.

The pitch of narrative terror throughout this tale becomes itself a metaphor for the experience of perception: "It was not that I feared to look upon things horrible, but that I grew aghast lest there should be

nothing to see." Poe's doctrine of single effect ensures that the claustrophobic vision, here so vividly represented, will be deeply felt if not
implicitly shared by his readers. As Iser would say, "textual structures
. . . depend on the degree in which the text establishes itself as a correlative in the reader's consciousness." "Any successful transfer," he
says further, "depends on the extent to which this text can activate the
individual reader's faculties of perceiving and processing" (*Act of Reading* 107). Poe seems implicitly aware of these concerns, and his tale is
structured so as perfectly to rise to their challenge.

The language of the tale, moreover, works in two distinct ways. As a
metaphor for the horror of perception, Poe's devices have renewed
force simply because they are analyzed in such detail.

> The vibration of the pendulum was at right angles to my length.
> I saw that the crescent was designed to cross the region of the
> heart. It would fray the serge of my robe—it would return and
> repeat its operations—again—and again. Notwithstanding its
> terrifically wide sweep, (some thirty feet or more,) and the hiss-
> ing vigor of its descent, sufficient to sunder these very walls of
> iron, still the fraying of my robe would be all that, for several
> minutes, it would accomplish. And at this thought I paused. I
> dared not go further than this reflection. I dwelt upon it with a
> pertinacity of attention—as if, in so dwelling, I could arrest *here*
> the descent of the steel. I forced myself to ponder upon the
> sound of the crescent as it should pass across the garment—
> upon the peculiar thrilling sensation which the friction of cloth
> produces on the nerves. I pondered upon all this frivolity until
> my teeth were on edge. (*TSEAP* 2:691–92)

Here a conventional device, reminiscent of dozens of ticking clocks in
the Gothic novel, is given new expressive life. What is more, every step
towards more fully understanding the horror of the situation leads automatically to a more horrified state of mind. Poe tantalizes the reader
with this state of affairs by suggesting the ultimate physical torment
that the gradual rending of the robe implies. The metaphorical implications of Poe's description, however, are entirely dependent on the
minuteness of the description itself. That is, the clearly metonymic
function of language is here not only complementary but necessary to
its full metaphorical function. Every detail that Poe adds in order to
make the perception convincing heightens its metaphorical significance.

While such moments of unity are apparent in the Gothic novel, they never offer the raison d'être for an entire tale, as Poe's doctrine of single effect suggests that they do here. Metonymy begins to assume metaphorical function, with the result that every detail of the tale moves in two directions at once. Poe saw the tale form as the answer to the kind of disjunction that haunted the Gothic novel. Traditional notions of character, setting, and even plot were for him detrimental to the affective force of a tale. In a review of Bulwer-Lytton's *Night and Morning*, for instance, he says that plot "at best . . . is but a secondary and rigidly artistical merit, for which no merit of a higher class—no merit founded in nature—should be sacrificed" (*CWEAP* 10:121). By so stating his case, Poe seems to equate the "artistical" with the un-natural and to suggest that his own structural procedure is more subtle and more profound. In his own most successful works, "plot" as such is neither mechanical nor inert, but rather it becomes an element fully complementary to and inseparable from the structure of effect. Here, however, he disparages plot as a way of demonstrating one of the fal-lacies upon which the Gothic novel foundered; Gothicists, too, sacri-ficed higher merits to the demands of structural complexity. For Poe, coherence exists in the more natural, and indeed the more impene-trable, realm of subjective impression.[13]

Poe's doctrine of single effect suggests what his alternative basis of narrative structure will be. Anticipating twentieth-century reception theory, Poe feels that in the imaginations of his readers, the story is likely to be created for him. He is committed, he says in a review of *Sheppard Lee*, to a kind of writing that consists in a variety of points—

> principally in avoiding, as may easily be done, that *directness* of expression which we have noticed in *Sheppard Lee*, and thus leaving much to the imagination—in writing as if the author were firmly impressed with the truth, yet astonished at the im-mensity, of the wonders he relates, and for which, professedly, he neither claims nor anticipates credence. (*CWEAP* 9:138–39).

In stressing the importance of the teller of the tale, Poe is answering a question that the Gothic novelists barely articulated. In *Sheppard Lee*, as in the works of Ann Radcliffe some forty years earlier, the super-natural was explained. In other works, for instance those of Lewis and Maturin, the supernatural often seems merely accepted. In focusing on the teller of the tale, Poe shows how the supernatural can be made convincing without rendering the work absurd. The Gothic novelists do indeed seem to be struggling toward such a technique at various points in their works, but nowhere are they as successful as Poe in choosing the proper filter through which the story should come to the reader.[14]

Only in the tale can the personal nature of this transaction be fully appreciated. In the tale our relation to the teller becomes more important than anything that happens, if only because our faith in him or her is what assures us that improbable events are actually happening. May talks of the "receptive" mode of experience, which the tale is particularly structured to evoke, and the "I-Thou" nature of narrative perception in short as opposed to long fictions (333).[15] Tales, that is, depend on an intense and personal relation between narrator and reader. This narrative intensity is an aspect of the nature of the tale that Poe, Hawthorne, and James fully exploit. And while of course the narrator of a novel is also crucial, there is not usually the intensely direct relationship of reader to teller to tale as it exists here. May ascribes "this intense focussing for the totality of the narrative experience" to a "mythic" quality inherent in the short story form (335); Frye speaks of the "glow of subjective intensity" in the tale and also suggests the mythic sources of romance (*Anatomy* 304). Poe creates his own mythology in his tales, a mythology which has his own suffering-horror as its source.[16]

Poe delineates the nature of this technique as his review of *Sheppard Lee* continues. It consists, he says,

> in minuteness of detail, especially upon points which have no immediate bearing upon the general story—this minuteness not being at variance with indirectness of expression—in short, by making use of the infinity of arts which give verisimilitude to a narration—and by leaving the result as a wonder not to be accounted for. It will be found that *bizarreries* thus conducted, are usually far more effective than those otherwise managed. (*CWEAP* 9:139)

Rather than take refuge in imprecise diction and euphemistic detail, as the Gothic novelists seem to do in their most bizarre moments, Poe insists on less fudging and more concrete detail as a way of making the context of the bizarre more immediately acceptable to the reader and thereby rendering the bizarre itself a matter of fact. That is why, as so often happens in Poe, we have at some moments no description at all and at others an entire catalogue of seemingly insignificant details.[17] Moreover, as I have said, Poe's use of detail, at its best, defies conventional limits of linguistic organization and provides a true unity of effect only vaguely apparent in the Gothic novel.

The reality that Poe seeks most centrally to evoke is that with the greatest affective potential. The threatening nature of the experience of one of Poe's tales is itself more important than any of the myriad interpretations that can be brought to bear on it. For interpretations are but an alien intellectualization of what Poe states so clearly in the language of his tales.[18] Poe's effects are not alienated from language in this way. For the sheer power of Poe's evocation of a nightmare world that remains partly unexpressed is what makes his tales so compelling. "The author," Poe says in his review of Hawthorne, "who aims at the purely beautiful in a prose tale is laboring at great disadvantage. For Beauty can be better treated in the poem. Not so with terror, or passion, or horror, or a multitude of such other points" (*CWEAP* 11:109). For Poe, the tale is an aid in creating such effects. Terror, passion, and horror can determine the form of a tale and define its meaning. The tale, in other words, allows these effects to become ends in themselves. By admitting and even giving a theoretical basis to such rationale, Poe set Gothic fiction in the only direction that could lead to literary sophistication. He created a form that could embody the Gothic intention in an integrated way. The Gothic tale is a literary form that is true to itself in a way that the Gothic novel could never be.

In his own tales, Poe demonstrates his particular sense of how the Gothic dream can best be articulated. Affective techniques, which make simple tales such as "The Pit and the Pendulum" irresistibly powerful, add a level of complexity to his greatest tales. In a work such as "The Fall of the House of Usher," Poe outlines the terms whereby the Gothic will achieve its most powerful effects. Like the internal and intensely subjective nature of the tale, horror itself becomes involved in a metaphorical structure that has as its tenor not the merely objectively horrifying aspect of human experience but the very specifically subjective horrors of his readers themselves. Horror and passion, therefore, are not mere abstractions in Poe's tales but deeply felt and carefully articulated entities, which have behind them the full force of experience.

> During the whole of a dull, dark, and soundless day in the autumn of the year, when the clouds hung oppressively low in the heavens, I had been passing alone, on horseback, through a singularly dreary tract of country; and at length found myself, as the shades of the evening drew on, within view of the melan-

choly House of Usher. I know not how it was—but, with the first
glimpse of the building, a sense of insufferable gloom pervaded
my spirit. (*TSEAP* 2:397)

The first sentence of "The Fall of the House of Usher" thus creates
a mood of "gloom" even before it presents a subject. Narrative distance
is diminished because this mood assumes priority before the narrator
has introduced himself. The narrator's "I" only then emerges to lead
the reader through the eerie wanderings of this sentence and finally to
the House of Usher itself. This is Poe's narrative technique throughout:
The first-person narrator records his experiences in a syntax that recreates those experiences so as to make the reader their subject. He
seems to see and to reflect, but the "I" is consumed in the structure of
the rhetoric, and we find ourselves in direct confrontation with subjective impressions that could be our own. Poe transforms the uncanni-
ness of the "I-Thou" narrative configuration of other tales by thus challenging our assumptions about the nature of narrative and by insisting
that our involvement is total. The uncertainty with which the narrator
articulates his observations becomes our own uncertainty about the
nature of our relation to what is transpiring there. It describes, moreover, the nature of the effect that the tale evokes. "I know not how it
was": The "insufferable gloom" of the tale can never be rationally interpreted. But it increasingly becomes the tale's only rationale. Kristeva's *crying-out theme* here becomes the basis of the narrative itself
(141).[19]

We can judge the success of Poe's tale design by looking directly at
its Gothic effects. Again, his use of the narrator provides an important
focus. After he has presented the opening impression of the House of
Usher he describes his own response: "There was an iciness, a sinking,
a sickening of the heart—an unredeemed dreariness of thought which
no goading of the imagination could torture into aught of the sublime"
(*TSEAP* 2:397). Our concern is not just that with one remark Poe effectively undercuts the "artistical" Radcliffean Gothic perspective;
more importantly, he is suggesting his method of achieving real Gothic
power. The narrator describes a *feeling* and distinguishes it from a literary response. Poe is trying to recreate such a feeling in his readers
as the tale proceeds. Where earlier Gothic writers try, for the most part,
to affect their readers directly through the horrors they describe (as in
the grotesqueries of Lewis), Poe uses indirection as a more sophisticated affective device, which depends on the immediacy with which
the reader substitutes his or her own responses for those of the narrator.

Through this narrative filter Poe renders the central setting of the tale—the house itself—intriguingly menacing. The narrator understands the house as a sign of the morbid decay it contains. He tries to explore its recesses but becomes hideously baffled, however, and must always settle for a description that only his subjective response invests with meaning. If Poe distils what is best about the depiction of setting in the Gothic novel—that is, the use of setting as metaphor for internal states—he also begins to suggest the final usefulness of metaphor as an interpretive tool. It is the power of suggestion rather than the power of meaning that creates the force here.

In other words, metonymical relations begin to take precedence over metaphorical ones, a necessary correction to Gothic flights of metaphor that remain suspended from narrative context in earlier works. Instead, Poe offers the consciousness of the narrator as the medium by means of which this odd transformation takes place. The results are as unsettling as they are irresistible.

The first paragraph closes with a description of how for the narrator "a black and lurid tarn . . . remodelled and inverted images of the gray sedge, and the ghastly tree-stems, and the vacant and eye-like windows" (*TSEAP* 2:398). Setting is here "remodelled" into the elements most gruesomely affecting, which are described ("black and lurid," "ghastly," "vacant and eye-like") so as to unsettle. The reflection in the tarn is like the reflection in the narrator's consciousness: Ordinary reality assumes an unfamiliar ghastliness that determines *how* as well as *what* we see.

Very shortly the nature of narrative control becomes clear:

> I have said that the sole effect of my somewhat childish experiment—that of looking down within the tarn—had been to deepen the first singular impression. There can be no doubt that the consciousness of the rapid increase of my superstition—for why should I not so term it?—served mainly to accelerate the increase itself. Such, I have long known, is the paradoxical law of all sentiments having terror as a basis. And it might have been for this reason only, that, when I again uplifted my eyes to the house itself, from its image in the pool, there grew in my mind a strange fancy—a fancy so ridiculous, indeed, that I but mention it to show the vivid force of the sensations which oppressed me. I had so worked upon my imagination as really to believe that about the whole mansion and domain there hung an atmosphere peculiar to themselves and their immediate vicinity—an atmosphere which had no affinity with the air of

> heaven, but which had reeked up from the decayed trees, and
> the gray wall and the silent tarn—a pestilent and mystic vapor,
> dull, sluggish, faintly discernible, and leaden-hued. (*TSEAP*
> 2:399–400)

The dynamics of this passage are paradigmatic of the narrative technique throughout the tale. Todorov would suggest that the doubt that
the narrator casts over his observations is an element of the fantastic.
Other critics have given scientific evidence that certain marshes emit
a gas akin to that noted by the narrator. According to Poe's own statement of affective technique, however, the force of the narrator's hesitation is certainly to cause us to hesitate, but then to lead us to a more
automatic belief; because the narrator doubts his own observations
and gives them little credence, we are reassured that he is not simply
a madman and that we can trust his responses. "Self-reflexivity as a
mode of exercising narratorial authority," Chambers says in a discussion of "The Purloined Letter," "has over duplicity the signal advantage that it *cannot* be deceptive. . . . It is as if . . . it remains for the
narrator to incorporate into his own art of narration the advantages of
artistic indirection with the certainty of effect inherent in artistic self-
designation" (65). Poe is a master of the self-reflexive narrator, and his
effects are precise and carefully gauged. Hawthorne uses a similar
technique in "Rappaccini's Daughter," as does James in "The Turn of
the Screw." In these tales we find that there is a genuine ambiguity
about what has occurred and a sense that the narrator has been in full
control—or is being controlled by the Gothic nature of his or her situation.

Furthermore, the process the narrator describes—that of disbelief
somehow heightening superstition—works on the reader as well. Poe
encourages the reader to be skeptical here, only because that skepticism will later work to his advantage. For now, he allows the "pestilent
and mystic vapor" subtly to undermine our sense of things. "Dull,
sluggish, faintly discernible, and leaden-hued": Just such a strange
film is cast over everything in the tale, and gloom assumes an objective
presence.

More important still is the narrator's insistence on self-consciousness, superstitions, impressions, sensations, fancy, and imagination.
The tale is, in other words, a product of the narrator's response to this
eerie setting. Poe insists on precision here because it allows him the
greatest expressive license. The natural becomes imbued with the
supernatural because the narrator, as oppressed by the sensations of
the moment as he is, is so careful to delineate the stages of his own

response. Within the mind of the narrator an objectively baffling experience becomes subjectively familiar, analogy gives way to identity, and the unknown begins to have personal significance. This significance is what is valuable here, not the precise meaning that gives rise to that significance.[20]

When the narrator resorts to direct description, he does so in a way that intensifies the Gothic nature of the setting while implying an unconventional Gothic dimension:

> The room in which I found myself was very large and lofty. The windows were long, narrow, and pointed, and at so vast a distance from the black oaken floor as to be altogether inaccessible from within. Feeble gleams of encrimsoned light made their way through the trellised panes, and served to render sufficiently distinct the more prominent objects around; the eye, however, struggled in vain to reach the remoter angles of the chamber, or the recesses of the vaulted and fretted ceiling. Dark draperies hung upon the walls. The general furniture was profuse, comfortless, antique, and tattered. Many books and musical instruments lay scattered about, but failed to give any vitality to the scene. I felt that I breathed an atmosphere of sorrow. An air of stern, deep, and irredeemable gloom hung over and pervaded all. (*TSEAP* 2:401)

This passage works to heighten the atmosphere of gloom through the strangely *un*detailed inventory of Gothic features. The windows are "long, narrow, and pointed"—that is, "Gothic"—and "inaccessible." The last quality lends a certain eeriness to the description. The "feeble gleams of encrimsoned light" intensify this eeriness, as do the "dark draperies" and the furniture, "profuse, comfortless, antique, and tattered." None of these things is presented to create a vivid visual image of the room; they are simply intended to evoke an impression. In a novel we would demand more specifically referential detail. In a tale we are satisfied once the affective impression has been achieved. Difference is what we are looking for here, just enough details to establish the "defamiliarizing" tone of the tale and to carry us into a world somehow different from our own.[21]

This passage suggests a further Gothic technique, however, which resides in its most central clause: "The eye . . . struggled in vain to reach the remoter angles of the chamber, or the recesses of the vaulted and fretted ceiling." As in the Gothic novel, the question of perception is crucial. But here the emphasis has shifted from a fear of the object that might be lurking in the darkness to the act of seeing itself. There is nothing but darkness in these distant recesses, but we (who have become the perceiving subject) can never know that for sure. Poe here merely adumbrates a technique that reaches paramount importance in the work of Hawthorne and James; for Poe it is still primarily a technique designed to heighten the atmosphere. But even here the eye struggling to see implies the most basic issue of Gothic fiction: How do we know what to believe in these works—how can we see? In epistemological terms, we remain throughout most of Poe's fiction in as oppressively gloomy a chamber as that depicted here.[22]

The narrator's struggle to see to the corners of this chamber is analogous to his attempts to see into the deepest recesses of his host's consciousness. His exploration of the house itself comes to represent his examination of Roderick Usher. This strikes us most clearly when we note that the deepest recess of the house is a vault that becomes the burial crypt for Usher's sister, Madeline. In the crypt as well, we come to feel, lie Usher's darkest secrets. So, as the narrator gets closer to this crypt, as he penetrates deeper and deeper into the house, he is penetrating the heart of Usher's madness. His obsession with Usher and his/its secrets suggest a fascination with the boundaries of self and its relation to this threatening other. Kristeva would propose that the narrator's preoccupations are a sign of his outcast status and that in pursuing Usher he approaches the sources of his own form of madness (5–7). The tale is a record of that quest and its narrative consequences.

The scope of the tale allows a step-by-step progression in this dual advance, a progression that is as excruciatingly deliberate as it is inevitable. In this progression lies Poe's particular version of dramatic suspense. The movement is so intense that it appears static and, as a result, critics have missed this aspect of the tale. Such intensity would not be possible in a longer work—it simply could not last. What Poe does here with so restricted a setting, however, is to make every detail heighten the suspense while seeming simply decorative.

Usher's artistic endeavors are described so as to make this clear:

> A small picture presented the interior of an immensely long and rectangular vault or tunnel, with low walls, smooth, white, and without interruption or device. Certain accessory points of the design served well to convey the idea that this excavation lay at an exceeding depth below the surface of the earth. No outlet was observed in any portion of its vast extent, and no torch, or other artificial source of light was discernible; yet a flood of intense rays rolled throughout, and bathed the whole in a ghastly and inappropriate splendor. (*TSEAP* 2:405–6)

This depiction of a vault that has emerged from Usher's imagination foreshadows the vault that figures later in the tale; it also suggests Usher's state of mind. Here, the setting is effective as an image of interiority because of the minuteness with which Poe has depicted it externally. Thus we can see what Poe meant by "minuteness of detail" in his review of *Sheppard Lee*. Because the image is rendered with care, it is literally convincing. Then once we have accepted it, it begins to reverberate with "deeper" significance.[23] The shift, moreover, from this product of Usher's imagination to the real vault, which also becomes a metaphor for that imagination while at the same time a literal place, just as the physical details of this picture can be literally described, suggests the degree to which the tale has begun to dissolve the conventional distinctions of object and subject. We can only understand this painting subjectively, not because of its metaphorical associations but because of its metonymic role. Gothic intensity arises from our inability to make easily such distinctions in this tale. Instead we feel victims of a world that always remains but never fully was objective. Kristeva says that "when the boundary between subject and object is shaken, and when even the limit between inside and outside becomes uncertain, the narrative is what is challenged first" (141). Narrative is already becoming unnaturally intense.

The Gothic novelists rarely create this intensity; nor do they often understand this aspect of setting. They either describe the setting perfunctorily, or use it to make a particular impression. Poe describes only that which, when depicted in detail, will contribute to the total effect. We never sense ourselves being manipulated, as we sometimes do in the Gothic novel, because with Poe there is no respite from manipulation: We are in an airtight chamber ourselves.

Setting, then, works primarily, if not solely, as an affective device. Descriptions such as those I have quoted function in two distinct yet, Poe insists, complementary ways. As in a novel, these descriptions seem to develop a "realistic" context for the experience that is being described. Not only do the house and its contents stand for a broader and more fully human world, the narrative technique of hesitation and confusion makes the reader's acceptance of those terms of identification more automatic. Poe thereby expands the superficially metonymic function of language in his tale and gives it a range of meaning otherwise unavailable in so brief a space. At the same time, the language of these descriptions can and must be understood metaphorically, even though the tenor of Poe's metaphorical vehicle remains indistinct. There can be no doubt in any reader's mind that the tarn and the vault will return to haunt more fully and articulately. For the moment, however, the metaphorical suggestiveness of these descriptions, itself heightened by the narrative mood, expands their "significance" and lends them an eerie power. In order to explore the source of this power the reader must first define the literal meaning of the descriptions, but that meaning is fully dependent on their metaphorical function; the exploration, therefore, leads in a circle, and the reader ends again confronting his or her own fears.[24]

Character portrayal is equally determined by affective concerns. Some critics have seen this as a failing in "Usher." For instance, Jacobs says that:

> Poe's theory of unity works in "Usher," but it works at the expense of certain qualities many of us today have been taught to expect in fiction. Roderick Usher, for instance, is not so much a convincing character as he is a pictorialization of theme. . . . Since Usher's fears are revealed more by description than by dramatic action, there is little conflict and almost no tension or suspense. The story can be regarded as mechanical—utterly contrived. (164–65).

In this case, Jacobs ignores the virtues of the defects he decries. Roderick Usher may indeed be a "pictorialization of theme," but in recognizing that he need not be anything more to achieve the affective ends of the tale, Poe was offering a useful corrective to certain meaningless attempts at character development in the Gothic novel. Poe focuses interest so as to maximize affective potential, without introducing anything irrelevant or contradictory. Other writers such as Brontë, Hawthorne, and James create fully convincing characters, as part of their affective technique, within the terms that by implication Poe establishes.

Poe here again depends on the presence of the narrator to create a convincing impression of these vaguely sketched beings. His description of Usher's fears does all that is necessary to invoke the sense of mystery and portentousness that Poe desires. Poe's "showing" is rather close to "telling" here because he has established a sound enough context for accomplishing his affective ends. Critics who ask more from Poe's characterization misunderstand his technique. The tale does ultimately stand closer to a picture than to a complex action. Poe means it to be as nearly immediate an experience as possible: Anything that would inhibit this immediacy would be detrimental to his desired effect. The nature of pictorialization for Poe, as we have just seen in discussing the picture of the vault, is by no means static or two-dimensional. Again and again Poe freezes action to look at it more closely, and in doing so opens up the "action" in both metonymical and metaphorical directions.

Consider the dynamics, for example, of the presentation of the catalogue of Usher's physical attributes. Usher is said to have had "a cadaverousness of complexion; an eye large, liquid, and luminous beyond comparison; lips somewhat thin and very pallid . . . hair of more than web-like softness and tenuity," but the narrator watches these features themselves change subtly:

> And now in the mere exaggeration of the prevailing character of these features, and of the expression they were wont to convey, lay so much of change that I doubted to whom I spoke. The now ghastly pallor of the skin, and the now miraculous lustre of the eye, above all things startled and even awed me. The silken hair, too, had been suffered to grow all unheeded, and as, in its wild gossamer texture, it floated rather than fell about the face, I could not, even with effort, connect its Arabesque expression with any idea of simple humanity. (*TSEAP* 2:401–2)

Again the narrator's tone creates the nature of the reader's response. The manner in which he articulates the change in Usher is more important than the details of the description themselves. The "and now" with which the passage begins heightens the narrator's sense of change. This is repeated in "The now ghastly pallor of the skin, and the now miraculous lustre of the eye," so that when he goes on to say that these "above all things startled and even awed me" we can begin to feel the power he means to convey. As the picture of madness, Usher defies interpretation. The narrator's attempt to sympathize and comprehend, however, opens an even greater abyss of meaning than would otherwise be the case. His response heightens the bizarre and the inhuman in Usher as a way of distancing us from him through fear and urging us to understand him through even closer examination.

Of Madeline we have an even more fleeting sensation than we have of Roderick. Usher speaks of his being the last of his ancient race. "While he spoke," the narrator tells us, "the lady Madeline . . . passed slowly through a remote portion of the apartment, and, without having noticed my presence, disappeared. I regarded her with an utter astonishment not unmingled with dread—and yet I found it impossible to account for such feelings" (*TSEAP* 2:404). Again, the whole cause for any emotional sensations whatsoever resides in the response of the narrator. And this time he does not even call on physical details for support: Just a feeling causes "utter astonishment not unmingled with dread." In the dynamics of a tale rarely more than a "feeling" is needed to engage us. We rely on the narrator for information and we are subject to such tantalizing remarks. We are affected because the narrative level of the tale is so persuasive, not because there is anything inherently complex or ultimately convincing in the character passing before us.

Roderick and Madeline exist in a different realm from characters in a novel. Far from being meant, like Emily St. Aubert, to catch our sympathy in themselves, the Ushers are created to provide a human coefficient for the growing sense of madness in the tale. The narrator himself is the only one depicted with any of the depth of development we expect from a novelistic character. But we already understand the degree to which the narrator's depth is an affective ruse: We have been seduced into a narrative situation that has our engagement as its only end.[25]

Consider for instance the passage which begins the climactic phase of the tale. Madeline Usher has died and the narrator describes what simply seems like Roderick's breakdown. It has affected him as well, if we are to judge from "the wild influences of his [Usher's] . . . fantastic yet impressive superstitions":

> It was, especially, upon retiring to bed late in the night of the seventh or eighth day after the placing of the lady Madeline within the donjon, that I experienced the full power of such feelings. Sleep came not near my couch—while the hours waned and waned away. I struggled to reason off the nervousness which had dominion over me. I endeavored to believe that much, if not all of what I felt, was due to the bewildering influence of the gloomy furniture of the room—of the dark and tattered draperies, which, tortured into motion by the breath of a rising tempest, swayed fitfully to and fro upon the walls, and rustled uneasily about the decorations of the bed. But my efforts were fruitless. An irrepressible tremor gradually pervaded my frame; and, at length, there sat upon my very heart an incubus of utterly causeless alarm. Shaking this off with a gasp and a struggle, I uplifted myself upon the pillows, and, peering earnestly within the intense darkness of the chamber, hearkened—I know not why, except that an instinctive spirit prompted me—to certain low and indefinite sounds which came, through the pauses of the storm, at long intervals, I knew not whence. Overpowered by an intense sentiment of horror, unaccountable yet unendurable, I threw on my clothes with haste (for I felt that I should sleep no more during the night), and endeavored to

arouse myself from the pitiable condition into which I had
fallen, by pacing rapidly to and fro through the apartment.
(*TSEAP* 2:411–12)

We do not respond to this passage as we would to a similar passage in
a novel, because Poe has conditioned us to take our emotional cues
from the narrator. We barely know anything about him but how he
responds to things, yet his response continues to impress us powerfully.
In a novel we might not be satisfied with such insubstantial alarms.
But Poe has convinced us that the "sentiment of horror" can become
an affective device itself. The technique of this tale heightens the affective possibilities because the narrator has been our only filter of
experience. The tale itself complements this passage because never
have we had empirical checks beyond narrative testimony. In a novel,
no matter how it is narrated, the form demands a certain degree of
objective realism. Here realism is primarily subjective, and objective
fact recedes into the distance. Indeed, in a singularly ingenious moment, Poe even has the narrator entertain the quite Gothic "objective"
features of the room as a cause for his feeling. "But my efforts were
fruitless." What he has done, in effect, is to have offered us a conventional Gothic reading of the scene—mere fear on account of the surroundings—and disqualified it as a way of suggesting just how profound his feelings must be.

The narrator articulates these feelings of unaccountable horror and
renders them intelligible by means of a certain public identity, but they
convey meaning only by our identification with his private responses.
Deepest personal horrors are represented, then, in a way possible only
where such a subjective focus is at work. For the tale this is all the
narrator needs to be. We do not need his history or his expectations.
He merely conveys directly to us the moment-to-moment horrors that
would otherwise take pages to dramatize. We hardly worry, it seems to
me, what happens to the narrator; he merely dramatizes the effect.

Of course, we do not experience the narrator this way, any more than
we really feel the literary limitations of Roderick and Madeline. Poe's
technique has insured that nothing more is needed. In contrast to odd
and often imprecise character development in the novels of Lewis or
Maturin, Poe demonstrates how little can suffice if it is presented with
the emotional response of the reader in mind. One does not notice the
limitations of Poe's characterizations because in this tale they only
serve to heighten the effect. Later writers, to be sure, learned to make
characterization an affective device in itself, but Poe's technique suggested the terms upon which such development could be based.

We can appreciate Poe's technique more fully as it operates in the final passages of the tale. As the ultimate crisis approaches we are left strangely distant from Usher's interior response. Instead, we experience the narrator's fears, listen to him read from a romance, and anticipate the signs of disaster on Usher's countenance as the narrator describes them. This is a technique familiar in "Usher," but how different, for instance, from a novel such as *The Monk*, where Lewis depicts Ambrosio's final fears in such blazing detail.[26] Usher's fears are left undepicted, just as he is left as a near-caricature, because the reader's own imaginative response is meant to provide the details of the growing horror. This pervasive drama of the scene encourages the reader to participate as fully as the characters.

As the tale draws to a close, we witness the narrator's increasing attentiveness as he reads about horrid shrieks and hears them at the same time:

> Oppressed, as I certainly was, upon the occurrence of this second and most extraordinary coincidence, by a thousand conflicting sensations, in which wonder and extreme terror were predominant, I still retained sufficient presence of mind to avoid exciting, by any observation, the sensitive nervousness of my companion. I was by no means certain that he had noticed the sounds in question; although, assuredly, a strange alteration had, during the last few minutes, taken place in his demeanor. From a position fronting my own, he had gradually brought round his chair, so as to sit with his face to the door of the chamber; and thus I could but partially perceive his features, although I saw that his lips trembled as if he were murmuring inaudibly. His head had dropped upon his breast—yet I knew that he was not asleep, from the wide and rigid opening of the eye as I caught a glance of it in profile. The motion of his body, too, was at variance with this idea—for he rocked from side to side with a gentle yet constant and uniform sway. (*TSEAP* 2:414–15)

The narrator gives us a careful "glimpse" of Usher's physical appearance so as to suggest the interior horror and to leave us to imagine its dimensions. Usher does not need to be more than this list of physical attributes. The limited perception that Poe offers brings us closer to the inherent horror of the situation than could an itemized portrayal, such as those readily available in the Gothic novel, because the most horrifying emotions cannot be delineated: Once they are named they become less powerful. The few signals we are given—the trembling lips, the dropping head, the swaying—lead us to anticipate imaginatively the kind of private horror that lies beyond description. The most powerful effects are left unspecified (indeterminate) because Poe knows that his affective technique has led us to the point of creating them for ourselves. For Iser, reading ("consistency-building") is "a living process in which one is constantly forced to make selective decisions. . . . This is what causes the reader to be entangled in the text-'gestalt' that he himself has produced" (*Implied Reader* 291). Poe's muffling of specificity and heightening of suggestion is gauged precisely to maximize this kind of entanglement. We create the horror, that is, and then we experience it.

The technique is similar in the scene in which all the Gothic elements of the tale are brought to a climax. The tale does not primarily depict an action; it merely intensifies effects until they explode in the final scene. As tension builds, we do not anticipate the fate of Roderick and Madeline as anxiously as we anticipate what effect the outcome will have on ourselves. We have come to fear the impact of the tale, and our experience of the Ushers becomes the measure of such foreboding. The strange and infectious abjection of the narrator assumes its own narrative force here and supplants the central characters as our primary focus of interest. Horror, that is, becomes an end in itself. By this strange reversal, the fate of the Ushers becomes less important than the effect of this final scene. We await the ending with such nervous intensity because every detail in the tale has led us to a fever pitch of anticipation. Since effect is Poe's central concern, narrative details take second place to our response to them. Thus not only is the nature of the plot subtly transformed, but also the conventional instincts toward interpretation are misdirected. Affect precedes event.

As the narrative becomes increasingly fraught with the emotional pressure that has been building up in the tale, Roderick hysterically suggests that his sister is still alive and that she is now on her way to "upbraid [him] for [his] haste":

> *"Madman! I tell you that she now stands without the door!"*
>
> As if in the superhuman energy of his utterance there had been found the potency of a spell—the huge antique panels to which the speaker pointed, threw slowly back, upon the instant, their ponderous and ebony jaws. It was the work of the rushing gust—but then without those doors there *did* stand the lofty and enshrouded figure of the lady Madeline of Usher. There was blood upon her white robes, and the evidence of some bitter struggle upon every portion of her emaciated frame. For a mo-

ment she remained trembling and reeling to and fro upon the
threshold —then, with a low moaning cry, fell heavily inward
upon the person of her brother, and in her violent and now final
death-agonies, bore him to the floor a corpse, and a victim to
the terrors he had anticipated. (*TSEAP* 2:416–17)

All the Gothic features of house and character are here brought into
cataclysmic complement. The scene answers all our emotional expectations—it is fully terrifying—and yet we cannot explain it. There is a
logic to the scene, but it is the logic of emotions rather than of reason.
If Roderick is the "victim of the terrors he had anticipated," so are we.
That is, this scene and the subsequent collapse of the house satisfy the
emotional demands of the tale. This is all we can ask.

The meaning of the final encounter between Usher and Madeline is
left unspecified. Critics have interpreted it in various ways, but Poe
refuses to articulate their relationship here, or to tell us whether or not
we are looking at a ghoul.[27] Our confusion serves his purposes exactly.
We experience a tremendous amount of emotion without really *knowing* what it is about. We cannot: Incest would be too mundane,
vampirism too bizarre. The cause of this dissolution must remain
unexpressed—then with the narrator we feel the madness of the inexplicable. "From that chamber, and from that mansion, I fled aghast"
(*TSEAP* 2:417). In explaining a breakdown of divisions such as that we
have experienced here, Kristeva suggests that narrative itself becomes
affected: "If one wished to proceed still further along the approaches
to abjection, one would find neither narrative nor theme but a recast-
ing of syntax and vocabulary—the violence of poetry, and silence"
(141). Poe's final rhetorical flourish indicates this kind of outcry, and
the collapse of narrative pretension at the end of the tale suggests the
violence of its impact. The narrator is for once confounded. If Poe has
been successful, we share that response with the narrator. The house
collapses because of a force that lies beyond our power of comprehension. The horror, then, cannot be accommodated. It reverberates in our
consciousness as something inexplicable, but grand.

Poe's "effect" is more compelling than our nervous embarrassment
at the revelations of Radcliffe or disgust at the horror of Lewis or Maturin. The tale's dimensions leave more room, paradoxically, for things
to remain unsaid. Novelistic discourse establishes a pattern of expli-
cation and closure. Poe, however, throws the veil over his narration at
the close, so that the "meaning" in some sense remains a mystery.[28]
Even at the close we are struggling to see what has affected us so powerfully. It is not that Poe wants to keep anything from us, but that he
wants to give us as much as possible.

Poe's theory of the Gothic tale, then, involves an absolute and un-qualified acceptance of the affective nature of Gothic fiction. The tech-niques I have outlined all arise out of Poe's dictum of the single effect, which depends on an undiluted acceptance of the nature of the work at hand. This very simple concern eluded the Gothic novelists. In trying to create works with the depth, breadth, and sophistication of novels, they very nearly fail, and in many cases do fail miserably. Poe, however, has managed to save the Gothic from any demands uncom-plementary to it. True novelistic sophistication can only proceed from this seemingly unnovelistic stance.

Terror, passion, and horror are the "issues" Poe sees as most fruit-fully evoked in the tales. To put that another way, he sees the tale as providing the most successful expression of that emotional trinity. I think now we can begin to understand just how that is true. The tale releases the writer from all those novelistic demands that were detri-mental to the Gothic novel. No feature need be introduced into the tale unless it works to heighten the effect. What "issues" Poe develops, such as the madness of Roderick Usher, clearly serve an affective pur-pose equal in importance to any other of the tale's more "interpretive" concerns. The sophistication of "The Fall of the House of Usher" is in every case an affective sophistication.

Primary among Poe's techniques are those having to do with narra-tive perspective. Almost every technical felicity in "Usher" involves a carefully planned narrative maneuver. So with Poe's other tales: even where he does not employ a first-person narrator, as in "The Masque of the Red Death," "The Cask of Amontillado," or "The Tell-Tale Heart," the teller of the tale—the sober and unfaltering voice that re-ports the unbelievable or horrifying so unabashedly—is central to its affective nature. The "Gothic" concern of the later two works comes to depend on the mental state of the narrator himself. Poe is perhaps the first tale-writer to demonstrate the affective power of paranoia so brilliantly. Even though we realize that the narrators are mad, we are incapable of resisting the horrifying force of what in their madness they relate. Narrative unreliability becomes a central feature in Amer-ican Gothic fiction and indeed at length emerges as the only technique compatible with novelistic realism.

The intensity of Poe's tales depends not only on their shortness, but also, as this study of his technique has shown, on their ability to exploit formal assumptions basically different from those that had worked to disrupt the Gothic novel. Conceptions of setting, character and action are substantially different in Poe's tales from what a novel would seem to demand. Certainly they are different from what the Gothic novelists attempt. Poe's clear statement of primary concerns was necessary to correct the befuddled state of Gothic fiction that confronted him. Because Poe clarifies the nature of Gothic expression and establishes the affective terms that technical devices must satisfy, later Gothicists are free to explore the Gothic possibilities of techniques that have the force of hollow convention in the Gothic novel. That is, rich character portrayal and realistic description of setting come to be recognized as affectively useful devices in the tales of Hawthorne and James, in part because Poe has liberated such devices from the assumptions of the novel. These writers demonstrate the manner in which the Gothic tale could become the sophisticated literary form that Poe's experimentation has made possible.

5

Hawthorne's Gothic Garden

Poe's appreciation of the tale as a literary form might help to explain his early admiration for Hawthorne, "a man," in his words, "of the truest genius" (*CWEAP* 11:113). For as different as they are from Poe's macabre imaginings, Hawthorne's tales are as committed to exploring the nature of Gothic effect and as theoretically experimental, both in conception and execution. Poe and Hawthorne approach the question of Gothic fiction from distant perspectives, but as a detailed analysis of "Rappaccini's Daughter" will demonstrate, Hawthorne was no less profoundly concerned with the mechanics of terror or the formal challenge that Gothic fiction made inevitable. Hawthorne's answer to the very questions that a contemporary such as Poe knew how to ask places him foremost among American Gothicists. Hawthorne's terror resides in scenes less outwardly sensational than those of Poe. The macabre and bizarre are no less present, however, for remaining beneath the surface. Hawthorne describes fictional procedure, after all, as "burrowing," during which indeed he leaves little horrific potential unexplored (*CEWNH* 11:4).

Hawthorne's fictional method centers then on that area of experience that the Gothic novelists first examined. The inability to reconcile subjective and objective responses to experience becomes in Hawthorne's work a more profound and instructive confusion than the Gothic novelists were able to articulate. As traditional distinctions break down in Hawthorne's tales, the reader is left without the empirical points of reference that even the Gothic novelists were careful to provide. The result is a more powerful and all-encompassing Gothic vision than the novelists' framed and circumscribed events were able to create. Hawthorne's concept of the tale is one that answers the confusion of many of the Gothic novels with the single-minded allegorical

intensity that is for Frye the key to the narrative subjectivity of romance and for more recent theorists the hallmark of the non-novelistic
development of talelike forms.[1] What Hawthorne does in a tale like
"Rappaccini's Daughter" is to establish from the first moment an
extraordinary relationship between narrator and reader, which makes
the tale both a voyage of discovery and a kind of self-confrontation.
The tale he tells is harrowing enough, but it becomes more harrowing
in the manner in which we are trapped into apprehending it.

In discussing Gothic effect in general, Poe praises "chiaro'scuro . . .
that blending of light and shade and shadow, where nothing is too
distinct, yet where the idea is fully conveyed" (*CWEAP* 14:89). He
might be describing Hawthorne here.[2] In his turn, Henry James
praised Hawthorne's tales for what he called their "picturesqueness,
their rich duskiness of colour, their chiaroscuro" (*Hawthorne* 60).
James well understood that he was describing no mere surface effect.
Chiaroscuro is an artistic way of describing the curious half-light of
Hawthorne's tales, a technique that has been much discussed. But it is
worth remembering that the epistemological anxiety that dimness
causes can also reflect the ontological anxiety that formal suspension
both nurtures and exploits. If Walpole's first articulation of the Gothic
enterprise included the attempt to suffuse the world of factual experience with the reddened glow of subjective interpretation, Hawthorne
has responded with a form that infuses what is common with what is
truly strange in order to upset our sense of fictive "reality."

In order to accomplish this neo-Gothic effect, however, Hawthorne
employs a grammatically complex and rhetorically subtle mode of literary discourse that substitutes a nearly fully effective Gothic textual
procedure for the isolated and ineffective Gothic "content" of earlier
works. Converting the binary opposition between objective and subjective states, so paramount in the English Gothic novel, into a fictional construct that refuses to give value to such distinctions, Hawthorne establishes a basis for Gothic anxiety that reaches beyond his
texts to encompass all manner of "literary" preconceptions.[3] In other
words, Hawthorne uses form itself as a Gothic element in his tales,
and our inability ever to know precisely where we are is a measure of
his success in this regard.

In tales such as "My Kinsman, Major Molineux," "Young Goodman
Brown," or "The Minister's Black Veil," we very quickly become aware
of a narrative procedure that traps us in our own attentiveness. We look
for ways to explain narrative inconsistencies or obfuscations, and in
doing so we commit ourselves to a mode of interpretation that is often
reductive and always self-indicting. If metaphor sends us in search of

absent and inaccessible truth, allegory seems more absolutely to demand a translation, from the literal facts of the tale to a mystical other
realm that we often call "meaning." But what are these "facts" on
which our judgment is based? We recall Iser's notion that "consistency-building is the indispensable basis for all acts of comprehension"
(*Act of Reading* 125) and his insistence that in literary texts there are
no "facts," but rather "a sequence of schemata, built up by the reper-
toire and the strategies, which have the function of stimulating the
reader himself into establishing the 'facts'" (141). Allegory, as I shall
indicate, is one of these strategies, which in Hawthorne's greatest tales
traps us between levels of meaning and forces us to become our own
Gothic villains.

Has Goodman Brown's wife been lost to Satanic power? That is, is
Faith available to him, or must he despair? Is Mr. Hooper hiding his
own guilt or mirroring ours? Is Aylmer pursuing an unattainable ideal
or destroying his only solace? Hawthorne's tales tease us with multiple
meanings (see Bensick ix–x), but in doing so they establish the insig-
nificance of any one meaning and the all-importance of our own complex and self-exposing relation to the text.

Michael Colacurcio has shown at length how deeply concerned with
the history, indeed the moral history, of New England, Hawthorne
really was. Writers such as Crews and Lesser have emphasized instead
the disturbing sexual uneasiness that so many of the tales reveal. Other
critics have emphasized Hawthorne's religious imagination and his
formal ingenuity. But we do not have half-a-dozen different versions
of the tales. We have one version that multiplies meanings as it multiplies readers, never disappointing those who seek seriously to find
something there. It is the nature of Hawthorne's affective form, in
other words, to create an indeterminacy that encourages closure in
private and personal terms. That is the first clear product of his tale
form. But it is not the only product, as we shall see.

Walter Benjamin claims that allegory "is a schema; and as a schema
it is an object of knowledge . . . at one and the same time a fixed image
and a fixing sign" (184). In Hawthorne's fiction, allegory is never so
fixed that we can avoid interpreting the surface before imagining the
meaning. The result is a constantly shifting and continual realigning
of the relation between the meaning and interpretation, with the result
that we can never be sure of what we know and must remain only
vaguely aware of what we think. As knowledge and thought become
more fixed—and fixing—however, they determine the measure of our
own private haunting. Benjamin says further that "in the allegorical
image of the world . . . the subjective perspective is entirely absorbed

in the economy of the whole" (234). What that means for Hawthorne is that our collective subjective responses become the tale and determine its Gothic power.

In "My Kinsman, Major Molineux," for instance, Robin's crisis of contextualization, his inability to read the signs in his surroundings, lead him to a harrowing yet liberating confrontation with a deposed but defiant relative who stares at him from out of the horror of his "tar-and-feathery dignity" and challenges him with a face as "pale as death, and far more ghastly" (*CEWNH* 11:228). Robin's expectations have met with contempt and ridicule, and his search produces a mockery of his most private ambitions. But this grim and dangerous encounter liberates him from those limiting reductions with which he encountered this new world and opens him instead to the thrill of reawakened potential. Similarly, as we approach these tales with our own preconceptions, again and again we will find ourselves cornered in a fictional dead end and hear the titter of authorial mockery behind the sententiousness of the narrator. And to the degree that the claustrophobia becomes oppressive and the mockery derisive, we find ourselves in a Gothic mode, for all the world like a dungeon of Maturin or a monastery of Lewis. But here it is not the external trappings of the situation that make it Gothic, but the very terms of our own expectation and response. If we are lucky, as very often Hawthorne assures that we are, this experience becomes in Jauss's sense liberating, and we find ourselves experiencing the world, and the world of fiction, in a new way (Jauss 40–42).

Poe, whose own Gothic technique was so distinctive, is finally insensitive to Hawthorne's affective subtlety. He objects to both ambiguity and allegory in Hawthorne's tales, features that give them their eerie power. We have to approach the first of these offenses—Hawthorne's ambiguity—rather indirectly. It has been noted that Poe was somewhat superficial in his reading of Hawthorne's tales. Robert D. Jacobs cites Poe's comments about the "moral" of "The Minister's Black Veil," for instance, to imply that "Poe demanded a fairly obvious meaning in the short tale, but one which was suggested, not stated. . . . There should be no ambiguity, no unresolved potentialities of interpretation" (326). It would perhaps be more accurate to say that Poe is uninterested in interpretations that turn the surface detail of his work into a shimmering symbolism and direct attention away from the vivid and horrifying concrete images he depicts. The collapse of the House of Usher is more powerful than the abstract interpretations that have been suggested as substitutions for that pile of rubble.

Poe's reading of "The Minister's Black Veil" elucidates the distance between himself and Hawthorne in this regard. Poe says that "The *moral* put into the mouth of the dying minister will be supposed to carry the *true* import of the narrative; and that a crime of dark dye, (having reference to the 'young lady') has been committed, is a point which only minds congenial with that of the author will perceive" (*CWEAP* 11:111).

Hawthorne's use of Hooper's veil, however, is by no means as precise in its significance as Poe makes it sound. Indeed, the veil serves a Gothic function as certainly as the veil in *The Mysteries of Udolpho* (see Allen). In that case, however, the veil hides what is merely the image of physical horrors, while in this case the horrors are made to seem metaphysical. Radcliffe is willing only to titillate her readers with the possibility of something frightening, while Hawthorne wants to shake his more deeply.

When Hooper is on his death bed he speaks the "moral" to which Poe alludes:

> "Why do you tremble at me alone?" cried he, turning his veiled face round the circle of pale spectators. "Tremble also at each other! Have men avoided me, and women shown no pity, and children screamed and fled, only for my black veil? What, but the mystery which it obscurely typifies, has made this piece of crape so awful? When the friend shows his inmost heart to his friend; the lover to his best-beloved; when man does not vainly shrink from the eye of his Creator, loathsomely treasuring up the secret of his sin; then deem me a monster, for the symbol beneath which I have lived, and die! I look around me, and, lo! on every visage a Black Veil!" (*CEWNH* 9:52).

Far from diminishing the Gothic force of the tale, it seems to me, this "moral" draws out its greatest affective potential. For Poe, the minister's relationship with the "young lady," so obviously hinted at at the beginning of the tale, is the key to meaning. But such a reading is closer to Radcliffe's Gothic technique than to Hawthorne's. In the former there is satisfaction and relief in finding out what is behind the veil; in the latter, no such satisfaction is offered. Poe is wrong to feel so secure. Hawthorne moves ambiguity beyond a simple momentary effect to a more general ambiguity of interpretation, which in turn heightens the Gothic power of his tale.

Mr. Hooper's final speech neither affirms nor denies Poe's reading; but from our experience of other tales, we can be certain that distancing and compartmentalizing are dubious practices in determining

Hawthorne's "moral." Poe has contextualized the meaning of the veil and deprived it of its metaphorical resonances. Mr. Hooper has perhaps focused only on the metaphorical: He cites "the mystery which [the veil] obscurely typifies" and speaks of secret sin. The dichotomy of interpretation thereby created, however, can but lead to misinterpretation. I say this because we are again in a situation where neither the purely metonymic nor the purely metaphorical interpretation of experience will yield a fully satisfying reading. Hooper has instead articulated the horror of the clash between the private and the public—the metaphorical and the metonymical—that has destroyed his humanity and rendered him a fatal omen. The veil remains a mystery at the close of the tale—quite unlike the analogous device in Radcliffe—as a challenge to our own powers of understanding and interpretation. If we find ourselves caught in the obvious trap of articulating either personal or social crimes, we are left like Poe to struggle with the horrifying implications of our own projected imagining. If, on the other hand, we understand the horror in the ambiguous terms that Hawthorne has provided—an ambiguity, that is, between the value of private experience and the ruthless publicizing activity of the social world—we are no less susceptible to the Gothic effect of the tale, nor can we in smugness distance ourselves from the minister's final indictment.

In "Young Goodman Brown," as well, we are led into a situation that resolves itself only in the most unresolvable ambiguity. The form of Hawthorne's tale shifts the terms of interpretation and casts "facts" in such a shadow that we can never be certain of the grounds of our response. "Had Goodman Brown fallen asleep in the forest, and only dreamed a wild dream of a witch-meeting?" (*CEWNH* 10:89), the narrator asks near the close of this famous tale. The question is inevitably rhetorical, but the meaning of the tale depends on our response. We can answer neither yes nor no. Instead we must accept the implication of both possible responses. Yes: Goodman Brown has fallen asleep in the forest and poured forth in dreams the depths of his own desperate sense of isolation and guilty wickedness. No: Brown has been but the instrument of a vision and a truth larger than himself and broader in its desperation, a vision within which the despairing Brown is but the occasion for an expression of wickedness and sin. In other words, either the private world is fraught with the unspeakable or the public world is a mere tissue of falsehood and corruption. But why need we choose when the two readings are in fact complementary?

At the intersection of these vertical and horizontal planes, of course, we have nothing more than Brown's conscious self: "A stern, a sad, a darkly meditative, a distrustful, if not a desperate man, did he become, from the night of that fearful dream" (*CEWNH* 10:89). The gloom with which the tale closes is not something from which we can easily distance ourselves. The "meaning" of the tale cannot exist in any realm beyond that of this final gloom. To refuse Brown sympathy—to judge him—is to participate in the wickedness that he decries; to sympathize, on the other hand, is to acknowledge what he has so keenly felt. We step, that is, into Brown's very position, meditative and distrustful.

This reversal represents the triumph of Hawthorne's Gothic ambiguity. The degree to which we attempt to "make sense" out of such endings is the degree to which we are ourselves implicated in Hawthorne's own version of Gothic gloom. It is not enough to say that Goodman Brown represents a certain type of Puritan (Colacurcio 296–97). Historical distancing is too easy here: It undermines the full effect of the tale, which is to force us to share in Brown's vision in the forest—in which a good portion of the community is implicated in nefarious practices—and to reason with him about the rectitude of human nature. This is not a satire on gloomy Puritanism, but a vision of the meaning of despair—not a meaning "out there," but a meaning within each and every reader of the tale. And such meaning for Hawthorne challenges the very form of the tale itself.

Poe's other objection to Hawthorne, the one that addresses all the tales we have thus far considered, is directed at his use of allegory. James criticizes Hawthorne on the same point. Poe feels that allegory "must always interfere with that unity of effect which to the artist, is worth all the allegory in the world" (*CWEAP* 13:148). James is rather more delicate: "Hawthorne . . . is nothing if not allegorical, and allegory, to my sense, is quite one of the lighter exercises of the imagination" (*Hawthorne* 62). While both of these judgments perhaps sound sensible, we should study Hawthorne's allegorical technique more carefully before subscribing to them.

In "The Birth-mark," Aylmer's own allegorical interpretation of the birthmark comes dangerously close to revealing the rigid limitations of his own response to his wife and the treacherous implications of this misinterpretation. In dreaming that to pierce this blemish would be in essence to pierce Georgiana's heart, Aylmer betrays his own base motives in resenting this mark of imperfection, but this does not stop him from pursuing a series of experiments designed alchemically to purify his wife's being.[4]

Allegorical interpretations reverberate with insistent regularity in this tale. I have mentioned Aylmer's own interpretation of the birthmark; Georgiana herself imagines it a charm. "Georgiana's lovers were wont to say, that some fairy, at her birth-hour, had laid her tiny hand upon the infant's cheek, and left this impress there, in token of the magic endowments that were to give her such sway over all hearts" (*CEWNH* 10:38). The mark, meaningless in itself, becomes such a profoundly suggestive signifier that Georgiana's life must be sacrificed to its power. Hawthorne, then, is not employing a simplistic and transparent system of allegory, as certain critics including Poe and James would seem to suggest, but an intricate and complicated analysis of the nature of allegory and the Gothic implications of attempting to create meaning where none exists. Hawthorne's allegory becomes a "fixing sign" (Benjamin 184) in the sense that our desire to interpret the central image pulls us more intricately into the narrative. In so doing, Hawthorne fixes the limits of our own imaginations within the abyss between primary and secondary levels of meaning. Hawthorne deconstructs the allegorical dichotomy, that is, and places us in the midst of the resulting indeterminacy of the tale.

The narrator offers no assistance in coming to terms with Georgiana's sacrificial commitment because his allegorical technique involves the reader directly in the Gothic workings of the tale. It is impossible for the reader not to become wary of Aylmer's drive for perfection. At the same time, however, Georgiana's willing devotion has the structure of a response that is to be applauded. Georgiana's desire to please tempts the reader to interpret her as an extension of Aylmer and her death as a measure of his failure. After Georgiana has been chemically treated, "the parting breath of the now perfect woman passed into the atmosphere, and her soul, lingering a moment near her husband, took its heavenward flight" (*CEWNH* 10:56). Aylmer's measure of perfection deftly becomes a feature of objective discourse. It matters not that we know Aylmer to be wrong.

About Georgiana we have never known anything at all:

> [H]ad Aylmer reached a profounder wisdom, he need not thus have flung away the happiness, which would have woven his mortal life of the self-same texture with the celestial. The momentary circumstance was too strong for him; he failed to look beyond the shadowy scope of Time, and living once for all in Eternity, to find the perfect Future in the present. (*CEWNH* 10:56)

The sacrifice of a human life is oddly absent from these closing lines of the tale because Aylmer's attempt to contain that life within his own power of intellectual interpretation has failed. Failed too perforce are our own attempts to approach Georgiana allegorically and give meaning to her situation, her physical flaw, her self. If Aylmer was unable "to find the perfect Future in the present," how much more culpable are we, outside the space and time of the tale yet still unable to see beyond the narrow confines of the mind that gives it structure.

Allegory in the conventional sense, then, fails in this tale to provide meaningful terms for interpreting human experience. As soon as we try to articulate the "moral" that Hawthorne has provided, we find language incapable of encompassing both Georgiana's complex and disturbing otherness and the simple fact of Aylmer's scientific failure. We find ourselves uttering broad statements about Aylmer's refusal to accept mortality, sexuality, his physical nature, the emotional attachment to his wife, and so on. We interpret experience, in other words, from the narrow and distorted perspective of this malevolent scientist, when in fact the only allegorical certainty of the tale is that no human experience can be contained within the limits of even the most profoundly intelligent interpretation. Georgiana's soul takes its heavenward flight in final defiance of all attempts to make her mean.

In Hawthorne's partly facetious preface to "Rappaccini's Daughter," the narrator describes that tale as a translation from the works of M. de l'Aubépine, and proceeds to criticize this author for those very qualities to which Poe and James object: "His writings," he says, "might have won him greater reputation but for an inveterate love of allegory, which is apt to invest his plots and characters with the aspect of scenery and people in the clouds, and to steal away the human warmth out of his conceptions" (*CEWNH* 10:91–92). The immediate impression of such an admission would be that "reality" is lacking in Hawthorne's tales, and that, of the two authors, Poe would stand more clearly in the line of emerging Gothic realism. Poe, we have seen, deals in real human feelings. What about Hawthorne? As this preface continues we can begin to understand his stance: "He generally contents himself with a very slight embroidery of outward manners,—the faintest possible counterfeit of real life,—and endeavors to create interest by some less obvious peculiarity of the subject" (*CEWNH* 10:92).

Recent "historical" readings of Hawthorne, such as those by Bell, Colacurcio, and Bensick, have shown us that this "slight embroidery" is enough to suggest a rich and careful cultural consciousness, by no means "counterfeit" or peculiar. Bensick has suggested that we take the historical setting of "Rappaccini's Daughter" more seriously than his narrator does and in doing so produce a reading both coherent and convincing.[5] This historical approach to Hawthorne puts the lie to such narrative abnegation as we encounter in this preface and proves that Hawthorne was no mean historian. But surely that is not the end of the matter. Narrative self-abnegation is not a sign of Hawthorne's limitations; it is his technique for creating a narrative situation which best suits his Gothic intention.

"Occasionally, a breath of nature, a rain-drop of pathos and tenderness, or a gleam of humor will find its way into the midst of his fantastic imagery, and make us feel as if, after all, we were yet within the limits of our native earth" (*CEWNH* 10:92). What is this but a restatement of Walpole's original conflict? Fantasy here deprives the fictions of their human warmth and novelistic realism. This ironic perspective causes us to question the terms of this distinction and to wonder whether Hawthorne has not found a technique that will answer the dichotomy that beset Gothic fiction from the first. In any case, we recognize an elaborate narrative charade, not certainly for the purpose of ridiculing this narrator, but for the more effective ruse of seducing us into an easy acceptance of what is one of the most harrowing of his tales. The narrative technique complicates our involvement by seeming to simplify it. Throughout this tale, Hawthorne makes his text more "readable," in Chambers's terms, with the result that it fixes us in our attempt to fix its meaning.[6] For Hawthorne, this procedure becomes "Gothic" precisely to the degree that our reading of this text matters not in fantastic but in human terms. In demanding readability, that is, we trap ourselves in the gruesome destructiveness of our own response.[7]

The reality that Hawthorne is working to create, then, is not entirely dependent on external concerns. In his tales, setting and scene interest him less in themselves than as the material with which the narrator engages to tell us his tale. The narrative tone creates an uneasiness that defies Gothic convention. The Gothic novelists use the most extreme devices imaginable to express extreme states of mind. Poe creates a world that barely touches our own. His characters inhabit a world of private fantasy. James, as we shall see, locates his Gothic experiences in an insistently everyday realm. Hawthorne's confession of an allegorical technique allows him to describe an everyday world and at the same time invest it with the horror of a Poeian fantasy. As the reader rejects the seemingly simple, objective world in the spirit of allegory and searches his own subjective response for the "meaning" of the tale, he accomplishes an important stage in the union of subjective and objective, which was part of Walpole's original Gothic intention. Insofar, that is, as the external, objective setting becomes interpreted and invested with "deeper" meaning, it comes to stand for a nightmare of which we are our own authors. Hawthorne directs us beyond the surface of his tales, then, as a way of confronting us with the horror of common experience.

Allegory emerges therefore as the technique whereby the reader can most easily recover the horror of his own experience in fiction. It is not just that Hawthorne's allegories can be ambiguous, but that that ambiguity is the very basis of his allegorical technique. All Hawthorne can express through allegory must be expressed in a negative structure: We sense an absence of truth in the literal and search for it in the symbolical. The symbolical, however, defies the limitations of definition and forces us to confront either ruthlessly meretricious "readings" or an ultimate inability to express any meaning whatsoever. In either case, the allegory has trapped us in a search for a truth that remains absent as profoundly as the need to seek it is present in the tale. Hawthorne turns the tale form inside out as a means of tapping its Gothic potential.

Benjamin tells us that "Evil as such . . . exists only in allegory, is nothing other than allegory, and means something different from what it is" (233). "Rappaccini's Daughter" plays on this notion of allegory and encourages us to search for the meaning of evil in the terms of our own response. The tale form aids Hawthorne in achieving the horror of this enterprise. The tale readily offers itself for Hawthorne's Gothic transformation. Because we necessarily understand a tale to have subjective significance, as opposed to the objective significance inherent to novel form, we are not likely to resist the temptation to transform the objective detail of the tale into terms with subjective import for ourselves. In a novel, the external world is rendered tangible by means of detailed description and becomes formally satisfying both in itself and as the background for represented action. In a tale, on the other hand, the external world becomes but a means to some more profound end: Objective details lose the rhetorical force that they have in the novel and come to seem, as they do in Hawthorne's tales, to be standing in for a world more powerful and real. It is in our search for *this* world that Hawthorne lures us into his Gothic landscape.

Historical readings of tales such as "Rappaccini's Daughter," while they correct endless attempts to fix meaning psychologically or religiously, are in the end no more satisfactory. To say that Goodman Brown has behaved as his historical counterpart would have behaved in the face of "spectral evidence" (Levin), or that Mr. Hooper "stands primarily as Hawthorne's figure of that potentially exhaustive and incipiently solipsistic sort of self-reference into which a powerfully heightened or Puritan . . . sight of sin can be discovered all ironically to lead" (Colacurcio 332), or that Beatrice Rappaccini is a latent carrier of syphilis (Bensick 109–12), is to use history as a way of fixing meaning. If the historical signposts are as clear as these critics say they are, surely they are like the signposts in *Wuthering Heights*, which seem to give clear directions but in fact lead us to a world beyond the limits of physical space. History for Hawthorne has a rhetorical force insofar as it can heighten and intensify the affective range of his tale. To say that history therefore determines meaning in these tales is to misinterpret Hawthorne's Gothic technique and to reduce the power of his tale to the sophistication of his sources. It has taken so long for historical readings to be introduced because history is lost in subjective response, and that is as Hawthorne thinks it should be. The reader's act of interpretive subversion plays into the hands of an author like Hawthorne, who is able as a result both to use the surface details of his work more freely than would be possible in a novel and to calculate their effects in a manner peculiarly his own. So where earlier Gothic novelists found the tangible world getting in their way, Hawthorne urges us beyond the tangible world to "something truer and more real, than we can see with the eyes, and touch with the finger" in order to leave us confronting an abyss of meaning (*CEWNH* 10:120).

Hawthorne sets this tale in the sunny but faraway world of Renaissance Padua: "A young man, named Giovanni Guasconti, came, very long ago, from the more southern region of Italy, to pursue his studies at the University of Padua" (*CEWNH* 10:93). If we think this narrative vagueness represents a casual attitude toward the setting on Hawthorne's part, Bensick demonstrates beyond doubt that the historical details within the text are accurate and pointed. Nonetheless, the mode of the opening is one not of precise historical investigation but rather of vague and romanticized historicism. Before we assign this technique to a pernicious narrator, as Bensick would want us to, let us consider where it leads us in the tale. Simply to know that Hawthorne checked his historical facts for plausibility by no means establishes his willingness to sacrifice effective narrative structure to the less obvious historical validity. The narrative procedure has its own Gothic rationale.

At first it seems that there is none of the first-person immediacy of Poe's best tales, nor any of his penchant for the properly atmospheric. But, as the opening paragraph proceeds, both of these assumptions are challenged:

> Giovanni, who had but a scanty supply of gold ducats in his pocket, took lodgings in a high and gloomy chamber of an old edifice, which looked not unworthy to have been the palace of a Paduan noble, and which, in fact, exhibited over its entrance the armorial bearings of a family long since extinct. The young stranger, who was not unstudied in the great poem of his country, recollected that one of the ancestors of this family, and per-

haps an occupant of this very mansion, had been pictured by
Dante as a partaker of the immortal agonies of his Inferno.
(*CEWNH* 10:93)

Throughout these opening lines there is deliberate vagueness about
time and place, a "high and gloomy chamber," an "extinct" family, and
a reference to the *Inferno*. If a historically-minded critic can stop and
track these allusions down, so much the better; but even more to the
point, it seems to me, are those readings which capture the ominous
atmosphere and the uneasiness, which depend on vagueness and the
power of allusion.[8] There is no need yet to turn on the narrator. He has
suffused a long list of historical markers with a gloom that history can
evoke only in the imagination. Indeed, he appeals to our imaginations
in an attempt to create an intellectual and emotional bond with his
readers. This is the opening paragraph of a tale, the narrative technique announces, and unsettling things are in store. We are being seduced by the narrative and trained as readers of this tale at the same
time. We are alive to a setting and a mood. That is what is important
here. If we are being seduced, it is into a relatively safe and only
vaguely threatening world.[9] We are being put into the mood for a
haunting.

As the paragraph continues to its conclusion we see that such suggestions are neither idle nor uncalculating:

> These reminiscences and associations, together with the ten-
> dency to heart-break natural to a young man for the first time
> out of his native sphere, caused Giovanni to sigh heavily, as
> he looked around the desolate and ill-furnished apartment.
> (*CEWNH* 10:93)

Not only have the terms of the tale already been set, but an important
aspect of its technique has been demonstrated as well. For although
Giovanni is not the narrator of this tale, we realize that he becomes the
focal point of interpretive perceptions and that his responses will com-
pel us to search for meaning where it may not objectively inhere. He
thus becomes both the transmitter and the transformer of events in this
tale, much as Poe's narrator controls the experience of his tales. But if
we see more than Giovanni sees, it is from a narrative perspective that
encourages us to doubt whether we have seen anything at all. The
distancing effect of the opening of the tale merely places us in a world
that almost immediately we are struggling to see more clearly than
Hawthorne allows us to. Giovanni's vision is limited, and his responses

are subject to error. Throughout the tale we are forced to consider these facts and to deal with them as we can. As we do so, we become authors of the tale to which we are responding.[10]

"The role of the reader," Iser tells us, "emerges from [an] interplay of perspectives [such as narrator, characters, plot line], for he finds himself called upon to mediate between them" (*Act of Reading* 33). In "Rappaccini's Daughter," we find ourselves in the position of having constantly to decide among a number of alternatives in each of these areas. The cosy titillation of the opening gives way to a narrative procedure that insists on allegorical interpretation at the same time that it makes such interpretation impossible.

Clearly Hawthorne's technique represents a reaction to that of the Gothic novelists, who present an all-or-nothing proposition, in which we must totally dismiss or totally accept supernatural experimentation. In some ways his technique can be seen as a reaction to Poe as well. In Poe's tales we struggle to see with a sense of the threat of what is absent. Our dread remains primarily direct and emotional. More often Poe's technique is to heighten the verisimilitude of the narrator so that we tend to "believe" his report. Hawthorne, in this tale, is more indirect: He creates an omniscient narrator and then limits his omniscience, thus forcing us to confront the difficulty of understanding what is going on. In fact, Hawthorne emphasizes narrative disbelief as a way of making us epistemologically anxious. To relieve this anxiety, we push toward interpretive certainty, thereby falling into the trap Hawthorne has set for us.

Giovanni's first observation of Rappaccini's garden is a purple passage that stands out as brilliant description. How different it is from a euphemistic Radcliffean description or an ominous Poeian one. The effects here are subtle and refined, not because the narrator is effete but rather in order to lure us into the seductive trap of the narrative. Giovanni notices that "it might once have been the pleasure-place of an opulent family; for there was the ruin of a marble fountain in the centre, sculptured with rare art, but so wofully shattered that it was impossible to trace the original design from the chaos of remaining fragments" (*CEWNH* 10:94). This description cries out for interpretation, not from a specifically historical perspective (whose garden was it?) but from a moral or cultural one (what does this opulence and decay, art and chaos, *mean?*). The latter perspective is surely that from which the story is traditionally read. The only problem with it at this moment is that it leads nowhere. The description creates a distinctive mood, but if we begin searching for allegorical interpretations we will be foiled. For the water "continued to gush and sparkle into the sunbeams as cheerfully as ever" (*CEWNH* 10:94). The scene is as enticing as it is appalling, seeming overdetermined but in fact radically indeterminate. "All about the pool . . . grew various plants, that seemed to require a plentiful supply of moisture for the nourishment of gigantic leaves, and, in some instances, flowers gorgeously magnificent" (*CEWNH* 10:95). If allegorically disposed, we will again probe this lush and verdant foliage for "deeper" meaning. The last phrase, in particular, suggests an overabundance of some kind, a profusion, even decadence. To the degree that we have already become involved in Giovanni's fate, we hunt the garden for signs of its danger.

And we are very quickly rewarded: "One plant had wreathed itself round the statue of Vertumnus, which was thus quite veiled and shrouded in a drapery of hanging foliage, so happily arranged that it might have served a sculptor for a study" (*CEWNH* 10:95). The plants in their profusion suggest a threat: Here in enveloping the presiding god of the seasons, they have rendered the representative of life a veiled and shrouded corpse. Surely, an attentive reader feels a twinge of fear for Giovanni here. The garden, we say to ourselves, is somehow fatal. By allowing ourselves to interpret the description in this way, we set ourselves up to be betrayed by our own responses.

The crux of interpretation is figured forth in the person of Beatrice Rappaccini, the mysterious woman who wanders in the garden beneath Giovanni's window. Before Beatrice appears we have come, with Giovanni, to view the garden as a strange and forbidding place. It is tended by Rappaccini, "a tall, emaciated, sallow, and sickly-looking man," who walks among his flowers as "one walking among malignant influences, such as savage beasts, or deadly snakes, or evil spirits" (*CEWNH* 10:95–96). This description is surely meant to encourage a sense of danger, both for Giovanni and for the reader; and it is worth noting that there is a range of malignancy, from the mere outward threat of the beasts to the subtle internal poison of the snakes, and ultimately to the spiritual undoing of the evil spirits. Rather than creating a complementary effect, however, this range of dangers offers us almost too many alternatives. Giovanni's "imagination" is at work here, creating possibilities that are threatening and strange.

Such subtlety continues as the narrator goes on to interpret Giovanni's experience of the garden in terms far from transparent in their implication: "Was this garden, then, the Eden of the present world?—and this man, with such a perception of harm in what his own hands caused to grow, was he the Adam?" (*CEWNH* 10:96). These lines have been interpreted variously, but we must remember that it is impossible to distinguish between Giovanni and the narrator here.[11] These are not words that the narrator puts in Giovanni's mouth, but the youth's own imaginative reaction to the scene and figure before him. It suggests Giovanni's frame of mind—his readiness to project his own terms of response on the puzzling scene. Like Goodman Brown or Aylmer, he attempts to translate experiences into terms that he can understand. In this case, the terms of his response are telling: He contrasts the "present world" to the world of innocence in Eden, and labels this gardener as corrupt as Adam was innocent. He betrays a gloominess of temperament as a result, and to the degree that we participate in this response, we do as well. The form of the rhetorical question of course encourages our involvement and commits us to a stance that may later return to haunt us. We are being schooled to approach experience hermeneutically and to move beyond appearance to "reality." An allegorical reading, that is, encourages us to see Rappaccini as evil. The nature of that evil depends on our understanding of the question. But whether his evil is social, or scientific, or metaphysical ultimately matters less than our readiness to interpret him as a malignant force. Our confusion encourages rather than diminishes this response because it is easier to turn on Rappaccini than to live without knowing where we are. Besides, Giovanni senses this malignancy as well, and as readers we are readily convinced to go along with him—even if that means, as here, following a path fraught with danger.

When Beatrice first enters this world she is simply "a young girl, arrayed with as much richness of taste as the most splendid of the flowers" (*CEWNH* 10:97). No sooner has she appeared, however, than this analogy with the flowers is extended to include a certain poisonous malignancy of her own. At least this is what it seems to our hero:

> Yet Giovanni's fancy must have grown morbid, while he looked down into the garden; for the impression which the fair stranger made upon him was as if here were another flower, the human sister of those vegetable ones, as beautiful as they—more beautiful than the richest of them—but still to be touched only with a glove, nor to be approached without a mask. As Beatrice came down the garden path, it was observable that she handled and inhaled the odor of several of the plants, which her father had most sedulously avoided. (*CEWNH* 10:97)

What is crucial in this passage is not Beatrice's poisonous nature, but the indirectness with which the narrator presents it to us. "Giovanni's fancy must have grown morbid," "the impression which the fair stranger made upon him," even "it was observable": Nowhere is there a direct statement of the truth that Giovanni's responses seem to imply. Because the narrator offers no aid, we are forced to determine for ourselves how we shall relate to Giovanni's struggle to perceive. Everything is left to Giovanni's observation, and objective fact becomes uncertain.

It seems to me fruitless to indict the narrator at moments like these. He stands back and allows the natural interaction of character, situation, and reader. Hawthorne's famed ambiguity works to involve his readers more directly in the tale, as they seek to interpret a fact that is not even clearly established. We recall that Iser sees a literary "fact" as something created by the readers. In distinguishing "meaning" and significance, moreover, Iser gets at the heart of the kind of problem we face in this situation. He says that "classical norms of interpretation rob the reading experience of a vital dimension in equating meaning with significance," and he insists that the "search for meaning that has dogged approaches to post-classical literature has caused a great deal of confusion, precisely because the distinction between meaning and significance has been overlooked" (*Act of Reading* 151). What happens in "Rappaccini's Daughter," typically for Hawthorne, is that the tale pushes us into a search for meaning, which in turn creates the significance of the tale. For Iser, "Significance is the reader's absorption of the meaning into his own existence" (151). In the case of the tale before us, we could say that significance is the measure of our inability to establish meaning without distorting the terms that the tale offers for establishing it.

Here, as elsewhere, the Gothic technique of the tale functions hermeneutically. When experience does not fit into any of Giovanni's interpretive structures, he is quick to imagine a disaster of "Gothic" proportions. He becomes haunted by his own situation for the reader: There is just enough ambiguity about what Giovanni sees to make it impossible for the reader to make up his or her mind how to take it. Very early on we begin to realize that at least part of the horror of the tale is the horror of deciding just what we can know and on what basis we can know it. Hawthorne's narrator encourages this hesitation because it ensures our search for an allegorical interpretation in which meaning seems more clear but ultimately more horrible. That is not enough, however, to keep us from attempting to interpret, or misinterpret, this world.

As Benjamin says, "The allegorical outlook has its origin in the conflict between the guilt-laden physis, held up as an example by Christianity and a purer *natura deorum*, embodied in the pantheon" (226). Already we are aware of this conflict in "Rappaccini's Daughter": Giovanni looks into a beautiful garden and guiltily thinks of sin. And in our own response to the tale, we look for a way of embodying that sin in the meaning we create.

Giovanni's own sense of the ominous leads him to an indirect mode of scientific inquiry, which involves Signor Pietro Baglioni, a genial professor who serves Hawthorne perfectly as an affective ploy. The archenemy of Rappaccini, Baglioni is all too happy to offer a severe indictment of the scientist: "He cares infinitely more for science than for mankind. His patients are interesting to him only as subjects for some new experiment" (*CEWNH* 10:99). All that has gone before leads us to jump at this response (as Giovanni seems to) as an explanation for the disturbing events we have "witnessed." There is a narrative warning to counsel us against such a response ("the youth might have taken Baglioni's opinions with many grains of allowance, had he known that there was a professional warfare of long continuance between him and Doctor Rappaccini, in which the latter was generally thought to have gained the advantage" [*CEWNH* 10:100]). I submit that we realize the import of this warning only in retrospect, so great is our need to have an answer to the questions the tale has raised. Bensick has suggested that we should take the narrator at his word and look into the "black-letter tracts" (100) that spell out the nature of the conflict between Rappaccini and Baglioni. What she finds in them is a bitter conflict between Paraclesian and Aristotelian science and a medical controversy that we would characterize today as homeopathic versus alopathic. Rappaccini deals in poisons, Baglioni in antidotes (see Bensick 44–73). But at this point in our reading, or even rereading, we are in no position to explain Giovanni's uneasiness and our own confusion in these terms. The tale may find a source for its effect in such a controversy. More important is the distrust of Rappaccini that the poison theory instils and the uneasiness that our doubts about Baglioni inspire. We are trapped, like Giovanni, between our fears and our prejudices. There is no way, not even an historical one, to get beyond them.

When Giovanni returns to his lodgings, he looks into the garden and, as he had "half-hoped, half-feared, would be the case" (*CEWNH* 10:101), Beatrice appears. He is attracted to her even more than he was before: "Her face being now more revealed than on the former occasion, he was struck by its expression of simplicity and sweetness; qualities that had not entered into his idea of her character" (*CEWNH* 10:102). Giovanni's "idea" is here challenged by an impression of sweetness and simplicity. In direct contrast to the intrigue and confusion of the encounter with Baglioni, we have the straightforward innocence of the girl herself. Of course that innocence may only be apparent, but the impression it creates for Giovanni is enough to make him qualify his mental picture of her. If his hopes and fears are in conflict here—his attraction to Beatrice and his suspicions about her nature—he finds her person to be in itself pure. In other words, Giovanni is puzzled about his relationship to *another* here and experiences all the doubts that someone trapped in his own ego would be expected to experience.

Giovanni is suffering from the peculiar psychological horror that Kristeva describes as abjection. It arises from the fact of the opposition between I and Other, an opposition she calls "violent but uncertain" (7), tantamount in certain cases to a kind of psychosis. Giovanni is hopelessly trapped between desire and repulsion (see Crews 118–24), so busy creating a response to Beatrice that he does not really attend to who she is. Now he notices that she *"seemed to have indulged* a fantastic humor in heightening, both by the arrangement of her dress and the selection of its hues" [my italics] a resemblance to the most pernicious flowers. The ambiguity inherent in the phrase I have italicized continues to develop a sense of epistemological confusion. This ambiguity grows as Giovanni watches a lizard die from a drop of moisture from a flower—as it "appeared" to him—and a butterfly crumple from Beatrice's breath. "'Am I awake? Have I my senses?' said he to himself. 'What is this being?—beautiful, shall I call her?—or inexpressibly terrible?'" (*CEWNH* 10:102–3).

This exploration of subjectivity and its inherent abjection before whatever lies beyond it is perfectly suited to the rationale of the tale. Even without a first person narrator, Hawthorne limits the tale to a single perspective and challenges us with the definite limits of knowledge and understanding that perspective affords. Èjxenbaum says that "the story must be constructed on the basis of some contradiction" (4), and the contradiction here is between Giovanni's subjective response and an objective truth with which the tale tantalizes us but never provides.[12] The form of subjectivity itself is the only meaning there is.

Hawthorne's ambiguous presentation of events causes us to share in Giovanni's confusion. We are forced to attempt an interpretation of these circumstances and thereby confront the possibility of an absence of meaning beyond Beatrice herself. Giovanni cannot "call" Beatrice one thing or another—cannot define her—because he does not know her. But he proceeds to assign her a meaning of his own. Hawthorne calculates his presentation so that we join Giovanni in his endeavor and even move beyond him in our ruthless desire to create a world of literal correspondence. Hence, Hawthorne creates a Gothic device out of the very act of reading. "Rappaccini's Daughter" is about as close as Hawthorne comes to outward Gothic—an old house, a garden, a villainous scientist—but even here it is not these things themselves, but the transformation that the human consciousness plays upon them, that makes them Gothic.

Jauss has said that a literary work can "reverse the relationship of question and answer and in the medium of art confront the reader with a new, 'opaque' reality that no longer allows itself to be understood from a pregiven horizon of expectations" (44). When that happens, the reader becomes uneasy, and in his uneasiness he searches for "the questions that will decode for him the perception of the world and the interpersonal problem toward which the answer of the literature is directed" (44). But in doing so, we as readers are likely to perpetrate our own miscontructions, which have all the violence of Gothic imprisonment. For we distort the tale in our own need to establish its meaning.

Before considering this affective technique in greater detail, let us consider Hawthorne's use of setting as a narrative device. Hawthorne does not imitate Poe in his manipulation of scene: While Poe uses his description of setting to heighten tension and to reflect various states of mind, Hawthorne invests such description with an even more intricate involvement with the action. Settings come to participate in the action of a tale—insofar as the characters respond to them—in a way that for Poe would seem to undermine the single effect. Indeed, at times, they become a kind of substitute for action.

When Giovanni finally gains entrance to Rappaccini's garden, for instance, he is confronted with his own fears:

> The aspect of one and all of them [the plants] dissatisfied him; their gorgeousness seemed fierce, passionate, and even unnatural. . . . Several, also, would have shocked a delicate instinct by an appearance of artificialness, indicating that there had been such commixture, and, as it were, adultery of various vegetable species, that the production was no longer of God's making, but the monstrous offspring of man's depraved fancy, glowing with only an evil mockery of beauty. (*CEWNH* 10:110)

Obviously this garden is not just meant to scare us (although it does partly have that function) like a castle passageway in Radcliffe, a graveyard in Lewis, or a prison chamber in Maturin; nor does it have quite the passionate presence of *Wuthering Heights* or the eerily macabre impact typical of a Poe scene. Instead, the description engages us: Surely it seems to tell us something about the danger facing Giovanni, but it defies our attempts to tell exactly what that might be.

In one sense, of course, the garden is a projection of Giovanni's fears of the "unnatural" in Beatrice, and because we can accept its menacing nature without examining the description closely, it simply heightens our fears about what may befall him. If we look more closely, however, we must question the significance of phrases like "adultery of various vegetable species." Because we must search for the questions to which this odd statement is an answer (does the term merely suggest the "unnatural"? is someone other than Giovanni implicated? what is the nature of the evil Hawthorne is invoking?), our instinctive reaction in support of Giovanni is undermined and our complacent distance from the events of the tale is eroded. For in search of the right questions to ask, we are taken beyond the limits of the text and into the confines of our own responding consciousness. The "objective" description thereby becomes absorbed in the subjective, and its meaning ceases to be fixed in any literal sense.[13]

The nature of "character" in this tale is equally indeterminate and ultimately menacing. Paradoxically, the narrative distance from Giovanni, and as a result our resistance to him, diminish even as our sympathy for Beatrice grows. Again we find ourselves in a position that encourages interpretation and judgment but makes them both impossible. This situation is of course analogous to Giovanni's own. Hawthorne underlines the general state of confusion through narrative asides and descriptive reservations that call Giovanni's perceptions into question but heighten the sense of imminent danger. He makes the reader feel the discomfort of the situation as a way of infinitely postponing narrative interpretation and stands uncannily silent when Giovanni is in deepest turmoil. In order for such affective devices to engage the reader, however, Giovanni must be more subtly and, let us say, novelistically depicted than an analogous character in Poe's fiction. Poe's technique insists on narrative distance as the key to engaging his reader in the fate, for instance, of Roderick Usher. Poe deliberately keeps us from exploring the "reality" behind Usher's terror except insofar as it is expressed in outward, physical terms. Hawthorne, on the other hand, makes us as familiar with the thoughts of his central character, as is necessary to involve us in the intricate workings of his perceptual response to bizarre and threatening events. We still do not have a "full" character, in the sense that characters we encounter in James are full, but we do have a vivid sense of Giovanni's vulnerability and his fear in response to the threatening and unknown meaning of Beatrice. As a result, we react to Giovanni's predicament as well as with him in response to Beatrice.

The tale form allows this richness of character precisely because it

is affectively motivated. Giovanni's subjectivity becomes a familiar
ground because we must probe it to establish our own response. Giovanni's predicament, moreover, is more powerful to the degree that we
understand the intricacies of its development. In truth, we understand
very little else. Giovanni's confusion and his fear become the ground
of exploration, and they become the center of significance as well. For
whatever else we can or cannot interpret in this tale, Giovanni we
understand.

Professor Baglioni, moreover, offers us a scientific basis for all Giovanni's fears. He takes an unfocused anxiety and transforms it into
specific horrifying fact. His suggestion that Giovanni himself has
fallen prey to Rappaccini's experimentation is more than enough
scientific corroboration, despite narrative reservation, to justify our
fears. The garden, as in the passage quoted above, immediately becomes a fully terrifying Gothic setting. And Beatrice, as angelic as she
seems, comes to share in the general air of malignancy.

Hawthorne leaves Beatrice undeveloped for obvious reasons. She is
meant to remain a mystery to Giovanni and to us alike, but this is not
simply to heighten the tension of the tale. Every step we take toward
defining and judging Beatrice implicates us in Giovanni's final crime.
Not Beatrice herself, but his impression of Beatrice comes to haunt
Giovanni:

> Whether or no Beatrice possessed those terrible attributes—
> that fatal breath—the affinity with those so beautiful and
> deadly flowers—which were indicated by what Giovanni had
> witnessed, she had at least instilled a fierce and subtle poison
> into his system. It was not love, although her rich beauty was a
> madness to him; nor horror, even while he fancied her spirit to
> be imbued with the same baneful essence that seemed to per-
> vade her physical frame; but a wild offspring of both love and
> horror that had each parent in it, and burned like one and shiv-
> ered like the other. Giovanni knew not what to dread; still less
> did he know what to hope; yet hope and dread kept a continual
> warfare in his breast, alternately vanquishing one another and
> starting up afresh to renew the contest. Blessed are all simple
> emotions, be they dark or bright! It is the lurid intermixture of
> the two that produces the illuminating blaze of the infernal re-
> gions. (*CEWNH* 10:105)

These feelings are for Giovanni not in the least dependent on any
"truth" about Beatrice. The poison—the mixture of love and horror—

is "instilled" by Beatrice only in the sense that she is the occasion for Giovanni to nurture such feelings.[14] The hell that Giovanni finds himself trapped in is as powerful as any of the subterranean worlds of the Gothic novel. And yet he has created this Gothic world for himself. Similarly the reader, in sympathy with Giovanni or for reasons of his or her own, is also responsible for creating the particular Gothic force of the work. What is horrifying about Beatrice lies in our reaction to her. Hawthorne has internalized the Gothic, that is, and involved the reader in the horror to a degree unprecedented. Instead of being terrified by the Gothic experience, we become, with Giovanni, the agents of that terror. Recent clinical readings are no less ruthless than moral, religious, or sexual ones. As soon as we start to explain Beatrice, we implicate ourselves in her destruction.

Whereas in Radcliffe the hero defends the heroine from the terrifying assaults of the Gothic villain, here the Gothic villain and the hero have become one. Indeed, Giovanni's madness is self-inflicted. Or, at least, the horror generated from our sense of Beatrice's toxic potential becomes less significant as the horror of Giovanni's response increases. His fear is what is most horrible within the tale. No objectively horrifying situation can equal the brutal malignancy of his response.

That we are intimately involved is reemphasized every time we, with Giovanni, question Beatrice's innocence. Beatrice herself offers us the terms in which we might free her from our judgment. When it is clear that Giovanni is being drawn to her in spite of himself, she tells him to believe not what he hears about her but what he sees. On the basis of what he feels he has seen, he hesitates and presses her further: "Bid me believe nothing, save what comes from your own lips" (*CEWNH* 10:112). Her response is crucial:

> "I do so bid you, Signor!" she replied. "Forget whatever you may have fancied in regard to me. If true to the outward senses, still it may be false in its essence. But the words of Beatrice Rappaccini's lips are true from the depths of the heart outward. Those you may believe!" (*CEWNH* 10:112)

Beatrice is telling Giovanni literally that he has misinterpreted the signs of her malignancy and that what seems is not always what is. She invites him to ignore his fallacious interpretation of experience that has perforce been based on surface appearances and to attend instead to the essential truth that resides in her heart. Beatrice asks Giovanni to abjure his everyday "I-It" response to reality and to substitute an "I-Thou" response, which acknowledges otherness and accepts it. She asks him to participate in her experience rather than isolate himself as a manipulator of the object.[15] She asks him to accept her as herself.

In doing so, however, Beatrice emphasizes the nature of Giovanni's problem here. For her real nature is of course inaccessible to Giovanni and must be taken on faith. It may even lie beyond her own power of self-awareness and articulation. In that sense Beatrice is playing upon the central dichotomy of the tale—self and other—and she thereby heightens our sense of the potential horror that lack of knowledge threatens. Her words can be understood as popular superstition about the duality of experience or the center of significance in the tale. But in either case, we are powerless to settle for one reading or another, because something technically interesting almost immediately occurs to qualify our interpretation. Importantly separated from Giovanni here so that we can gauge our own response, alone we must confront the narrator's play on our impulses of faith and suspicion:

> But while she spoke, there was a fragrance in the atmosphere around her, rich and delightful, though evanescent, yet which the young man, from an indefinable reluctance, scarcely dared to draw into his lungs. It might be the odor of the flowers. Could it be Beatrice's breath, which thus embalmed her words with a strange richness, as if by steeping them in her heart? A faintness passed like a shadow over Giovanni, and flitted away; he seemed to gaze through the beautiful girl's eyes into her transparent soul, and felt no more doubt or fear. (*CEWNH* 10:112)

The aroma undermines our assent to Beatrice's protestation of innocence because it is the sign that we, like Giovanni, have been anticipating. The narrator's "as if," however, contradicts our first response, offers an alternative to the "poison" theory, and casts the problem of interpretation itself into high relief. Because the narrator has allowed us to react against Beatrice before checking this response, we are likely to dismiss his seemingly equivocal suggestion that Beatrice's words have been steeped in her heart as unconvincing narrative speculation. Analogy only confuses us here, but we know what is really going on, we say to ourselves with all the assurance of dramatic irony. Hawthorne's suggestion of an alternative to the "poison" theory is so weak that it ensures our believing in the poison all the more strongly. So, as the passage proceeds, we step even beyond Giovanni in our suspicion, and see him as a victim of the poisonous breath and mysterious spell. Our literary reaction, that is, the astuteness of our observation, indicts us even further here.

Hawthorne is of course heightening the significance of his tale by involving us in such a moment of dramatic irony. Further, our sense of understanding something that Giovanni has missed throws us into the situation with a greater enthusiasm for routing the ghosts. Most importantly, however, in separating us from Giovanni at this point, in encouraging us to see evil where he sees none, Hawthorne has worked us into the position that will render the denouement most powerful. We are forced to develop an anti-Beatrice stance that is not primarily influenced by a fear Giovanni articulates. We judge her for ourselves, perhaps even despite our desire to believe in her. This disjunction has in it all the makings of madness, and as the tale proceeds it indeed takes us further and further in the direction where madness seems most clearly to lie.

Because the "allegory" of Beatrice's poison and Giovanni's detoxification campaign works for Hawthorne as a substitute for conventional Gothic use of the supernatural, the author is free to present a tale that remains convincing on its literal level, even though the events it describes are unabashedly "marvelous." By using the narrator both as a focusing device and as a confused and confusing interpreter of events within the tale, Hawthorne manages to cast reasonable doubt on the bizarre at the same time as he persuades us of its actuality. The narrator's perception (as in Poe's "House of Usher") becomes a limiting and seemingly unsatisfying point of reference for us readers, which forces us to determine for ourselves the "meaning" of events within the tale. The narrator never presents the "proof" of Beatrice's poison, for instance, without pausing for some sort of narrative explanation. This is largely beside the point, however, because we are already interpreting the tale in a manner that ignores the literal in favor of the allegorical reading. We accept the literal description of events between Beatrice and Giovanni because of our certainty that a deeper "meaning" lies behind them. All the characters within the tale, as well as the narrator, encourage such a reading. We come to fear for Giovanni not simply because of the literal threat of poison, but also because of our sense of deeper, menacing implications inherent to the poison as an allegorical device. As the events of the tale reach a point of crisis, we feel both justified in our malevolent interpretation and appalled at its consequences. Either impulse is as profound, however, as the sense that we ourselves have been the victims of a narrative technique from which "meaning" infinitely recedes. Benjamin speaks of the "violence of the dialectic movement within . . . allegorical depths" (166): This tale pulls us between the literal and the figural and condemns us to the distraction of potential meaninglessness.

When Giovanni receives from Baglioni an antidote to what the latter has convinced him is Beatrice's poisonous potential, the terms of our discussion come into clearer focus. Giovanni first makes a tentative act of faith in Beatrice in which he refuses to acknowledge the realm of the literal events he has witnessed, which "dissolving in the pure light of her character, had no longer the efficacy of facts, but were acknowledged as mistaken fantasies. . . . There is something truer and more real, than what we can see with the eyes, and touch with the finger." If there is something more real, it barely sustains Giovanni, for very quickly he "fell down, grovelling among earthly doubts, and defiled therewith the pure whiteness of Beatrice's image." When Giovanni's growing faith falters, Beatrice begins ironically to become *his* victim: "Not that he gave her up; he did but distrust" (*CEWNH* 10:120).

After all, one critic says, Beatrice *is* enigmatic (Crowley 26). But that does not render the drama of Giovanni's response any less powerful. Bensick claims that the narrator trivializes the literal events of the tale and pushes us in the direction of a moral interpretation (67–71, 114–19). But an interpretation is, after all, what we want: It would have been impossible for Hawthorne to have made this tale as powerful as it is without this narrative presence to challenge us into searching for such meaning and to torment us with the possibility that none exists. Of course we end up interpreting the story for ourselves, but the narrator's exclamations here, so in keeping with the terms of the tale, determine just how we do so. Whether there is "something truer and more real" is what the tale is about.[16]

The problem for Giovanni, then, becomes his inability to provide a satisfactory interpretation of events that have turned him from the literal towards the indefinite realm of the allegorical. Fact, fantasy, and something more real than sense impression thus mingle in Giovanni's befuddled response to his experience. In searching for the truth behind the action of the tale, Giovanni attempts to substitute his understanding of experience for experience itself. Even the higher response implicit in Giovanni's evocation of "the pure light of her character" is an interpretation as out of touch with the real Beatrice as any of his fearful impressions. Giovanni's abjection is based on his inability to break down the walls of his own subjectivity.[17] Indeed Giovanni's response carries us into an unknown and meaningless realm that we too are happy to substitute for Beatrice, the shadowy other. It nonetheless becomes the basis for our encouraging Giovanni's final outrage.

Instead of separating ourselves from Giovanni at this moment of distrust, the transcendent suggestion seems to exonerate his desire for "some decisive test that should satisfy him, once for all, whether there were those dreadful peculiarities in her physical nature, which could not be supposed to exist without some corresponding monstrosity of soul" (*CEWNH* 10:120). Bensick is helpful in articulating the assumptions behind such a stance. "Giovanni," she says, "leaps to the realm of ontology" (16). She encourages us to see this equation as problematic and reminds us that "Beatrice never does clearly agree with Giovanni that their apparent common destructive physical power has a spiritual dimension" (78). But Giovanni's failure to trust Beatrice is a kind of poison of its own, and we hardly need the narrator to interpret for us his increasing threat. For inherent in his doubts are the very terms of Giovanni's failure. His assumptions about Beatrice are themselves a venomous response based on fear and suspicion. His desire to purge her of her poisonous nature is really a need to make her subject to his own limited vision. In attempting this transformation, Giovanni changes the terms of allegorical implication: "Again Giovanni sent forth a breath, deeper, longer, and imbued with a venomous feeling out of his heart; he knew not whether he were wicked or only desperate" (*CEWNH* 10:122). The narrator is making the point that only after Giovanni has determined, with our support, to test Beatrice do we witness his poison. Giovanni's desperation becomes the mirror of our own confusion here. As readers we are responsible for the "meaning" of the tale, but already we become increasingly uneasy about what our full responsibility will be.

When Giovanni thus threatens the life of a spider, we have no choice but to begin searching for a new set of allegorical terms with which to interpret events in the tale. If, as is likely, we begin to shift responsibility from Beatrice to Giovanni in this final movement of the tale; or, as is equally likely, we begin to sense the limitations of our allegorical response, we are really only following the affective path that Hawthorne has so carefully provided.

In the final interview between hero and heroine, Beatrice begins to admit to Giovanni the truth of her scientific breeding and of the loneliness of her existence, but he interrupts her with an impassioned accusation:

> "Accursed one!" cried he, with venomous scorn and anger. "And finding thy solitude wearisome, thou hast severed me, likewise, from all the warmth of life, and enticed me into thy region of unspeakable horror!" (*CEWNH* 10:124)

He goes on to call her hateful, ugly, loathsome and deadly—"a world's wonder of hideous monstrosity!" (*CEWNH* 10:124). Giovanni's "venomous scorn and anger" is enough to isolate us from him and to gain our sympathy for Beatrice, but we are kept from supporting her by her own admission that all of which he has accused her is true. So again we are confronted with the interpretive paradox that has been haunting us all along.

In challenging Giovanni's assumption that a poisonous body means a poisonous soul (one could ask in what but a literary realm such meaning would inhere), Beatrice articulates the paradox of meaning and demonstrates the ruthlessness of Giovanni's desire for precise and definite correspondence between experience and his interpretation of experience (see Bensick 74–92). The narrator then tells us that "after such deep love had been so bitterly wronged as was Beatrice's love by Giovanni's blighting words" (*CEWNH* 10:126), there is nothing left for Beatrice in this world. Like the heroine of "The Birth-mark," "she must pass heavily, with that broken heart, across the borders of Time— she must bathe her hurts in some fount of Paradise, and forget her grief in the light of immortality—and *there* be well!" (*CEWNH* 10:126). Surely such a statement has little value in an historical interpretation of the tale. These vague promises are more a measure of what Beatrice has lost than what she has gained. The narrator is forced to turn toward future hope rather than present consolation. But is that not at least part of the point? If Beatrice is beyond interpretation in her mere otherness, will she not be finally so in death? Perhaps for Giovanni that finality will come as a relief. For, with Baglioni, his real obsession is to put an end to his private anxiety.

Giovanni's offer of the "antidote" finally brings this action to completion. The antidote itself now exists as a sort of grotesque parody of our own response to Beatrice; and, ironically, it will offer her release from the greatest ills that beset her.[18] There is probably no doubt in our minds as Beatrice takes this drug that her gesture is one of self-destruction. Only Giovanni is ingenuous enough to think that it will "work." His stance, too, is a kind of parody of what we had been hoping for only moments earlier, reminding us of how great our own limitations have been. When Beatrice has taken the fatal draught she bids Giovanni farewell: "Thy words of hatred are like lead within my heart—but they, too, will fall away as I ascend. Oh, was there not, from the first, more poison in thy nature than in mine?" (*CEWNH* 10:127). Far from suggesting that Giovanni is in a state of incubatory syphilis (Bensick 103–4), Beatrice's analogy between words and things represents but another attempt to cross the abyss of meaning. The tale has finally proven, however, that to do so is an impossibility. We might note that Giovanni's isolation is now complete. What Beatrice offered him was a way out of the limitations of his own timid personality. That opportunity is lost. Giovanni is trapped now with the meaning—and the total meaninglessness—that his "test" has provided him. Whatever the "meaning" of this final scene, it rebounds on him. Gothic hero and Gothic villain have become one.

The tale actually ends with a confrontation between Rappaccini and Baglioni in which the latter cries out triumphantly over the scientist's loss. Aside from making us feel that we, with Giovanni and Beatrice, have all been the victims of a larger controversy, Baglioni's contemptuous words suggest that the very terms of our response to the tale have been inadequate to the complexities of experience it contains: "Rappaccini! Rappaccini! And is *this* the upshot of your experiment?" (*CEWNH* 10:128). These words ring in our ears at the end of the tale in haunting contrast to Beatrice's own soft challenge. Rappaccini is rightly accused, perhaps, but Baglioni's tone of triumph is so grotesquely misplaced that our feelings at the close of the tale are pushed in the direction of self-contempt.[19] We have been involved in an experiment ourselves, and in human terms we have failed.

Hawthorne's affective technique, then, has involved playing our own responses against us and, in a way, generating the Gothic horror of the tale out of our desire to give meaning to his allegory. Again, the tale form has been central to this technique. In the first place it allows Hawthorne the freedom to manipulate his allegory most affectively. The distance and tone of the tale opening make us more receptive to the *bizarreries* that follow. The freedom from novelistic restraints in terms of setting and character means that Hawthorne is able to manipulate those concerns simply to serve his affective ends. Most importantly, though, as we have seen, the tale is able to establish itself in relation to the reader so intimately as to involve our responses directly within its formal nature. In other words, the only meaning of the tale resides in the terms of our response to what transpires there. In a novel, the emotions that are raised most often keep us in attendance upon an action. In a tale the emotions almost begin to supersede the action and serve as an affective end themselves. Hawthorne combines an emotional and an intellectual response in order to force us to a realization of the nature of the horror inherent to human interaction. That we share in the violent nature of the hero of the tale is something that we are forced to feel, because of our own recognition of the impossible situation embodied in the tale's central paradox.

The tale form is significant here because it provides the context, in a way that for earlier Gothicists the novel could not, for the kind of ontological confusion that encourages this self-confrontation. A tale does not have to depend on the empirical verities that are central to a novel. Charles May says that "If the novel creates the illusion of reality by presenting a literal authenticity to the material facts of the external world . . . the short story attempts to be authentic to the immaterial reality of the inner world of the self in its relation to eternal rather than temporal reality" (328–29). May's conception suggests the area in which the tale confronts us and by means of which it creates our own response. It concerns itself with the meaning and power of subjectivity and with the significance of private rather than public values. The world is of secondary importance in a tale. Indeed, the force behind the tale form draws us from the world that we know. Out of the resulting state of insecurity emerge responses to circumstances that in a novel would only cause us to laugh. Hawthorne seduces us out of our very safe world by subtly transforming, through allegory, what seems like our own world into a realm where his affective intentions are in control; he engages us in outwardly ridiculous circumstances simply because we feel we can assign them meaning. Once our understanding has been so engaged he can use it to manipulate us into a position where our sympathy works against us. Then he confuses the allegorical focus we thought we had established and proves to us that what is most horrifying is in our own world after all. While the novel draws us gradually into its world, the tale, as Hawthorne employs it, seduces us quickly into a world that takes whatever dimension we create for it. There is neither the development of a novel nor the denouement. The extremely simple allegorical shape of the action makes the effects all the more profound. We are forced to look beyond the surface of the action and end up confronting only the limitations of our own response.

The Gothic horror of Hawthorne's tales works, as this analysis suggests, from inside out. Hawthorne burrows deeper even than Poe because the ultimate force of each of his tales resides in the reader. Poe terrifies us with situations, but with Hawthorne literature itself becomes Gothic matter. The allegorical nature of his tales forces us, as well, to interpret the tenor of the Gothic vehicle—in this tale the poison itself—in purely subjective terms. For where Hawthorne provides no meaning, we are quick to provide one. More important, however, is the fact that the tale thereby expands beyond its limited confines into the limitless reaches of our own private worlds. In a novel the world presented always remains out there, while in the best of tales it lies most deeply within.

Hawthorne's tale technique thus depends upon his leading the reader through a "literary" appreciation of a text to a more intimate involvement with it. This technique emerges from a very private sense of the nature of human experience, which finally Hawthorne enables us to share. His allegories may at first seem quaint to the modern reader, but in their quaintness lies their power: The inadequacy of the "morals" of these tales encourages us to supply the richness of Gothic implication. In doing so, we become implicated in their Gothic nature.

6

James's Ghostly Impressions

The greatest of Hawthorne's early critics and the one most sensitive to the nature of his achievement was, of course, Henry James. James learned a great deal from Hawthorne, and various aspects of James's work have been interestingly related to that of his predecessor.[1] From very early in his career James experimented with the tale form; therefore he was alive to the technique whereby Hawthorne had heightened the affective power of his own tales. In his study of Hawthorne for the English Men of Letters series, James describes those tales in terms that give us a crucial, if not surprising, insight into his interpretation of Hawthorne's technique:

> The charm—the great charm—is that they [Hawthorne's tales] are glimpses of a great field, of the whole deep mystery of man's soul and conscience. They are moral, and their interest is moral; they deal with something more than the mere accidents and conventionalities, the surface occurrences of life. The fine thing in Hawthorne is that he cared for the deeper psychology, and that, in his way, he tried to become familiar with it. . . . This air, on the author's part, of being a confirmed *habitué* of a region of mysteries and subtleties, constitutes the originality of his tales. (*Hawthorne* 64)

James echoes Hawthorne's own terminology here: *moral* interest, *something more* than conventionality, a *deeper* psychology; all these remind us of Hawthorne's affective technique and his manner of engaging the reader in Gothic experience. The "mysteries and subtleties" James found in Hawthorne's tales are vastly intensified in his own, especially in the ghostly tales, which include his most important examples of the form.[2] James's concern for "the whole deep mystery of man's soul and conscience" surfaces everywhere in his tales, rendering them intellectually and emotionally sophisticated. James's own rewriting of morality, his own handling of the conflict between Gothic experience and narrative convention, carry him beyond the formal difficulties that confounded his eighteenth-century predecessors and enable him to refine, if not revolutionize, the achievement of his American forebears. James was committed to integrating Gothic concerns into the novelistic tradition without diluting them in intensity or fierceness. It was possible for him to accomplish this goal because James understood the problems inherent in Gothic expression and knew how to create a narrative form precisely suited to the eerie formlessness of his material. If there is something cold—at times almost diabolical—about his Gothic enterprise, we must still admire the brilliance with which he makes his own version of horror so thoroughly harrowing.

James was from the first committed to the tale as a serious literary form. Throughout his career he made remarks such as that to be found in his *Notebooks* for Sunday, 19 May, 1899:

> But [Taine's] talk about [Turgenev] has done me a world of good—reviving, refreshing, confirming, consecrating, as it were, the wish and dream that have lately grown stronger than ever in me—the desire that the literary heritage, such as it is, poor thing, that I may leave, shall consist of a large number of perfect *short* things, *nouvelles* and tales, illustrative of ever so many things in life—in the life I see and know and feel. (*NHJ* 101)

A glance at his *Notebooks* reveals, however, that it was no easy task for James to create the "perfect short thing." He repeatedly finds himself faced with short tales expanding, through his developmental impulse, into *nouvelles* or short novels.[3] Control becomes the admonitory imperative throughout the *Notebooks;* moreover, we can watch him trying to "control" himself in his attempts to delineate the method of compression necessary to keep a particular work within certain bounds. This process of self-regulation for effect suggests a wariness on James's part. It also suggests a certain distance from those effects themselves. Perhaps it is this distance that allows James to gauge his effects so precisely. In the Preface to "The Coxen Fund," for instance, he says of the tale that as a "marked example of the possible scope, at once, and the possible neatness of the *nouvelle*, it takes its place for me in a series of which the main merit and sign is to do the complicated thing with a strong brevity and lucidity—to arrive, on behalf of the multiplicity, at a certain science of control" (*AN* 231). Here is the Jamesian revision of the doctrine of "single effect": "To do the complicated thing with a strong brevity and lucidity"—instead of narrowing his scope and presenting only one side of experience, James intends to acknowledge the multiplicity of his material, but still to represent it so that a single purpose is maintained. He associates brevity with strength and distinguishes *nouvelle* from novel as a way of marking out an area of (literary) experience for which the novel is unsuited.

"The Coxen Fund" itself, as well as James's reports on its progress in his *Notebooks*, illustrates this process. The strong first person narrator of this tale works in a way that would not be unknown to Poe:

> The formula for the presentation of it in 20,000 words is to make it an *Impression*—as one of Sargent's pictures is an impression. That is, I must do it from my own point of view—that of an imagined observer, participator, chronicler. I must picture it, summarize it, impressionize it, in a word—compress and confine it by making it the picture of what I see. (*NHJ* 160)

James's careful use of the term *impression*, suggesting as it does the subjective focus of earlier Gothic tales, begins to elucidate James's own technique. For James, an observer is a participator, and in an impression the creator and the observer meet. "When James writes [in the Preface to *The Ambassadors*] about 'the terrible *fluidity* of self-revelation,'" William R. Goetz tells us, "he is referring less to the problem of dramatic construction . . . than to the extratextual question of the relations between author, reader, and work."[4] But this question is not "extratextual" for James. Indeed, his elaborate system of Notes and Prefaces assures our engagement in the process of creation as well as the dramatic intricacies of "self-revelation." James is certainly as sensitive to the affective implications of his narrative structure as any of the writers we have considered. An impression, if finely wrought, is perfectly recreated in the reader. That is the basis of James's Gothic technique.

He speaks further in this entry about "condensed action," "*intensification*," and "summarized exhibition," all techniques crucial to the Gothic tale as I have described it. For James a tale could only be perfectly short by being perfectly realized as an impression. His description makes it sound as though he is doing what he does in novels in miniature, but condensation and intensification are telling expressions that begin to hint at the essence of James's conception of the tale. Condensation and intensification result in a world as uncanny as it is seductive and magical.[5]

In his study of Hawthorne, James speaks of "the magnificent little romance of *Young Goodman Brown*" as "not a parable, but a picture, which is a very different thing" (93). James emphasizes the visual in Hawthorne because as a picture the tale has greatest effect. This helps us further to distinguish Jamesian Gothic: A picture, vivid enough and carefully drawn, can create an impression as no amount of "meaning" can. James saw a picture not only as an objective artifact, but as an expression of the most intimate subjective vision. If Hawthorne suggests an inner reality that recedes as we pursue it, James's realities are so profoundly internalized that it is the exterior that threatens to recede.

Leon Edel quotes James (at twenty-two) as saying that "a good ghost story must be connected at a hundred points with the common objects of life," and that he preferred the "terrors of the cheerful country house and the busy London lodgings" to the clanking trapdoor ghosts of the Gothic romance (quoted in "Introduction," *Ghostly Tales* xxv). By defying Gothic convention in this way, James seems to suggest a deeper and more fully articulated sense of Gothic material, which could be brought into the realm of realist fiction, or in effect brought out in it, without losing any of its intensity. James's ghosts appear without disrupting the surface reality of his tales because "the common objects of life" have no meaning for him beyond the impression that they so compliantly help him to create. James does not devalue the real, as Hawthorne seems sometimes to do; rather, he insists that it is always more than realistic fiction has allowed it to be. Subjective and objective distinctions begin to fade in James's work because he already understands that such distinctions need to be deconstructed before a truly powerful Gothic fiction can emerge. He harnesses the horror that Kristeva describes as resulting from such a dissolution (141) and uses it for his own affective ends.

While earlier examples of the Gothic, according to Todorov, have as their "principle and explicit theme the hesitation of the protagonist, in James's work the representation of such hesitation is virtually eliminated, and only survives in the reader" (Todorov, "The Structural Analysis of Literature" 86). For Edel, this is James's "little expedient of inviting the reader to participate in the terror or hauntedness that he seeks to evoke" ("Introduction" xxix). These observations are by no means unjust, but they fail to explain the full extent of James's mastery of the Gothic. For it is not only that he engages the reader directly in the Gothic situation, but rather that he makes the Gothic situation a part of the reader, makes it "exist" in his or her consciousness as it has never before existed. He does this by refusing to give special value to specific readings or levels of meaning in his tales, while at the same time encouraging us to look for the key to meaning. But as he himself says of Hawthorne, these tales are not parables, they are pictures. He makes certain that they become pictures of ourselves.

Jauss says that "even the extreme case of an open-structured fictional text, with its quantity of indeterminacy calculated to stimulate the imagination of the active reader, reveals how every fresh response links up with an expected or supposed meaning, the fulfillment or nonfulfillment of which calls forth the implicit question and so sets in motion the new process of understanding" (69). For James, however, a "new process of understanding" begins with the author's attempt to defy the very concept of "supposed meaning" by means of a narrative that has no meaning but that which is constituted in the response of the reader. We can, of course, talk about the "meaning" of any of James's Gothic tales, but no articulation of meaning can take the place of the Gothic experience itself. James challenges such literary assumptions as a way of carrying us beyond ourselves into a public/private world both uncanny and, finally, liberating.

James describes this aspect of his Gothic technique as follows:

> With the preference I have noted for the "neat" evocation—the image, of any sort, with fewest attendant vaguenesses and cheapnesses, fewest loose ends dangling and fewest features missing, the image kept in fine the most susceptible of intensity—with this predeliction, I say, the safest arena for the play of moving accidents and mighty mutations and strange encounters, or whatever odd matters, is the field, as I may call it, rather of their second than of their first exhibition. By which, to avoid obscurity, I mean nothing more cryptic than I feel myself show them best by showing almost exclusively the way they are felt, by recognising as their main interest some impression strongly made by them and intensely received. (*AN* 256)

Here an effect we have observed in the most powerful Gothic tales is fully articulated. The greatest impression is conveyed by depicting the impression only, and allowing the reader to imagine the cause. The "intensely received" impression that James here describes as occurring *within* his tales gives rise to a response in the reader that direct presentation of the supernatural would make impossible.

James goes on to explain that there would be an inevitable thinness in the direct technique: "We want it clear, goodness knows, but we also want it thick, and we get the thickness in the human consciousness that entertains and records, that amplifies and interprets it" (*AN* 256). James then cites Poe as an example of a writer whose effects "coming straight, as I say, are immediate and flat." Hawthorne, one would imagine, approaches the richness James describes in a tale such as "Rappaccini's Daughter," but even Hawthorne does not quite recognize the affective possibilities that James attests to:

> The moving accident, the rare conjunction, whatever it be, doesn't make the story; . . . the human emotion and the human attestation, the clustering human conditions we expect presented, only make it. The extraordinary is most extraordinary in that it happens to you and me, and it's of value (of value for others) but so far as visibly brought home to us. (*AN* 257)

James hereby shifts the focus of Gothic fiction from the inhuman to the human and from the supernatural to the natural; or perhaps it would be more precise to say that he breaks down the division between such artificial distinctions. It is "how" to articulate the human element in Gothic that so baffles James's early predecessors. By rejecting the dichotomies that they so carefully establish, James liberates Gothic fiction from its position as a qualified form and places it within the great tradition itself. The "moral" force of James's Gothic tales is more than an intensification of that concern for "the deeper psychology" he recognized in Hawthorne. It is, instead, a transformation of the Gothic from a passive to an active form: "Only make the reader's general vision of evil intense enough," James says in the Preface to "The Turn of the Screw," ". . . and his own experience, his own imagination, his own sympathy . . . and horror . . . will supply him quite sufficiently with all the particulars. Make him *think* the evil, make him think it for himself, and you are released from weak specifications" (*AN* 176).

By evoking the reader's own horror, James avoids the pitfalls of conventional Gothic expression. The existence or nonexistence of ghosts is a moot issue in one of his tales, for ghosts and such conventional devices are understood as a means to an expressive end that lies in the reader's own response.[6] Unlike those writers, however, who, for instance, used the sublime as a technique for evoking a psychological reaction, James is not seeking a response to something that he articulates within the tale; rather, the reader must experience the tale so as to provide its detail him- or herself. Affective technique, therefore, has come as far as possible from Lewis's gruesome corpses and Radcliffe's waxen images. James is of course still trafficking in fear, but it is the fear of real as opposed to fear of imagined experience. It has no parameters beyond the individual experience of each reader; it is neither subjective nor objective, internal nor external, but merely an intense expression of who we are and how we know ourselves.

James's Gothic tales, in other words, provide a peculiarly Jamesian answer to the Gothic dilemma that Walpole articulated. Fact and fancy, reality and imagination, are blended in these tales with a subtley that renders them as inevitable as they are unnerving. Although their subtlety seems effortless, James can at times in the *Notebooks* be seen to be working out his conception of the Gothic tale and expanding our sense of the significance of the form.

"Owen Wingrave," for instance, concerns a tall, athletic-looking, but sensitive young man who reads Goethe's poetry on a bench in Kensington Gardens. He belongs to a family that has made the military its "religion," but he is himself unwilling to serve. We might at first ask where we are to find Gothic material in a tale about a young man who resists the army. James answers this question for us himself. In his *Notebooks*, we see James conceiving of an Owen who "fights, after all, exposes himself to possibilities of danger and death for his own view— acts the soldier, *is* the soldier, and of indefeasible soldierly race— proves to have been so—even in his very effort of abjuration"(*NHJ* 119).

James sensed, however, that such a tale needed "to be distanced, relegated into some picturesque little past when the army occupied more place in life—poeticized by some slightly romantic setting" (*NHJ* 120). James's impluse, then, was to "romanticize" his material to heighten its effect. But the terms of this distancing become even more suggestive as James develops his idea:

> Even if one could introduce a supernatural element in it—make it, I mean, a little ghost-story; place it, the scene, in some old country-house, in England at the beginning of the present century—the time of the Napoleonic wars.—It seems to me one might make some *haunting* business that would give it a colour without being ridiculous, and get in that way the sort of pressure to which the young man is subjected. I see it—it comes to me a little. He must die, of course, be slain, as it were, on his own battle-field, the night spent in the haunted room in which the

ghost of some grim grandfather—some bloody warrior of the
race—or some father slain in the Peninsular or at Waterloo—is
supposed to make himself visible. (*NHJ* 120)

James's idea to make the tale "a little ghost-story" seems at first to
suggest that the supernatural element was here extraneous to the original idea. But as James works out the story for himself, the supernatural emerges naturally as a means to express "the sort of pressure to
which the young man is subjected." But this pressure can by no means
be expressed in any other way. Here we see James working out the
form of the tale in terms that assure us that Owen's death is a metaphorical vehicle, which will lead us in our search for meaning into the
shadowy precincts of self-confrontation.

This simple suggestion in the *Notebooks* is rendered most powerfully
in the tale. Because Owen is of the heroic ilk, James avoids telling us
too much of the tale from that perspective. Instead, Spencer Coyle and
his wife provide the "human attestation" to the emerging Gothic interest of the tale, especially as the scene shifts to Paramore, the family
mansion, where familial pressure is being (officially) applied. They
note the "sinister gloom" of the place, and Mrs. Coyle even goes so far
as to call it "wicked and weird" (*HJSS* 332).

James is doing more than laying the groundwork for a haunting
here. He is demonstrating that Gothic fears and hysterical imaginings
are indeed part of an everyday world and need little more than an
"admirable" old house to excite them. The human element in the tale
insists that a house is more than a house, that its meaning is complicated by the terms of human perception. The uncanny is oddly available here as a way of apprehending experience. James is moreover
suggesting the kind of challenge Owen will be prepared to face: This
is what will happen, he seems to be saying, when a young man is
trapped between events and a demand for meaning.

Owen is peculiarly aware of "the house—the very air and feeling of
it." "There are strange voices in it that seem to mutter at me—to say
dreadful things as I pass," he tells his friends. "I mean the general
consciousness and responsibility of what I'm doing. . . . I've started up
all the old ghosts. The very portraits glower at me on the walls" (*HJSS*
336). Owen's expression of his predicament has no meaning without
its suggestion of the ghostly: His "general consciousness" becomes itself the metaphorical vehicle beyond which stand "all the old ghosts."
What has happened, then, is that James has so identified metaphorical
and metonymical structures in this tale that neither can exist without
the other. Everything about Owen's predicament implies a confluence

of the realistic and the uncanny. It remains for him to attempt to distinguish them.

James accomplishes more than a literalization of the ghostly metaphor. He also suffuses the literal itself with metaphorical implications. Owen must struggle with these ghosts as he struggles with his family. Each represents the other in an intimate and indestructible bond. The intensity of this situation is only increased when James introduces us to what otherwise would be an unthreatening, contextualizing, dinner party, which at first seems intended to introduce a few diverting characters to the family group. Owen's friend Kate Julian belies this impression, however, by taking the military issue so seriously as to retort "Ah let him prove it!" to Coyle's claim that Owen is at heart a fighting man (*HJSS* 345). Her remark is cryptic and suggestive enough to remind us that she is merely reasserting the challenge of the house itself, and that social relations will only intensify Gothic concerns.

When other guests such as Owen's friend Lechmere attempt to counteract this impression by talking about the haunted room, trying not to take it seriously, we are reminded of a Gothic technique that goes back at least to Lewis's tale of the Bleeding Nun, where defiance of the supernatural leads only to blatant victimization. But what was a mere means to an end in Lewis's hands is for James an end in itself as well. Lechmere and the others are clearly afraid of the "risk" that the haunted room implies—the risk not just of a ghostly presence, but of meaning itself. For if there are no ghosts, their fears and their challenges are merely self-reflexive and without objective meaning. Miss Julian herself leads the campaign to determine the nature of truth.

Through Lechmere we indirectly hear a report of her challenging Owen to pass a night in the haunted room. It is furthermore Lechmere's impression that Owen has already spent the previous night there and that "he *did* see something or hear something" (*HJSS* 350). Lechmere and Coyle confront this possibility helplessly. "Why then shouldn't he name it?" Coyle asks in defiance. "Perhaps it's too bad to mention," the young man suggests (*HJSS* 351). Lechmere's response is reasonable as well as alarming, but it is Coyle's that is more fully in touch with James's Gothic concern. By not naming what he has seen— that is, by not giving public expression to his private experience— Owen attempts to separate the metaphorical and the metonymical functions of language in the tale. He attempts to internalize the ghostly presence as a way of silencing it. The outcome is inevitable.

The long, culminating paragraph of the tale realizes this inevitability in terms that are by now familiar. Instead of witnessing Owen's supernatural confrontation, we are, with Spencer Coyle, trapped by the baffling architectural complexity of the house itself and unable to do more than let the fear possess us as it does our interlocutors. By insisting on the nature of the house itself, James is reminding us of his Gothic heritage. At the same time, however, the Coyles' homely inability to do more than chat about the situation and then succumb to sleep reminds us how very much this world is like our own. If we are tempted to suggest that James is therefore creating the same dichotomy of subjective and objective as his predecessors, though, events in the tale quickly remind us that for James such a dichotomy is not only unnecessary but untrue. Coyle wakes to an agonized cry for help, which at once gives meaning to the maze of corridors and brings life to the decrepit edifice:

> He rushed straight before him, the sound of opening doors and alarmed voices in his ears and the faintness of the early dawn in his eyes. At a turn of one of the passages he came upon the white figure of a girl in a swoon on a bench, and in the vividness of the revelation he read as he went that Kate Julian, stricken in her pride too late with a chill of compunction for what she had mockingly done, had, after coming to release the victim of her derision, reeled away, overwhelmed, from the catastrophe that was her work—the catastrophe that the next moment he found himself aghast at on the threshold of an open door. Owen Wingrave, dressed as he had last seen him, lay dead on the spot on which his ancestor had been found. He was all the young soldier on the gained field. (*HJSS* 352)

The full measure of the horror of the tale does not rest solely in the stricken pose of Kate Julian or even in the corpse of young Owen. Spencer is "aghast," as we should be, not just at the fact of Owen's death, but at the horror of the circumstances surrounding it. In fulfillment of our greatest fears, the metaphorical level of the tale has assumed an uncanny air of reality. Owen's death insists on the power of the forces working against him, forces we have come to understand as house, family, and tradition. These forces are "objectified" in the ghost we never see. Owen's corpse both brings strains of significance into focus and renders them inseparable. Tenor and vehicle, metaphor and metonymy, subjective and objective, inside and outside—all such dualisms are broken down, and we are left confronting the horror of a world in which boundaries are meaningless and subjective horror assumes public form. Donna Przybylowicz suggests that "when one brackets the natural world in order to examine the intricacies of the mind, what is revealed is the dialectic of self and other, of the differential relations between manifest and latent contents of the psyche" and that James's late texts emphasize "the relativity of all experience and . . . the functioning of the mind" (9). In his Gothic texts, it is especially true that mind and world are pathologically inseparable, and that self becomes threateningly exposed to the misconstructions of other. Still, the functioning of mind matters less in these tales than the horror that privacy finally implies. Mind ceases to function, in fact, when confronted with the implications of its own nature.

Owen dies a hero—both his sense of himself and the family claim are vindicated. Those who remain behind, however, are left confronting a world in which "catastrophe" can be fully articulated. Jamesian ghosts, then, reside in neither a purely objective nor a purely subjective realm. Todorov says that in James's tales "perception and knowledge take the place of the object which is, or is to be, perceived" ("The Structural Analysis of Literature" 86). Perception and knowledge are crucial in these tales; but as "Owen Wingrave" suggests, rather than replace objective experience, they become the field within which the complex nature of experience is realized.

If the ghost is a matter of fact in "Owen Wingrave" (for even if we wish to force the ghostly confrontation into Owen's private psyche, we must still acknowledge its objective power), and the issue of perception a secondary one, a tale like "Sir Edmund Orme" suggests a more complex but nonetheless single-minded presentation of Gothic concerns. The ghost in this tale is that of Sir Edmund Orme, a lover whom Mrs. Marden had jilted several years before. Now as she and the young man who narrates the tale are trying to win her daughter Charlotte's acceptance of his proposal of marriage, this ghost keeps appearing to them as some kind of warning. They both seem comfortable enough with the ghost, but their big fear is that Charlotte should see it. For Mrs. Marden this would imply that Charlotte has inherited her romantic guilt, and for the narrator that she has inherited her faithlessness. "I believe it will all pass," Mrs. Marden says to the narrator, "if she only loves you" (*HJSS* 164).

Our perspective on the ghostly situation, then, is the reverse of what it was in "Owen Wingrave." That is, we now see things on the side of those who bring their own haunted personalities, their own questioning faithlessness, to bear on an innocent girl. Like Giovanni in "Rappaccini's Daughter," these characters push toward a resolution of the question of whether or not Charlotte sees the ghost, just as they push toward a marital commitment from her. The ghostly obsession, however, displaces any direct interest in Charlotte, and, as in Hawthorne's tale, Charlotte is more a victim of experiment and speculation than she is an object of love. "I want to understand what I see" (*HJSS* 158), says the narrator, and out of that desire comes the Gothic force of the tale.[7]

Again, the ghostly material in the tale assumes a role beyond that of compartmentalized subjectivity. For a moment, the ghost becomes objective fact and, in so doing, challenges the world of privacy and subterfuge. It appears at those moments when Mrs. Marden has attempted to separate her subjective experience from the public world that she has created for her daughter. Such a dichotomy is false, and experience itself returns to "haunt" Mrs. Marden in the form of Sir Edmund Orme. Mrs. Marden and the ghost depart simultaneously: She dies suddenly once her secret has been revealed, and the ghost ends his visitations. Nevertheless, the ghost has liberated Charlotte from her enforced parochialism and offered her an authentic vision of reality. The idea that Charlotte has finally seen what is going on around her gives the tale a real Jamesian interest. The moral and psychological concerns are complex: James generates greater horror from the human relationships here because he has created a convincing ghost. What we perceive in this tale is how appropriate hauntedness can be as a means of talking about characters' relations to the past and explaining their actions in the present. James makes us recognize that such ghostliness is woven into human experience. Mrs. Marden was about to make her daughter the second victim of her lovelessness. The intrusion of a ghost into the world of this tale is for James a way of making us feel what things are really like in our own world. James's ghosts do not stretch our imaginations, they enrich our conception of who we are.

Such an appreciation of James's Gothic technique is useful in approaching his most widely known Gothic tale, "The Turn of the Screw." The clearest fact about this tale is that it has given rise to an overwhelming amount of critical exegesis. While the same is perhaps true of all great works of literature, rarely is it the case that critical discussion of a work hinges on a single issue so prominently. The issue, of course, amounts to whether or not the ghosts "really" exist in this tale—whether the children, Miles and Flora, are in fact threatened by supernatural presences or whether these presences are merely the hallucinatory projections of the governess who narrates the tale. The history of criticism of the work shows that for several years after the publication of the tale the governess was taken seriously and that an anti-governess faction sprang up in the thirties, largely thanks to Edmund Wilson, creating a critical controversy that has been raging ever since.[8] Shosana Felman has said, "If the strength of literature could be defined by the intensity of its impact on the reader, by the vital energy and power of its *effect, The Turn of the Screw* would doubtless qualify as one of the strongest—i.e., most *effective* —texts of all time" (143). In the realm of Gothic fiction, where effect is all, "The Turn of the Screw" remains unparalleled.

This critical heritage itself helps to illuminate the nature of "The Turn of the Screw." The disagreement over the tale arises from an ambiguity that is inherent to its affective technique. The tale is the record of an unnamed woman whose tenure as governess to two small children at Bly, an isolated country house, is fraught with fear and horror. At first her problems seem fairly simple. Miles has been sent home from school for reasons that neither the governess nor her companion, Mrs. Grose, the housekeeper, are able to comprehend. The governess is powerless to turn to the children's guardian, a man for whom she has developed a certain affectionate devotion, because he has very clearly stipulated that she is to handle all problems on her own. The problems become more serious, however, when the governess sees first one and then another "ghost" of previous servants at Bly. With Mrs. Grose's seeming encouragement she supposes them to be Peter Quint, former valet to the master, and Miss Jessel, her predecessor as governess. Mrs. Grose suggests that they were an evil pair, both in their own liaison and in their influence on the children. The governess becomes obsessed with the fear that these ghosts will appear to the children, and it gradually becomes apparent to her, in answer to these fears, not only that the ghosts have appeared to the children but also that the ghosts and the children are somehow in league.

At every stage of the tale the governess protests the veracity of her visions: "It was not, I am as sure to-day as I was sure then, my mere infernal imagination . . ." ("Turn" 50). But we are never allowed to see things as clearly as she does, nor are we left without doubt that perhaps the experience is in her imagination. We do see, however, her various methods of exposing the children's ghostly attachment, which only result in upsetting the children, or so it seems, and alienating Mrs. Grose. Her frenzy culminates in a final confrontation with Miles, which results in the boy's demise, dispossessed of the ghost, as she would have us believe, or simply frightened to death.

Freudian critics have made much of the sexual implications of the tale and the possibility that the governess's reactions are basically hysterical. "The one characteristic by which a 'Freudian reading' is generally recognized," Felman tells us, "is its insistence on the crucial place and role of sexuality in the text" (150). "The Freudian critic's job," she says, "is but to pull the answer out of its hiding place—not so much to give an answer *to* the text as to answer *for* the text: to be *answerable for* it, to answer *in its place,* to replace the question with an answer" (152). Felman, in other words, argues that "sexuality is the *division and divisiveness of meaning;* it is meaning *as* division, meaning *as* conflict" (158). But meaning in this sense, Felman says, can only fail to mean and must give rise to a conflict of interpretation like that surrounding "The Turn of the Screw" (159). We have already seen the degree to which an insistence on precise and rigid "meaning" has been a source of conflict in Gothic fiction and how a clash of interpretation has been one response to the unsettling narrative effect of the kind of horror that Gothic fiction produces. What Felman so wittily exposes as the collective hysteria of the critics of the tale is surely a measure of its uncanny power. The haunting power of "The Turn of the Screw" has no more specific a meaning than any of the *other*worldly hauntings I have considered. James uses the threatening possibilities of meaning, however, to render our own relation to the text so harrowing. As a result, the tale achieves what so many other Gothic works aspire to: It challenges our concept of reality itself.[9] In "The Turn of the Screw" the very nature of subjectivity is thrown into doubt, as is the basis on which we can establish our relation to the unknown.[10]

The plight of the governess is so familiar to us as readers of Gothic fiction that we can but wonder that such a controversy has been granted so marked a level of critical credence. The crisis that the tale explores is similar to the crises of other Gothic tales. James is so deft, however, in rendering the ghostly in realistic terms that it is impossible not to take the governess seriously, at least at first, and not to question her when she comes to be questioned. That there is no way of deciding her case is a critical commonplace. That this is precisely the measure of James's success in the tale has even yet not been fully explored.

Within the tale, subject and object are identified so intensely that they become almost interchangeable. "The moving accident . . . doesn't make the story," I have quoted James as saying, "the human emotion and the human attestation . . . only make it" (*AN* 257). In this case, human attestation represents an artistic fusion of the subjective and objective in the tale, at the same time that the governess narrates the story of what was for her the brutal struggle between them. The tale, that is, objectifies subjectivity and gives the object a subjective presence, while the governess attempts to determine her relation to both inside and outside, and therefore to "truth." Were she to address "The Turn of the Screw," Kristeva's terms of analysis would be more to the point than most others. Her analysis of "abjection" explores the psychological implications of the governess's obsession with such relations: "Owing to the ambiguous opposition I/Other, Inside/Outside—an opposition that is vigorous but pervious, violent but uncertain—there are contents, 'normally' unconscious in neurotics, that become explicit if not conscious in 'borderline' patients' speeches and behavior" (7). The governess inhabits this border region and makes her own abjection palpable for the reader in the terms that Kristeva describes.

"How can I retrace to-day the strange steps of my own obsession?" the governess asks ("Turn" 52), and we very quickly realize that nearly a century of critical controversy was anticipated in her own reaction to the situation at Bly. The ambiguity of events is not only a critical concern, it is present in the text itself:

> There were times of our being together when I would have been ready to swear that, literally, in my presence, but with my direct sense of it closed, they [the children] had visitors who were known and were welcome. Then it was that, had I not been deterred by the very chance that such an injury might prove greater than the injury to be averted, my exaltation would have broken out. "They're here, they're here, you little wretches," I would have cried, "and you can't deny it now!" The little wretches denied it with all the added volume of their sociability and their tenderness, just in the crystal depths of which—like the flash of a fish in a stream—the mockery of their advantage peeped up. ("Turn" 52)

The governess here articulates the problem for which critics have indicted her: She very clearly sees that her own effect on the children, were she to spring the ghosts on them, might in fact be worse than the influence of the ghosts themselves. She is frightened for the children as much as she is frightened by them. The ambiguity as to whether or not the children are in league with the ghosts is not an accident; it is exactly what James wants to heighten.[11] This odd situation gives rise to the real horror of the tale. For Felman,

> The governess naturally . . . postulates that the signified she is barred from, the sense of what she does not know, exists and is in fact possessed by—or possessing—someone else. Knowledge haunts. The question of meaning as such, which seems indeed to haunt the pages of *The Turn of the Screw*, can thus be formulated as the question: *"What is it that knows?"* (201)

Like Giovanni Guasconti, the governess is beset with an ontological crisis that results in the fusion of objective and subjective states in the tale, and in turn of the metonymical and metaphorical functions of language. This situation establishes the anxiety that pervades the tale. Earlier Gothicists, in experimenting with ghostly convention, used metaphorical and metonymical language alternately. James has here created a world in which the two are indistinguishable. Hence the mystique of "ambiguity" surrounding the tale: The ultimate Gothic effect is of course an inability to know what is true beyond the confines of private experience. Here private is public and vice versa. And while it would be nice, both for the governess and for us, to know the answer to the grand question she poses, the beauty of the tale is its defiance of such desires. For after all, what is truly horrifying about human experience in James's terms is that the subjective is the only objectivity we can know.

For the governess, the tale must seem to assume the form of an elaborate self-defense because her anxiety and confusion, again and again articulated in her narration, insist on the shape of proof. But of course she can prove nothing to herself nor to the reader. For in Miles's death her struggle ceases: Subjective and objective divide again into unfathomable duality, creating a void of meaning that is as impossible to cross as her experience is to interpret.[12]

In order to recreate her anxiety, the governess rightly focuses on the danger to the children and her fears on their behalf. As the passage quoted above makes clear, however, the fears are self-directed. That is, it is her responsibility to decide what to do about the children, and in deciding she must try to determine the limitations of her own perceptions or risk acting in a world in which such determinations are impossible. It is easy for the reader to share in this anxiety because James creates for us a position exactly analogous to that which the governess narrates. We are forced to determine the indeterminate relation of objective fact and subjective fantasy in the tale and to decide her culpability or innocence and the culpability or innocence of the children. Such decisions are potentially as horrifying as the decisions she herself makes. We must face the crisis she faces and judge for ourselves; that is, if the governess does not do what is best for the children, what would we do in her place? The tale involves us to the degree that whether or not the ghosts exist we believe that the children are in danger. Psychologically we are implicated in that danger ourselves, for we are incapable of seeing any more than the governess sees.

In thus participating in the experience of Bly, we recreate the tale's great achievement: its harrowing resolution of subjective and objective states. We interalize the governess's plight and understand the terms of her obsession intimately. That is why so many readers resent critical attacks on the governess and indeed why so many critics exult in them. For by condemning the governess, critics condemn our own pleasure in a tale that has so perfectly avoided the linguistic and structural pitfalls of its predecessors. Moreover, such condemnation seems to deprive us of our own experience of this struggle between the public and the private, which James has been so careful not to resolve. We almost dread that he will.

We can discover the nature of this dread in "The Turn of the Screw" by examining the closing pages of the tale, where James's affective technique is most vivid. Felman says that "in this final chapter the entire effort of the governess aims at *reading* the knowledge of the child, and thus at naming truth and meaning" (209). When the governess finds herself alone with Miles after Flora and Mrs. Grose have fled Bly, she confronts him over the disappearance of the letter she had written to the uncle:

> My grasp of how he received this suffered for a minute from something that I can describe only as a fierce split of my attention–a stroke that at first, as I sprang straight up, reduced me to the mere blind movement of getting hold of him, drawing him close and, while I just fell for support against the nearest piece of furniture, instinctively keeping him with his back to the window. The appearance was full upon us that I had already had to deal with here: Peter Quint had come into view like a sentinel before a prison. The next thing I saw was that, from outside, he had reached the window, and then I knew that, close to the glass and glaring in through it, he offered once more to the room his white face of damnation. It represents but grossly what took place with me at the sight to say that on the second my decision was made; yet I believe that no woman so overwhelmed ever in so short a time recovered her command of the *act*. It came to me in the very horror of the immediate presence that the act would be, seeing and facing what I saw and faced, to keep the boy himself unaware. . . . It was like fighting with a demon for a human soul, and when I had fairly so appraised it I saw how the human soul–held out, in the tremor of my hands, at arms' length–had a perfect dew of sweat on a lovely childish forehead. ("Turn" 84–85)

The fierce split of her attention, with which the governess begins the final chapter of "The Turn of the Screw," signals the Gothic crisis as I have described it. In her hands she holds one tangible, seemingly objective version of reality; without the window there stands a profoundly threatening different, seemingly subjective presence attempting to assert itself. But for the governess these two worlds are dangerously confused and hideously inseparable. Quint's "white face of damnation" expresses this confusion perfectly: Damnation works as both a metaphor for the influence of the unseen on the seen, and as a metonymic suggestion of how this experience connects to our own sense of things. By so transforming his sentinel-like presence, the governess renders action both necessary and impossible. We too feel the necessity of action and the horror of having to act. For action will define one's relation to these conflicting forces in a permanent and possibly devastating way. This is the kind of paralysis Kristeva describes as abjection: "There looms, within abjection, one of those violent, dark revolts of being, directed against a threat that seems to emanate from an exorbitant outside or inside, ejected beyond the scope of the possible, the tolerable, the thinkable" (1).

When the governess says that "it was like fighting with a demon for a human soul," she is using metaphorical language that is absolutely identical to her real situation. She is trapped, that is, in a situation that defies the distancing of metaphor, or rather substitutes equivalence for analogy, ultimately baffling her search for truth. Inside and outside are confused both literally and figuratively here.[13] The governess's "very horror of the immediate presence" draws her into a battle as vivid and desperate as any I have considered. What does it mean to say that these are her hysterical imaginings? Does not the power of the scene emerge from the governess's need to discover the truth of her experience and her terror at confronting it? Felman speaks of "the madness of interpretation" surrounding the tale. She says that "while it points to the possibility of two alternative types of reading, it sets out, in capturing *both* types of readers, to eliminate the very demarcation it proposes" (227). But that is precisely what it does first within the tale to the governess herself; it eliminates the kinds of demarcation that would make it possible for her to escape the horror that this collapse of boundaries make inevitable: "It was for the instant confounding and bottomless, for if he *were* innocent what then on earth was I?" ("Turn" 87). This "bottomless" fear—this abyss of meaning that opens before the governess at her moment of crisis—is what the tale is all about.

The events at the close of the tale confound our own increasing desire for meaning and resolution. The nearly physical interaction between Miles and the governess remains impossible to untangle. Miles bursts out in a "white rage," either of fury or of fear. His frantic searching is either in a spirit of disbelief or exposure. His invective jeer ("You

devil!") could be directed at the governess or at Quint; and it could be
uttered in sheer terror, or in recognition that she has found him out.
The governess reads his inability to see Quint as a sign that she has
triumphed. "I have you," the governess says to signal her possessive
triumph, and yet she speaks of the moment as one of loss: "With the
stroke of the loss I was so proud of he uttered the cry of a creature
hurled over an abyss" ("Turn" 88). She seems to know that in liberating Miles from Quint she has lost him as well. She catches him and
holds him for a minute before she realizes that Miles has succumbed
to his own liberation. And his death leaves us ever to wander in the
darkness of our own confusion.

The affective technique of "The Turn of the Screw" could thus be
said to involve us in the subjective horror of an experience and to insist
that we take that subjectivity as fact. We are therefore confronted with
our own inability to explain, or explain away, the Gothic experience.
The degree to which we push for a resolution to this confusion, the
very degree to which we desire that resolution still, is the degree to
which we are part of the horror of the tale.[14]

This tale could be said to expand the subjective nature of discourse
and through its use of language to involve the reader in its Gothic
nature. The governess articulates a horror of her own, but that becomes encompassed in our experience of the tale with her as a function in it. James has taken the doctrine of "single effect" and extended
it beyond the devices within the work to the work itself.[15] That is, the
whole experience of the tale is meant to be its own climactic event.
Affect becomes everything: What the tale has accomplished in affective terms is all that it means, and our own horrifying confusion becomes what the tale is "about." Nothing exists in the tale except to
complicate our feelings about what transpires there. It is "an *amusette*
to catch those not easily caught" (*AN* 172), and all the details of our
experience of the tale are but the bait for the epistemological crisis that
we experience as the ultimate horror of this tale and of Gothic fiction
in general.

James did not, however, leave the form of the tale in such a subjective
wilderness for posterity. In his final Gothic tale he went on to show
that experiences of Gothic proportions need not lead to destruction
and dilemma. In other words, in what is in some ways his most deeply
personal Gothic tale—the one that comes closest to his own experience—James suggests the manner in which horror can be confronted
and accommodated within a world of what I have been calling novelistic dimension. He presents the Gothic confrontation in a way that we

can finally understand, and in doing so, to speak in less theoretical terms, he shows us how we can live with the unknown.

In "The Jolly Corner," as Leon Edel tells us, James "created one of his finest phantoms–the ghost of a man in search of himself, and of that side of himself which he has repudiated" (*HJSS* 721). But the phantom itself is not only what is fine; the fineness exists rather in the tension-fraught anticipation of the "presences" that Spencer Brydon feels in the abandoned New York home of his childhood, to which he has returned after a life abroad.[16] The confrontation with these presences—with the life that might have been—forms the basis of the action in this tale, but the excruciating anticipation is in some ways an end in itself: and there the full force of Jamesian interest resides.

> It had begun to be present to him after the first fortnight, it had broken out with the oddest abruptness, this particular wanton wonderment: it met him there—and this was the image under which he himself judged the matter, or at least, not a little, thrilled and flushed with it—very much as he might have been met by some strange figure, some unexpected occupant, at a turn of one of the dim passages of an empty house. (*HJSS* 730)

Note the subtlety of James's technique. An unspecified "it" haunts a description of wonder until that wonder itself becomes analogous to the confrontation with a ghost. For James even the method of relating the tale—a method far less obvious than the mood-setting of Poe or even Hawthorne—embodies his Gothic concerns. Form and subject, style and content, become one, just as the states he describes become an indeterminate realm consisting of both subjectivity and objectivity. We are not surprised, then, when James transforms analogical language into a version of the real:

> The quaint analogy quite hauntingly remained with him, when he didn't indeed rather improve it by a still intenser form: that of his opening a door behind which he would have made sure of finding nothing, a door into a room shuttered and void, and yet so coming, with a great suppressed start, on some quite erect confronting presence, sometimes planted in the middle of the place and facing him through the dusk. (*HJSS* 730)

Spencer Brydon first introduces the ghostly presence in language, as a metaphorical expansion of experience, and then finds himself substituting tenor for vehicle, literalizing the metaphor and confronting the

ghostly without its distancing effect.[17] Within the house, as subjective and objective experience become suffused, the languages of metaphor and metonymy become virtually interchangeable. Experience is
handled so deftly in the tale that, when a ghost does finally appear,
whether or not it has an objective presence is an insignificant concern.

Przybylowicz says that in his late works James "begins . . . to experiment with the idea of the deconstructed, fragmented self and to concern himself with the interrogation and disintegration of accepted values and institutions. The whole notion of 'reality' no longer exists"
(21). She says of Spencer Brydon as well that his "frenzied pursuit of
ontological disequilibrium" (23) leads him from the "natural-fact-
world" to an "imaginary realm of phantasy" (117). It is true that the
experience of this tale challenges our sense of the everyday world; but
unlike earlier Gothic works, it insists on retaining the "natural-fact-
world" both in Brydon's private experience and in the narrative structure of the tale. James does not therefore abandon the uncanny power
of the "I-Thou" mode here. Rather, he challenges the very distinctions
between tale and novel that I have been making. What is most haunting about this tale, in other words, is the degree to which the everyday
world is not sacrificed to effect but rather transformed by it.

The one character who exists as a finely drawn *ficelle* to bring out
Brydon's inner experience could serve to dismiss the ghostly presence
with her cool rationality. But instead Alice Staverton, observing and
testing Brydon's ideas as she does, works primarily to intensify and
support the formal achievement. She becomes as intimately involved
in the haunting as he—she sees and accepts the ghost of what he
"would have been"—and as a result she has the singular distinction of
being able to contextualize the Gothic nightmare, just as James's language has been doing all along. The harrowing self/other dichotomy,
elsewhere so destructive, here seems only helpful and supportive. Alice
saves Brydon because she can see the truth about him; in fact, she sees
this ghost before he does:

> "Well, *I've* seen him."
> "You—?"
> "I've seen him in a dream."
> "Oh a 'dream'—!" It let him down.
> "But twice over," she continued. "I saw him as I see you now."
> "You've dreamed the same dream—?",
> "Twice over," she repeated. "The very same."
> This did somehow a little speak to him, as it also gratified
> him. "You dream about me at that rate?"

"Ah about *him!*" she smiled.

His eyes again sounded her. "Then you know all about him." And as she said nothing more: "What's the wretch like?"

She hesitated, and it was as if he were pressing her so hard that, resisting for reasons of her own, she had to turn away. "I'll tell you some other time!" (*HJSS* 738)

Of course this is meant to heighten suspense, but at the same time it shows us how unsensational James can be. There never seem to have been two less likely subjects for a haunting. Yet the very concerns that oppress each of them separately, and in their relationship to one another, are the material out of which Jamesian ghosts are made. For Kaston, such conversations are the sign of mutuality in late James: By building on these fragments of understanding, characters begin to understand.[18] Alice emphasizes the *alter* of Brydon's alter ego, partly to underline the crucial difference, as he will discover, but also as a means of suggesting just what kind of a personal threat such a presence can be. She seems to understand the nature of Brydon's abjection and to offer him solace as an escape from its terms. The horror of his situation could come between them, as any reader familiar with James expects, but in this case, somehow, it draws them together. No characters in Gothic fiction learn to approach one another so directly.

The nature of this communion depends chiefly on the setting in which the story is laid. The house on the "jolly corner" is a cause of mutual concern to hero and heroine. It represents the vestiges of a past age—the time, at least, before life had changed them. ("They had communities of knowledge, 'their' knowledge [this discriminating possessive was always on her lips] of presences of the other age . . ." [*HJSS* 729].) The house offers them a sentimental reflection on the life that might have been ("'Oh,' he said, 'I *might* have lived here; . . . I might have put in here all these years. Then everything would have been different enough—and, I dare say, "funny" enough'" [*HJSS* 733]). "The great gaunt shell" takes on a personality of its own, "as . . . some lifelong retainer's appeal for a character" (*HJSS* 731), and that is the basis of the haunting that ensues. We understand that it comes to represent the "past" for both of them, and as such it haunts them with the possibilities of a different present.

The physical house almost seems to aspire to the state of metaphor. The "great grey rooms," as physically oppressive as they can be, indeed very quickly become the mental landscape that all Gothic settings aspire to. That James effects this transformation is not surprising, and has been often remarked.[19] What is more interesting, though, is the method whereby James breaks down the distinction between interior and exterior states here:

> He always caught the first effect of the steel point of his stick on the old marble of the hall pavement, large black-and-white squares that he remembered as the admiration of his child-hood. . . . This effect was the dim reverberating tinkle as of some far-off bell hung who should say where?—in the depths of the house, of the past, of that mystical other world that might have flourished for him had he not, for weal or woe, abandoned it. On this impression he did ever the same thing; he put his stick noiselessly away in a corner—feeling the place once more in the likeness of some great glass bowl, all precious concave crystal, set delicately humming by the play of a moist finger round its edge. The concave crystal held, as it were, this mysti-cal other world, and the indescribably fine murmur of its rim was the sigh there, the scarce audible pathetic wail to his strained ear, of all the old baffled foresworn possibilities. What he did therefore by this appeal of his hushed presence was to wake them into such measure of ghostly life as they might still enjoy. (*HJSS* 740)

James focuses on a precise physical detail, just as the memory would recreate a former home, and uses that physical detail to ring in the past.[20] Depths of house, past, and mystical other world clearly reside in the same imaginative place. The delicacy of the image that James suggests is appropriate because of the narrative delicacy with which he sets these wheels in motion. A tap of steel on marble becomes a "dim reverberating tinkle" and then a "scarce audible pathetic wail." Bry-don's imagination transforms the house into his memory—it is as clearly an interior landscape for him as it is for the reader. The "moist finger" is Brydon's own, playing on his inner consciousness, as it is James's playing on the tension of the situation. The emphasis here is on "impression": both the one Brydon creates and the one created in him. The wail that springs out of the place in his imagination is the measure of his suffering. The place, in Kristeva's terms, cries out for him. The "stylistic intensity" here represents Brydon's horror, what Kristeva calls "the incandescent [state] of a boundary-subjectivity" (141), which in other contexts has been the uncanny experience of a mystical presence. Here it is the void of memory.

Setting, then, in its very physicality, becomes the springboard of the imagination. James had praised Hawthorne's subjects for their "picturesqueness, their rich duskiness of colour, their chiaroscuro" (*Hawthorne* 60), and in this tale we can see him putting such effects to use himself. Light and dark assume metaphorical significance, and the house becomes the medium for self-discovery:

> With habit and repetition he gained to an extraordinary degree the power to penetrate the dusk of distances and the darkness of corners, to resolve back into their innocence the treacheries of uncertain light, the evil-looking forms taken in the gloom by mere shadows, by accidents of the air, by shifting effects of perspective; putting down his dim luminary he could still wander on without it . . . and . . . visually project for his purpose a comparative clearness. (*HJSS* 742)

Physical and mental processes are identified here to such an extent that each has metaphorical potential for the other. This linguistic balance intensifies descriptions in both directions. Brydon presses on with a determination to know what other Gothic heroes have fled in fear of. By so equating the public and the private, James not only heightens the Gothic nature of this quest but interprets it exclusively in its own terms. When Brydon loses confidence, therefore, and experiences fear, it is not fear that takes the form of the house, but rather the house that takes the form of fear:

> The house, withal, seemed immense, the scale of space again inordinate; the open rooms, to no one of which his eyes deflected, gloomed in their shuttered state like mouths of caverns; only the high skylight that formed the crown of the deep well created for him a medium in which he could advance, but which might have been, for queerness of colour, some watery under-world. (*HJSS* 753)

"Seemed," "created *for him*," "might have been": Although James insists on the subjective nature of the Gothic experience here, there is none of the ambiguity of "The Turn of the Screw." We understand the Gothic nature of Spencer Brydon's world strictly in terms of his own relation to it.

In the Gothic novel, the Radcliffean heroine, for instance, seems dwarfed by the dimensions of her surroundings, and she is terrified. Here Brydon expands the dimensions of the house by means of the importance he places on the impending confrontation. The narrative analogies that emerge in this description, such as "it might have been, for queerness of colour, some watery under-world," suggest more clearly Brydon's own sense of his Gothic quest. In Radcliffe, then, the sources of the Gothic are objective and isolated, while James makes them inseparable from the inner experience of his character. We are not free to step back and analyze the Jamesian Gothic experience, because its objective reality is indistinguishable from Brydon's subjective interpretation of it. As a result, we have no escape from its Gothic intensity. Indeed, James has created an affective situation that so undermines our distance from the Gothic experience that our only alternative is to experience it exactly as Brydon himself experiences it in this scene.

The Jamesian Gothic character is more luridly exposed than any I have considered. We experience Brydon's response to his situation directly and with more unmediated intensity than we experience anything in Gothic fiction. "Some impressions strongly made . . . and intensely received" remain the key to James's Gothic technique. Here we see such a technique developed to its fullest. Instead of standing back in amazement at Frankenstein or Heathcliff, puzzling over the stupor of Roderick Usher, or even finding ourselves alienated from the judgment of Giovanni Guasconti, we feel with Brydon each turn in the passageways of his search for himself. Even the intensely engaging nature of James's other tales seems pallid beside the intensity of this inner confrontation. Far from defusing the force of the tale, this technique heightens the degree to which the reader becomes involved in it. We come to know Brydon intimately, so that we can experience the force of his fear more fully.

James makes us familiar with the workings of Brydon's mind so that we can appreciate the dimensions of his terror and experience his Gothic nightmare as our own:

> . . . an appearance produced, he the next instant saw, by the fact that the vestibule gaped wide, that the hinged halves of the inner door had been thrown far back. Out of that again the *question* sprang at him, making his eyes, as he felt, half-start from his head, as they had done, at the top of the house, before the sign of the other door. If he had left that one open, hadn't he left this one closed, and wasn't he now in *most* immediate presence of some inconceivable occult activity? It was as sharp, the question, as a knife in his side, but the answer hung fire still and seemed to lose itself in the vague darkness to which the thin admitted dawn, glimmering archwise over the whole outer door, made a semicircular margin, a cold silvery nimbus that seemed

> to play a little as he looked—to shift and expand and contract.
> (*HJSS* 754)

The technique of the opened door in itself is so simple that it is almost laughable. We do not laugh, however, and this is a signal that James has so intensely involved us in Brydon's plight that such simple effects have become profound. The panic of Brydon's response is something we can feel intensely. The movement from exterior detail to interior reaction has been intensified to the point of hysteria, while at the same time we watch, for Brydon and for ourselves, the hard surfaces of the house become suffused with the silvery nimbus of dawn. Mental and physical states are reaching the climax of such a process of suffusion as well: The play of Brydon's mind colors the scene as much as does the play of dawn light.

Because we have been able to see Brydon from the outside, with the help of Alice Staverton, as well as to know him from within, there is a dual process at work here. Emotionally we fear the ghost as Brydon has come to fear it. We also know instinctively, much as Alice Staverton knows, that this confrontation must take place, and, again like Alice, we know its significance. No interpretation is required here, because the tale interprets itself. James has so linked the metaphorical and metonymical functions of language that although meaning remains absent and indeterminate in this overdetermined text, its significance is implicit within the tale and articulated in the terms in which the tale is told. This is not "meaning" in the sense of a "detachable message" (Iser, *Act of Reading* 7), but rather "the referential totality which is implied by the aspects contained in the text and which must be assembled in the course of reading"; and which according to Iser must be combined with "the reader's absorption of the meaning into his own existence" (151). In "The Jolly Corner," there is no abyss of interpretation and little possibility of interpretive distortion: The tale offers us no alternative but to understand it in its own terms. The ghostly confrontation is the reality that the tale proposes, and we accept it.

If this confrontation casts a negative shadow over similar moments in the Gothic novel—one need only think of the lockstep progress of the Bleeding Nun and Lewis's bald assertion of her ghostly presence ("God Almighty! It was the bleeding nun!") to generate such a feeling—it is only because James's narrative technique offers a convincing solution to the problem of direct supernatural portrayal. Spencer Brydon "sees" a ghost, and we see it with him. "Rigid and conscious, spectral yet human, a man of his own substance and stature waited there to measure himself with his power to dismay" (*HJSS* 755).

Everything in the tale has led us to anticipate this confrontation, an objective presentation of subjective experience as well as a subjective understanding of the objective, and we are not disappointed.

We do not stop to question whether or not the ghost is "real," because it stands so clearly before us and we accept it as an expression of Brydon's struggle with himself. He is responsible for the ghost, literally and figuratively; and that is exactly how we understand it. That it is not what Brydon expected ("It was unknown, inconceivable, awful, disconnected from any possibility . . ." [*HJSS* 756]) suggests the degree to which it is "one of those violent, dark revolts of being, directed against a threat that seems to emanate from an exorbitant outside or inside" (Kristeva 5). Brydon is as deeply horrified as is possible, and we understand, for ourselves, what that horror implies. The alter ego has made its devastating point. When Spencer Brydon finally "sees," it is a moment of vision for us as well.[21]

And, one might add, for Alice Staverton, who, at the moment of the ghost's appearance (he appears to her in another dream), knows that Brydon knows, at last, what he would have been. "It had brought him to knowledge, to knowledge—yes, this was the beauty of his state" (*HJSS* 758). The closing pages tell us the full extent of this knowledge. That the ghost was more horrifying than Brydon ever imagined is the final measure of the power of self-deception. We share the extremity of Brydon's horror because James has caused this sudden subversion, for him and for us, of our control. This experience is not totally devastating because of Alice Staverton's reassuring refusal to abandon the hero and her faithful presence at his side.

"You brought me literally to life" (*HJSS* 758–59), Brydon tells her. She becomes his tutor ("Isn't the whole point that you'd have been different?" [*HJSS* 761]), his mother (as she holds him to her breast), his lover (as she fully accepts him). For Brydon she offers a rebirth unusual in James's world:

> "I *could* have liked him. And to me," she said, "he was no horror. I had accepted him."
>
> "'Accepted'—?" Brydon oddly sounded.
>
> "Before, for the interest of his difference—yes. And as *I* didn't disown him, as *I* knew him—which you at last, confronted with him in his difference, so cruelly didn't, my dear—well, he must have been, you see, less dreadful to me. And it may have pleased him that I pitied him." (*HJSS* 762)

Her understanding is both literal and figurative response. And because Alice herself equates them, we find ourselves confronting a heightened sense of reality here. Brydon, like so many Gothic heroes, panics at the fact of difference. But Alice redeems that difference with her love.

This denouement is in some ways a reversal of the ultimate Gothic concern of works like "Rappaccini's Daughter" or "Sir Edmund Orme." Alice sees the horror and yet is not horrified by what she sees. She does not push to understand, she merely lovingly accepts; and this is the key to the salvation her love offers. At the same time James has surpassed the inherent awkwardness of these earlier Gothic effects. Epistemological confusion enhances the affective technique there. Hawthorne's allegorical perspective keeps us a certain distance from final explanations. Beatrice's "poison" affects Giovanni in a way we can never fully understand; indeed our efforts at understanding are the very source of Gothic power. The power of "The Jolly Corner," however, arises out of an acceptance of Brydon's plight. He has at no time alienated us. As the story closes, we understand him as a man who has had to face the dreadful truth about his inner self but who is at the same time liberated from the horrifying confines of the private. Gothic fiction as well ceases to inhabit the realm of private fantasy and emerges as a form with profound public significance, liberated again from the limits of formal conventionality.

"Such compositions as 'The Jolly Corner,'" James says, "would obviously never have existed but for that love of 'a story as a story' which had from far back beset and beguiled their author" (*AN* 252). The "story" of "The Jolly Corner" is more than a sensationalistic rendering of a man's inner search. James uses his ghostly effects to expand the expressive possibilities of fiction without subverting the fictive concerns that are most important to him. With James we have witnessed the full legitimization of the Gothic. He has seamlessly incorporated ghostly effects into serious fiction, without either diminishing the power of the Gothic or diluting the seriousness of his work. The keystone to this technique is of course the form of the tale. There the "story" remains unencumbered of everything but its bare essentials. *Impressionize*, says James, and it is because the impressions he creates are so powerful that his tales achieve such greatness.

> The charm of all these things for the distracted modern mind is in the clear field of experience . . . over which we are thus led to roam; an annexed but independent world in which nothing is right save as we rightly imagine it. We have to do *that*, and we do it happily for the short spurt and in the smaller piece, achieving so perhaps beauty and lucidity; we flounder, we lose

breath, on the other hand—that is we fail, not of continuity, but of an agreeable unity, of the "roundness" in which beauty and lucidity largely reside—when we go in, as they say, for great lengths and breadths. And this, oddly enough, not because "keeping it up" isn't abundantly within the compass of the imagination appealed to in certain conditions, but because the finer interest depends just on *how* it is kept up. (*AN* 171)

How it is kept up in "The Jolly Corner" and the other tales I have considered is not only through our excitement at the hands of a deft manipulator of the Gothic, but also through our understanding of what concerns are most intensely his own:

> Essentially . . . excited wonder must have a subject, must face in a direction, must be, increasingly, *about* something. Here comes in then the artist's bias and his range—determined, these things, by his own fond inclination. About what, good man, does he himself most wonder?—for upon that, whatever it may be, he will naturally most abound. Under that star will he gather in what he shall most seek to represent; so that if you follow thus his range of representation you will know how, you will see where, again, good man, he for himself most aptly vibrates. (*AN* 253–54)

Nowhere is this more apparent than in James's own Gothic tales. He uses the form to clarify areas of concern which pervade his work. As a result the tales themselves assume a seriousness that their powerful effects do not belie. James's tales most clearly show us that the Gothic can offer serious fiction an expanded literary vocabulary for the expression of the most deeply human concerns.

While James's tales achieve a level of sophistication outside the ken of early Gothic visionaries, they do at the same time offer a practical so- lution to the challenge of Walpole's Gothic dream. Walpole sought to create a form that would blend two modes of literary discourse. With James such a blending is finally accomplished, not just in terms of literary convention, but also in accordance with the truth of human experience. For James develops a form that combines the haunting forces of an unreal and subjective world with an objective fictional world both palpable and real. In James's tales the unreal is granted legitimacy because it is more than merely metaphorical. It becomes a part of the human context. James thereby teaches us the degree to which the Gothic is part of human experience and indeed instructs us in the Gothic dimensions of our own natures. We understand his tales not as sensationalistic pieces acting on us from without, but as deeply moving works that affect us most powerfully from within. They are so powerful because they convey directly in emotional as well as intellectual terms the very concerns James seeks to evoke. The didacticism of these tales is at heart emotional: Whatever we come to know as a result of the Jamesian Gothic experience, we have first been made to feel.

The ultimate achievement of Gothic fiction, therefore, is to raise such purely emotional affective concerns to a level of sophistication that liberates them from the realm of the sensational and earns them a place in the literary canon. James's tales demonstrate the kind of affective sophistication a Gothic writer can aspire to: In his works there is nothing that is not perfectly commensurate with the truth of the situation he is depicting. He haunts us with the Gothic force of the world we know. James sees no need to distance his ghosts beyond the human consciousness that apprehends them. Nevertheless, his tales strike the chord that his Gothic predecessors were straining toward. For what do ancient castles, monks, prisons, or murderers express beyond the truth they convey about human emotions? James evokes all the ghostliness of the Gothic by suggesting that we consider the motivation for these metaphors in the first place. Here the uncanny potential of the tale form is fully realized. When Buber talks about the uncanny moments that disrupt our settled assumptions about the nature of experience (*I and Thou* 34), he could be talking about the kind of intensity we witness in these tales.

The measure of Gothic success lies not in any objective inventory of props and devices, James would say, but in the power of emotion generated in tales such as "The Turn of the Screw" or "The Jolly Corner." These tales truly have the harrowing power of the epigraph to this study, because they make their appeal exactly where our emotions are most vulnerable. When we begin to lose faith in our own ability to distinguish what is real, we are in a Gothic world ourselves. Walpole's Gothic dream becomes a reality in James's fiction because James makes it a reality for every one of us. The Jamesian Gothic metaphor has as its tenor not only the consciousnesses of the characters within his tales, but also the consciousnesses of those reading them. There is a reality that realism can only capture—paradoxically—by means of an impression of ghostliness; as a result of this ghostliness we are led into a more direct and a more horrifying knowledge of ourselves.

Notes

Introduction

1. See, for instance, Robert D. Hume, "Gothic versus Romantic": "But in general [the Gothic novel] can be seen as one symptom of a widespread shift away from neoclassical ideals of order and reason, toward romantic belief in emotion and imagination. Horace Walpole saw his novel as part of a resurgence of romance against neoclassical restrictions" (282).

2. The most important Gothic studies include works that employ psychological, structural, and phenomenological methodology. See, for instance: Mario Praz, *The Romantic Agony*; Tzvetan Todorov, *The Fantastic: A Structural Approach to a Literary Genre*; and Maurice Lévy, *Le Roman "Gothique" Anglais*. In my own discussion of Gothic fiction, I make free use of these studies and of such other critical works as are helpful in determining the critical heritage of the Gothic and those features of Gothic expression that make this heritage inevitable. Of particular use in achieving these ends are Kiely's *The Romantic Novel in England* and Napier's *The Failure of Gothic*. I am also indebted to such studies as Sedgwick's *The Coherence of Gothic Convention* and Wilt's *Ghosts of the Gothic*, as well as to the feminist analyses of Auerbach, Doody, Kahane, and Restuccia. My debt to these and other crucial Gothic studies will be apparent as I proceed. Further, no one can write about Gothic fiction without mentioning those "histories" that have given the genre an identity. I am grateful for the information available in such studies as: Summers, *The Gothic Quest*; Birkhead, *The Tale of Terror: A Study of the Gothic Romance*; Varma, *The Gothic Flame*; Punter, *The Literature of Terror*; and Day, *In the Circles of Fear and Desire*. My own study does not claim the historical inclusiveness of these works but will offer a theory of Gothic that can usefully supplement these studies, especially the most recent.

3. See *Yale Edition of Horace Walpole's Correspondence* 1:88; also Kiely 27.

4. For a similar description of Gothic inconsistency, see Napier 5–7.

5. See Engell, *The Creative Imagination* 69; Bate 129–59; and Kiely 9–11.

6. For a discussion of Akenside in context, see Engell 44.

7. For a thorough discussion of the use of the supernatural in eighteenth-century poetry, see Spacks, *The Insistence of Horror*.

8. Quoted in Monk 74 and Weiskel 14–15.

9. The most important study of Burke and Burkean aesthetics remains Monk 84–100. More recent studies include: Kiely 12–17; Weiskel, especially 87–99; Engell 70–71; and Ferguson.

10. Burke bases his discussion of terror and the sublime, for instance, on etymological considerations: "Several languages bear a strong testimony to the affinity of these ideas. They frequently use the same word, to signify indifferently the modes of astonishment or admiration and those of terror " (97–98).

11. In her discussion of Burke, Ferguson suggests that "the sublime tradition constitutes itself as a phenomenology of perception *about* aesthetics and psychology but not *of* them (in their usual extensions)." She goes on to say that "the overwhelming mountains and bottomless abysses which we take to be the identifying marks of the sublime are beside the point even if we treat them symbolically, because the sublime tradition, like any other essentially phenomenological account of perception, cares less about what we see or that we see than about how we see" (64).

12. For a discussion of such conventions, see Sedgwick 9–36.

13. Also see Sedgwick, *Between Men* 92–96.

14. See Reid, *The Short Story* 25; also Marder.

Chapter 1

1. See Iser, *Act of Reading* 41, for a useful revision of Holland's notion of the precedence of psychoanalytic meaning.

2. On the topic of Isabella's anxieties and their relation to the castle, see Kiely 40. Holland and Sherman (282–83) and Kahane (337–42) discuss the Freudian implications of the castle.

3. Hume 284; also see Howells: "We realise that [the Gothic novelists] are important and memorable for they made the first experimental attempts to write a new kind of fiction which dealt primarily with emotional and imaginative awareness" (1).

4. See Napier 9–72 for a discussion of the recurring limitations of the Gothic form.

5. Lewis, *The Monk* 404ff.; Maturin, *Melmoth the Wanderer* 285ff.

6. See Jakobson 90–96. If the same is not true for Frankenstein's monster, that is because that monster's history is devised to turn sentimental appreciation into Gothic horror, a transformation accomplished deftly through the arrogant machinations of Frankenstein himself.

7. Sedgwick, *The Coherence of Gothic Convention* 12; also see Weiskel 112.

8. See Napier 56–62; Kristeva describes such narrative breakdown as the result of a collapse of division between subject and object, outside and inside; see *Powers of Horror* 140–41.

9. See Kiely 17—23; Napier 9–72.

10. Coleridge 357; Woolf 107–10.

11. See Sedgwick, "The Character in the Veil"; and Kahane,"The Gothic Mirror" 335–36. For Doody, "In Mrs. Radcliffe's novels we find the world of nightmare made into an objective art which is neither self-indulgent nor dogmatic" (563); see 563–71. Also see Wilt, especially 126–44, for a discussion of the ways Austen in *Northanger Abbey* imitates, rather than parodies, *Udolpho*.

12. For a theoretical discussion of the "marvelous," see Todorov, *The Fantastic* 42–52.

13. *Act of Reading* 49–50. Iser is responding primarily to Lesser and Holland.

14. This notion of "sub-universes" comes from William James's chapter on "The Perception of Reality," in *The Principles of Psychology* 2:293–95. See May 331.

15. See Kristeva (7–8, 140–41) for a discussion of the narrative implications of this breakdown.

16. See Burke 106: "The mind is hurried out of itself, by a croud of great and confused images; which affect because they are crouded and confused."

Chapter 2

1. Kristeva says, in her *Powers of Horror*, that "what we designate as 'feminine,' far from being a primeval essence, will be seen as an 'other' without a name, which subjective experience confronts when it does not stop at the appearance of its identity" (58–59). With these words, Kristeva summarizes much of what has been written about this novel from the Freudian and feminist perspectives. By discussing the "two-sided sacred" and the nature of "the signifying process" itself, she offers useful insight into the Frankenstein myth.

2. See Hodges for a discussion of Shelley's ability to "subvert patriarchal narrative conventions" (155); also Levine, "*Frankenstein* and the Tradition of Realism"; and Dunn. For Dunn, "*Frankenstein* structurally dramatizes the failure of human community and implicitly challenges the reductive inclusiveness of more conventional fictional forms" (408).

3. See Macovski on the nature of confessional structures in *Wuthering Heights* and Foster on confession in fiction as representative of "patterns of power, desire, guilt and obligation" (7).

4. Hodges has written interestingly about this dream sequence: "Through the agency of dream," Hodges tells us, "this [patriarchal] order confronts something it cannot fully account for, something it has excluded or repressed. Such a bringing to the surface of a troubling otherness . . . has been described [by Hélène Cixous] as an effect of women's writing. . . . The dream form of *Frankenstein*, then, might be seen as a transgression of the boundaries of patriarchal order" (159).

5. Many critics have discussed the anxiety of motherhood in *Frankenstein*. See, for instance, Moers, "Female Gothic"; and Johnson, "My Monster/My Self."

6. In discussing the seductive quality of narrative in *Frankenstein*, I am indebted to Chambers and to Newman. My own reading of Chambers leads me to slightly different conclusions from those of Newman, but her study has also been useful to me throughout. "There is a sense," Chambers tells us, "in which the maintenance of narrative authority implies an act of seduction. . . . This is never more the case," he says, "than when the narrative content is acknowledged to be fictional: . . . the 'point' of the narration can only lie then in its obtaining from the narratee a specific type of attention" (51).

7. Chambers says that certain texts are "*actively* seductive in their mechanisms for ensuring the appropriate form of reader involvement in the mode of understanding they assume to be crucial" (217) and that this narrative situation leads to a "double perspective" of narrator and narratee (218), which is in turn explained by "the duality of the storytelling situation itself" (219). Although Chambers uses his analysis of stories by Balzac, Flaubert, James, and Joyce to generalize about the nature of fiction, we can appreciate the special appropriateness of an analysis that again emphasizes duplicity and doubling.

8. In his book *Shelley's Mythmaking*, Bloom begins by distinguishing "I-Thou" and "I-It" poetic experience, using Martin Buber's terms of distinction. Percy Shelley creates an "I-Thou" relationship in his poetry, according to Bloom. Sometimes "the poet enters into a relationship with a natural Thou, the relationship itself constituting the myth"; at

other times, as "the Jews formulated the abstract, complex myth of the Will of God"; "similarly, from his concrete I-Thou relationships, the poet can dare to make his own abstractions" (8). For Bakhtin, "The most important acts constituting self-consciousness are determined by a relationship toward another consciousness (toward a *thou)*" (287).

9. Buber, *I and Thou* 34. See May, especially 333.

10. Iser tells us that "the intended reader, as a sort of fictional inhabitant of the text, can embody not only the concepts and conventions of the contemporary public but also the desire of the author both to link up with these concepts and to work on them— sometimes just portraying them, sometimes acting upon them" (*Act of Reading* 33).

11. For a discussion of narcissism in "Alastor," see Weiskel: "The narcissism of *Alastor* is . . . both incomplete and inverted. . . . Hence the fruitless search for a 'prototype': the narcissistic object cannot be recognized for what it is" (146).

12. I disagree with Newman's contention that the various narrators in *Frankenstein* "speak with an eloquence more expressive of a shared Romantic ethos than of differences in character" and that "the novel fails to provide significant differences in tone, diction and sentence structure that alone can serve, in a written text, to represent individual human voices"(146).

13. Certain critics have taken the Gothic heritage of *Frankenstein* more seriously than others. See, for instance, Kiely, chapter 8; Moers, "Female Gothic"; and Gilbert and Gubar 213–47.

14. Newman connects the story of Frankenstein's creature and Justine to Ambrosio's difficulties with Rosario/Matilda; see 151–52.

15. Lohafer discusses this "ontological gap" throughout her study, especially 52–57, where she considers "discontinuity" between real and fictive worlds.

16. In Todorov's terms, *Frankenstein* is simply marvelous. Shelley does not really cause us to doubt whether or not the creature exists. But *Frankenstein* is a marvelous work that nonetheless earns the right to Todorov's "fantastic" designation because it so perfectly convinces us of its own legitimacy, its rationale.

17. See Newman (155–57) for a discussion of this aspect of the creature's power; also Hodges: "His success at acquiring language is manifest in the eloquence of his narrative" (160).

18. For instance, Veeder talks about the "viability of the domestic ideal" in relation to the De Lacey family (210); Dunn speaks of the "domestic ideals" that this family represents and that become inaccessible to the creature. Dunn decides, however, that "this encounter of the Creature with the De Laceys comes as a hideous parody of sentimental fiction's blissful domestic scenes" (414).

19. Hodges suggests that in *Frankenstein* Shelley demonstrates "the inadequacy of the paternal narrative by opening it up to what it excludes" (156) and claims that "like Shelley herself, the monster asserts his desire to conform to the expectations of society" and that "what is repressed by society cannot be included on any terms without causing its maddening dislocation, or more positively, without causing its transformation" (161–62).

20. As an exception, see Griffin, "Fire and Ice in *Frankenstein*" 68–69.

Chapter 3

1. The most useful study in this regard remains that of Kiely (233–51). See also, Moers 99–107; Newman 141–44; Restuccia 257–61; Trickett; and Winsor. Also see Sedgwick, *The Coherence of Gothic Convention*.

2. See Kiely 17; Napier 1–8, and passim; see also Sedgwick 12–14 and Weiskel 112.

3. Anderson, Garrett, and especially Miller, in "*Wuthering Heights* and the Ellipses of Interpretation," all offer valuable insights into the formal nature of *Wuthering Heights*.

4. Most recent among these is Newman, who suggests that *Wuthering Heights* and other "frame narratives" are intended to show that "a story can be cut off from its origin in a particular speaker and tell itself in other speakers, who to some extent are shaped by it instead of shaping it" (142) and in so doing challenge basic tenets of narrative theory. I hope to show that they challenge tenets of novel theory as well.

5. Lockwood's narrative presence has been widely discussed. See, for instance, Knoepflmacher (84–96), and McCarthy.

6. The classic indictment of Nelly Dean is presented by Hafly. See also Mathison; Knoepflmacher 92–93; and McCarthy 56–59.

7. See, for instance, Kiely 238–40; Knoepflmacher 88–89; and McCarthy 51.

8. See Musselwhite for a similar description of the textual situation here.

9. Miller emphasizes a similar confusion in critical interpretations; see "*Wuthering Heights*," especially 89–92.

10. Knoepflmacher, with others, blames Lockwood's citified urbanity (88–89); while Macovski sees it as part of a larger pattern of "failed audition" in the novel (366–71); Newman suggests that narrative unreliability here is beside the point (143).

11. Jakobson 90; see also Weiskel 30; and Gillis 80.

12. In addition to those studies listed above in note 6, see also Musselwhite 157; and Macovski 373–74.

13. For a distinction of "I-It" and "I-Thou" modes of experience, see Buber 33–34; May 333; Bloom, *Shelley's Mythmaking* 8ff.

14. See Miller, "*Wuthering Heights*" 92–95.

15. Macovski discusses the work in similar terms, but the source for his analysis of "I-Thou" configurations in *Wuthering Heights* is not Buber but Bakhtin. For Bakhtin, "In dialogue a person not only shows himself outwardly, but he becomes for the first time that which he is . . ." (252). Macovski applies this description to all the speaking/listening pairs in *Wuthering Heights* (371–77), but what surely fits such a description more than any communication between Nelly and Lockwood or between them and the central characters is that between these central characters themselves, even, or primarily, when they are absent from one another.

16. The process whereby such thinking came to be labeled madness is provocatively discussed in Foucault; see especially 87–93 and the discussion of the relation of madness to passion found in chapter 4. For a post-Freudian reading of the passage that follows, see Homans 16–18.

17. Patterns of imagery are discussed, for instance, in Shorer, and Van Ghent 187–208.

18. See also Foster, *Confession and Complicity in Narrative*. He argues that confession is an attempt to objectify self, which establishes "patterns of power, desire, guilt and obligation" (7). Foster also says that "in the activity of interpretation, a reader will almost inevitably find the text to be a confirmation of his own thoughts . . ." (12–13).

19. Miller (92–93) bases his notion of the "uncanny" on that articulated in Freud's notion of the "unheimlich"—"nothing else than a hidden, familiar thing that has undergone repression and then emerged from it" (399). Todorov's notion of the "fantastic," although in his own terminology opposed to the "uncanny," is in certain respects similar to the sense of the "uncanny" that Miller uses here. See Todorov, *The Fantastic*, 24–40.

20. Useful discussions of the second generation of *Wuthering Heights* are included in Armstrong 257–62, Burgan 404–11, Eigner 96–99, Garrett 8, Knoepflmacher, *Laughter and Despair* 105–8.

21. Armstrong suggests that Hareton is a "typically Victorian way out of the dilemma

of a world thrown open to competition" and that "rather than unleashing popular energy, this protagonist's rise entails the harnessing and exhaustion of subversive forms of desire" (254).

22. Armstrong takes us further than other readings have: "A version of the middle-class hegemony itself is what perverts established traditions in the second half of Brontë's novel and brings Gothic devices [cited elsewhere as abduction, rape, incest, and necrophilia] to the service of realism instead of romance" (254).

23. "The short story breaks up the familiar life-world of the everyday, defamiliarizes our assumption that reality is simply the conceptual construct we take it to be, and throws into doubt that our propositional and categorical mode of perceiving can be applied to human beings as well as to objects," May says. "The short story, more than the novel, presents the world as I-Thou rather than I-It" (333).

24. For a more complete description of this notion of "defamiliarization" in the short story (or tale), see Èjxenbaum, especially 4.

25. See especially Leavis and Kettle 130–45. A useful answer to such studies is to be found in Grudin.

26. This discussion is much indebted to Ralph W. Rader, "The Coherent Incoherence of *Wuthering Heights.*"

Chapter 4

1. Ringe's *American Gothic* is useful throughout this and the remaining chapters of my study. Two other recent and important studies of American Gothic are those of Punter and Bell.

2. The most substantial study of Poe's critical theory is that of Jacobs; the most useful study of his tales is that of Thompson. See also Saxena.

3. For a full discussion of the conception and execution of "The Tales of the Folio Club," see Thompson 39–67.

4. Also see Mabbot's introduction for a discussion of Poe's sources (*TSEAP* 2:15–17).

5. Davidson, for instance, dismisses the early critics who found this tale seriously disturbing (499).

6. For a discussion of Poe's use of nightmare images in "Metzengerstein," see Saliba 93–106; and Hirsch.

7. Thompson suggests that a similar ironic technique is at work throughout the tales; see 52–54.

8. See his "Review of Twice-Told Tales by Nathaniel Hawthorne," *CWEAP* 11:106–7.

9. See Èjxenbaum 4; May 328–29. "The short story is short," May says, "precisely because of the kind of experience or reality embodied in it" (328). See also Fowler: "Size counts as a critical factor from a generic point of view" (62); and Friedman 167–86.

10. See Frye, *Anatomy of Criticism* 304–8.

11. See, for instance, Kiely 17; Napier 5–7; see also above, Introduction and chapter 1.

12. Kristeva says of Céline that his "narrative is a narrative of suffering and horror, not only because the 'themes' are there, as such, but because his whole narrative stance seems controlled by the necessity of going through abjection, whose intimate side is suffering and horror its public feature" (140). Kristeva speaks of "the pit where what speaks is a strange rent between an ego and an other—between *nothing* and *all* . . . a narrative between apocalypse and carnival" (141). Poe is exploring his own particular

abjection here and in "Usher." The stylistic intensity of his descriptions suggest "the unbearable identity of the narrator and of the surroundings that are supposed to sustain him," which leads to a "*crying-out theme*" of suffering-horror" (Kristeva 141). Poe is the master of suffering-horror in fiction, as "The Pit and the Pendulum" begins to demonstrate.

13. A much more sophisticated notion of "plot," that articulated, for instance, by R. S. Crane ("The Concept of Plot and the Plot of *Tom Jones*") suggests that the intelligent use of plot embodies a synthesis of action, character, and thought and thereby fully determines the nature of the work concerned. That Gothic works could be said to employ plots of this kind only after Poe's indictment of plot in these terms is a measure of earlier difficulties and a partial explanation of Poe's sense of plot as something external and secondary.

14. For a general discussion of this aspect of Gothic fiction, see Todorov, *The Fantastic* 24–40.

15. May bases these ideas on the work of Deikman and Buber. See pages 43–44 above.

16. Where such narrative intensity does assume importance in the novel, in such works as *Frankenstein* or *Wuthering Heights*, we find ourselves looking for terms with which to qualify our sense of these works as novels. "Gothic" is such a term.

17. See Jacobs 174–75 for a discussion of the aesthetic implications of Poe's use of detail. In an engaging article, Walter Evans argues that Poe defies his own theory of the tale in "Usher."

18. "The assumption that the right thing to do with a literary text is to interpret it," Chambers tells us, "has become in our present-day practice so automatic and unexamined that we scarcely recognize its significance as an indicator of our general social circumstances and of our alienated approach to language in particular" (12). Also see Iser, *Act of Reading:* "If interpretation consists in forcing the hidden meaning from a text, then it is only logical to construe the process as resulting in a loss for the author" (4).

19. Todorov excludes this tale from his category of the "fantastic" and alludes to several facts that "explain" the outcome of the tale (*The Fantastic* 47–49). I would agree with Todorov up to a point—there do seem to be explanations for the various bizarre occurrences at the House of Usher. But this just underlines Poe's Gothic power, for the impact of the story far surpasses the limits of the suggested explanations. See Stuart Levine (38–41) for a suggestion that the tale is "built out . . . from a central nameless shape of terror" (41). That terror is given a scientifically persuasive name in Butler's "Usher's Hypochondriasis." Hypochondria, Butler tells us, "offered a superb medical analogy to the romantic's concern with bonds between the internal, subjective realm and the external world of physical objects" (5).

20. "Meaning and significance are not the same thing, although the classical norms of interpretation . . . would have us believe they are. . . . The significance of the meaning can only be ascertained when the meaning is related to a particular reference" (Iser, *Act of Reading* 150).

21. Frank O'Connor distinguishes between the novel, which can "adhere to the classical concept of civilized society, of man as an animal who lives in a community," and the short story, which "remains by its very nature remote from the community—romantic, individualistic, and intransigent" (21; quoted in May 333).

22. The question of Poe's narrative ambiguity and the problem of "explanation" throughout the tale is explored interestingly by Voloshin. She says, for instance, that "The multiple interpretations suggested in the tale for unusual impressions and appearances work together to make the Usher world resist ordinary interpretation" (426).

23. See Beebe 128; Wilbur 267–68; see also Gargano.

24. "If reading removes the subject-object division that constitutes all perception," Iser says, "it follows that the reader will be 'occupied' by the thoughts of the author, and these in their turn will cause the drawing of new 'boundaries.' Text and reader no longer confront each other as object and subject, but instead the 'division' takes place within the reader himself" (*Implied Reader* 293).

25. "Narrative authority (posited on information to be conveyed)," Chambers says in a discussion of "The Purloined Letter," "has been replaced here by narratorial authority (based on the 'undecidability' inherent in artistic signs), and textual self-reflexivity has less the (narrative) effect of producing information than the (narratorial) effect of confirming the text's elusiveness" (66–67).

26. "Blind, maimed, helpless, and despairing, venting his rage in blasphemy and curses, execrating his existence, yet dreading the arrival of death destined to yield him up to greater torments, six miserable days did the villain languish" (*The Monk* 420). Try as Lewis might, the horrors here remain primarily physical.

27. Incest and vampirism are the most popular explanations for the final embrace and for the tale in general. See, for instance, D. H. Lawrence; Tate; and Kendall. See also David W. Butler 5–12. Bell offers the most interesting reading: "What matters here . . . is not what the story means in any particular reading but the status it gives to its hidden or submerged meaning in relation to its phenomenal language, its symbolic narrative form." What Bell sees as a struggle between narrator and tale could also be described as a struggle between tale and reader, which finds its only "meaning" in the latter (111).

28. As Iser asks, "What can one do with a meaning that has been formulated and put on display, having been stripped of all its mystery?" (*Act of Reading* 4).

Chapter 5

1. *Anatomy* 304–5. For the latter discussion, see, for instance, May 328–30; and Lohafer 10–24.

2. See Jacobs 182–85; Brodhead 29–42; Fogle 3–14; and Martin 12–13.

3. See DeMan 6–19 and 59–67, where a similar situation in Proust's *Swann's Way* is examined.

4. See Crews (156–57) and Mottram (187) for more specific "interpretations" of the blemish.

5. Bensick bases her rich and rewarding study on details of Renaissance medical practice.

6. Chambers 18–49. As in the case of other tales that Chambers discusses, "Rappaccini's Daughter" is "a 'readerly' text that uses the device of 'readability'—its power as fiction to determine the reading situation that makes sense of it—in order to criticize the notion of readability and the presuppositions concerning the nature of meaning it implies" (44).

7. Chambers says further, in his discussion of Marcel Schwab's "Les Sans-Gueule," that "the narrational tone of the storytelling is as self-assured and classical as the case related is unprecedented and baffling" and that "the meaning this technique conveys is one that subverts the possibility of meaning," contrasting authoritarian narrative "pressure to restore a situation of readability" and "a situation of weakened authority" (44–46). The narrative situation in "Rappaccini's Daughter" is even more complex than that described here, but I think it is already clear that neither simple rejection of the narrator nor powerful historical "explanations" convey the power of this remarkable tale.

8. Bensick offers chapter and verse of a historical reading here, even suggesting what

family it must be whose arms Giovanni recognizes (32–34), what Giovanni must be studying (44–45), and the precise date at which the action must be imagined to have transpired (31–33). Further, she argues that for the narrator "the concrete historical allusions in 'Rappaccini's Daughter' are simply a backdrop" (37) and that "critics have followed the translator's signal in establishing [the tale] as a fantasy" (40). Bensick dismisses a reading that sees such material as "only incidental to the work" because "we would have to concede that the tale is in a major way a failure" (38).

9. For Chambers, the narrative act is always an act of seduction (218–23).

10. De Jong reminds us that "Hawthorne's [narrators] do not solicit the reader's confidence by pretending to intellectual or moral authority; they present themselves as romancers looking for meaning in the events they relate" and suggests that "by constantly reminding the reader that Hawthornian romance is an artful blend of the Actual and the Imaginary, they challenge him to define reality" (359–60).

11. Most critical responses to these lines take their root in Male (54–57) and Boewe.

12. For Lukács, the tale is "the narrative form which pin-points the strangeness and ambiguity of life," in which "meaninglessness *as meaninglessness* becomes form; it becomes eternal because it is affirmed, transcended and redeemed by form"(51–52).

13. As Iser says, "indeterminacies . . . *demand* completion from our existing store of knowledge" (*Act of Reading* 177).

14. Bensick argues that this "poison" should be understood as syphilis and that Giovanni's fears are therefore justified. But Bensick's careful deductions bear no relation to a paragraph such as this in which "poison" is being used metaphorically. Were Beatrice actually infectious, this passage would be of little importance. But in fact it helps us establish a horror more harrowing than the clinical one that Bensick describes. For a further sampling of readings of Beatrice as "poison," see Crews 119–20; Male 59–60; and Brenzo. Crews sees the poison as the embodiment of Giovanni's sexual fears and Male says that the poison represents the corruption of Beatrice's mortal nature in contrast to her divine spirit. Brenzo suggests out that the real poison emerges from the fear, obsession, and unhealthy desire of the male characters in the tale.

15. See May 333; Buber 34.

16. Bensick (114) challenges the narrator's "there is something truer . . . ," but that claim is precisely what the tale is forcing us to prove for ourselves.

17. Kristeva suggests, "The constituting barrier between subject and object has here become an unsurmountable wall. An ego, wounded to the point of annulment, barricaded and untouchable, cowers somewhere, nowhere. . . . Where objects are concerned he delegates phantoms, ghosts, 'false cards': a stream of spurious egos" (47). Giovanni cannot accept the mystery of Beatrice's otherness and he must objectify it once and for all.

18. Bensick is particularly helpful on the notion of poison and antidote; see 74–92.

19. For a thorough discussion of the controversy between the scientists, see Bensick 44–73.

Chapter 6

1. See Bewley; R. W. B. Lewis; Poirier. The work of these critics provides a rich context for this study, but none of them addresses the particular concerns at issue here.

2. The conventional selection of eighteen tales is that made by Leon Edel in *Henry James: Stories of the Supernatural*. The tales included are: "The Romance of Certain Old Clothes," 1868; "DeGrey: A Romance," 1868; "The Last of the Valerii," 1874; "The

Ghostly Rental," 1876; "Sir Edmund Orme," 1891; "Nona Vincent," 1892; "The Private
Life," 1892; "Sir Dominic Ferrand," 1892; "Owen Wingrave," 1892; "The Altar of the
Dead," 1895; "The Friend of the Friends," 1896; "The Turn of the Screw," 1898; "The
Real Right Thing," 1899; "The Great Good Place," 1900; "Maud-Evelyn," 1900; "The
Third Person," 1900; "The Beast in the Jungle," 1903; "The Jolly Corner," 1908. Edel
uses the latest published edition of each tale.

3. For a discussion of the tale, the anecdote, and the *nouvelle* as generic distinctions,
see Vaid 1–10. The tale, for James, could be very short or relatively long. In this study, I
will consider examples that range from 10,000 words ("Sir Edmund Orme") to 44,500
words ("The Turn of the Screw"). Also see Good, and Cowdery, especially 19–34.

4. *AN* 321; Goetz 114.

5. Buber's *I and Thou* (33–34) informs my description here.

6. Todorov emphasizes this affective technique in his discussion of James's tales, and
suggests that the hesitation he has seen as crucial to the "fantastic" is in that James
made both the method of the tale and its subject. The hesitation is transferred from
character to reader, and the quest for the supernatural becomes replaced by a desire to
understand ("The Structural Analysis of Literature" 82–87).

7. Todorov's reading of the tale would take this statement on its own terms. In the
narrator's quest for understanding, he would say, resides the "fantastic" interest of this
tale. Indeed, the ambiguity about Charlotte's relationship to the ghost makes this concern somewhat engaging. But to make that the crucial interest of the tale is particularly
inhumane. In my reading of the tale, this ambiguity can be seen as a way of heightening
the effective force of far more central and powerful a concern. For whether or not Charlotte has seen the ghost, in terms of the action of the tale, we understand the ghost not
as a measure of narrative confusion but as a measure of Charlotte's victimization.

8. For a discussion of this controversy, see Willen. See also Sheppard; McElroy; and,
most importantly, Felman 141–247.

9. "The verb *to be* has lost one of its functions," Todorov tells us, "that of affirming
the existence or non-existence of an object" ("The Structural Analysis of Literature" 87).

10. "Madness is in a sense the final issue raised by the first-person narrator in James,"
Goetz says, ". . . this narrative method also raises fundamental questions of the artistic
imagination and narrative authority" (115).

11. Felman tells us that "'Knowing' . . . is to 'seeing' as the signified is to the signifier:
the signifier is the *seen*, whereas the signified is the *known*. The signifier, by its very
nature, is ambiguous and obscure, while the signified is certain, clear, and unequivocal.
Ambiguity is thus inherent in the very essence of the act of seeing" (200).

12. See Schleifer: "The void stands behind the world—behind nature and behind
language—ready to expose itself in the intensity of silence, in the forceful arguments of
absence" (309–10).

13. What Kristeva says of Céline could apply as well here as it has at other moments
of Gothic intensity: "Céline's narrative is a narrative of suffering and horror, not only
because the 'themes' are there, as such, but because his whole narrative stance seems
controlled by the necessity of going through abjection, whose intimate side is suffering
and horror its public feature" (140).

14. "Following [Edmund] Wilson's suggestions," Felman says ironically, "there seems
to be only one exception to this circle of universal dupery and deception: the so-called
Freudian literary critic himself. By avoiding the double trap set at once by the unconscious and by rhetoric, by remaining himself *exterior* to the reading-errors that delude
and blind both characters and author, the critic thus becomes the sole agent and the
exclusive mouthpiece of the *truth* of literature" (229). But of course such critics are as

implicated in the significance of "The Turn of the Screw" as those who read it as a simple ghost story.

15. In discussing "The Turn of the Screw," James says: "The grotesque business I had to make her [the governess] picture and the childish psychology I had to make her trace and present, were, for me at least, a very difficult job, in which absolute lucidity and logic, a singleness of effect, were imperative" (*Henry James: Letters* 4:86).

16. In discussing this tale and "The Beast in the Jungle," Goetz says that "What is striking is not that they internalize second consciousness but that they project the hero's own self, or part of it, onto an alter ego" (164). We have seen that such projection has been implicit in Gothic fiction all along.

17. On the imagery and implication of vacancy in the tale, see Auchard 50–51: "Here the voids are charged" (51).

18. Kaston 14; see also Yeazell 64–99.

19. See, for instance, Sheldon; and Buitenhuis 214–20.

20. Przybylowicz says that Brydon has "a mnemonic relationship to his past self" (125).

21. For an interpretation of this encounter as an "ordeal . . . of reading and writing," see Esch.

Works Cited

Akenside, Mark. *The Pleasures of Imagination. A Poem. In Three Books.* 1744. London: Dodsley, 1769.

Allen, M. L. "The Black Veil: Three Versions of a Symbol." *English Studies* 47 (1966): 286–89.

Anderson, Walter E. "The Lyrical Form of *Wuthering Heights.*" *The University of Toronto Quarterly* 47 (1977–78): 112–34.

Armstrong, Nancy. "Emily Brontë In and Out of Her Time." *Genre* 15 (1982): 243–64.

Auchard, John. *Silence in Henry James: The Heritage of Symbolism and Decadence.* University Park, PA, and London: The Pennsylvania State University Press, 1986.

Auerbach, Nina. *Romantic Imprisonment: Women and Other Glorified Outcasts.* New York: Columbia University Press, 1985.

Austen, Jane. *Northanger Abbey.* 1818. Vol. 5 of *The Novels of Jane Austen.* Ed. R. W. Chapman. Oxford: Oxford University Press, 1933.

Baillie, John. *An Essay on the Sublime.* 1747.

Bakhtin, Mikhail. *Problems of Dostoevsky's Poetics.* Ed. and trans. Caryl Emerson. Theory and History of Literature, no. 8. Minneapolis: University of Minnesota Press, 1984.

Bate, Walter Jackson. *From Classic to Romantic: Premises of Taste in Eighteenth-Century England.* 1946. Reprint. New York: Harper and Row, 1961.

Beattie, James. *Dissertations Moral and Critical.* 1783.

Beebe, Maurice. "The Universe of Roderick Usher." In *Poe: A Collection of Critical Essays,* ed. Robert Regan, 121–33. Englewood Cliffs, NJ: Prentice Hall, 1967.

Bell, Michael Davitt. *The Development of American Romance: The Sacrifice of Relation.* Chicago: University of Chicago Press, 1980.

Benjamin, Walter. *The Origin of German Tragic Drama.* Trans. John Osborne. London: NLB, 1977.

Bensick, Carol Marie. *La Nouvelle Beatrice: Renaissance and Romance in "Rappaccini's Daughter."* New Brunswick: Rutgers University Press, 1985.

Bersani, Leo. *A Future for Astyanax: Character and Desire in Literature.* Boston: Little Brown, 1976.

Bewley, Marius. *The Complex Fate: Hawthorne, Henry James and Some Other American Writers.* London: Chatto & Windus, 1952.

Birkhead, Edith. *The Tale of Terror: A Study of the Gothic Romance.* London: Constable, 1921.

Bloom, Harold. "Frankenstein, or the Modern Prometheus." In *The Ringer in the Tower: Studies in Romantic Tradition*, 118–29. Chicago: University of Chicago Press, 1971.

———. *Shelley's Mythmaking*. New Haven: Yale University Press, 1959.

Boewe, Charles. "Rappaccini's Garden." *American Literature* 30 (1958): 37–49.

Brenzo, Richard. "Beatrice Rappaccini: A Victim of Male Love and Horror." *American Literature* 48 (1976): 152–64.

Brodhead, Richard H. *Hawthorne, Melville, and the Novel*. Chicago: University of Chicago Press, 1976.

Brontë, Emily. *Wuthering Heights*. 1847. Ed. William M. Sale, Jr. Norton Critical Edition. New York: Norton, 1972.

Brooks, Peter. "Virtue and Terror: *The Monk*." *ELH* 40 (1973): 249–63.

Buber, Martin. *I and Thou*. 2d ed. New York: Scribner's, 1958.

Buitenhuis, Peter. *The Grasping Imagination: The American Writings of Henry James*. Toronto: University of Toronto Press, 1970.

Burgan, Mary. "'Some Fit Parentage': Identity and the Cycle of Generations in *Wuthering Heights*." *Philological Quarterly* 61 (1982): 395–413.

Burke, Edmund. *A Philosophical Enquiry into the Origin of Our Ideas of the Sublime and Beautiful*. 1757. 2d ed. 1759. Menston: Scolar, 1970.

Butler, David W. "Usher's Hypochondriasis: Mental Alienation and Romantic Idealism in Poe's Gothic Tales." *American Literature* 48 (1976): 1–12.

Cassirer, Ernst. *Language and Myth*. Trans. Susanne K. Langer. 1946. New York: Dover, 1953.

Chambers, Ross. *Story and Situation: Narrative Seduction and the Power of Fiction*. Theory and History of Literature, no. 12. Minneapolis: University of Minnesota Press, 1984.

Cixous, Hélène. "Castration or Decapitation." Trans. Annette Kuhn. *Signs* 7 (1981): 41–55.

Colacurcio, Michael J. *The Province of Piety: Moral History in Hawthorne's Early Tales*. Cambridge: Harvard University Press, 1984.

Coleridge, Samuel Taylor. *Coleridge's Miscellaneous Criticism*. Ed. Thomas M. Raysor. Cambridge, MA: Harvard University Press, 1936.

Cowdery, Lauren T. *The Nouvelle of Henry James in Theory and Practice*. Studies in Modern Literature, no. 47. Ann Arbor: UMI, 1986.

Crane, R. S. *Critical and Historical Principles of Literary History*. Chicago: University of Chicago Press, 1971.

———. "The Concept of Plot and the Plot of *Tom Jones*." In *Critics and Criticism*, ed. R. S. Crane, 616–47. Chicago: University of Chicago Press, 1952.

Crews, Frederick C. *The Sins of the Fathers: Hawthorne's Psychological Themes*. New York: Oxford University Press, 1966.

Crowley, J. Donald. "Hawthorne." *American Literary Scholarship: An Annual/1978*. Ed. J. Albert Robbins. Durham, NC: Duke University Press, 1980.

Davidson, Edward H. Introduction. In *Selected Writings of Edgar Allan Poe*. Boston: Riverside, Houghton Mifflin, 1956.

Day, William Patrick. *In the Circles of Fear and Desire: A Study of Gothic Fantasy*. Chicago: University of Chicago Press, 1985.

Deikman, Arthur. "Bimodal Consciousness." *Archives of General Psychiatry* 25 (1971): 481–89.

De Jong, Mary Gosselink. "The Making of a 'Gentle Reader': Narrator and Reader in Hawthorne's Romances." *Studies in the Novel* 16 (1984): 359–77.

DeMan, Paul. *Allegories of Reading: Figural Language in Rousseau, Nietzsche, Rilke, and Proust*. New Haven: Yale University Press, 1979.

Doody, Margaret Anne. "Deserts, Ruins and Troubled Waters: Female Dreams in Fiction and the Development of the Gothic Novel." *Genre* 10 (1977): 529–72.

Dunn, Richard J. "Narrative Distance in *Frankenstein.*" *Studies in the Novel* 6 (1974): 408–17.

Edel, Leon. Introduction. In *The Ghostly Tales of Henry James*, by Henry James. New Brunswick, NJ: Rutgers University Press, 1948.

Eigner, Edwin M. *The Metaphysical Novel in England and America: Dickens, Bulwer, Melville, and Hawthorne.* Berkeley: University of California Press, 1978.

Èjxenbaum, B. M. *O. Henry and the Theory of the Short Story.* Trans. I. R. Titunik. 1925. Ann Arbor: University of Michigan Press, 1968.

Engell, James. *The Creative Imagination: Enlightenment to Romanticism.* Cambridge, MA: Harvard University Press, 1981.

Esch, Deborah. "A Jamesian About-Face: Notes on 'The Jolly Corner.'" *ELH* 50 (1983): 587–605.

Evans, Walter. "'The Fall of the House of Usher' and Poe's Theory of the Tale." *Studies in Short Fiction* 14 (1977): 137–44.

Felman, Shoshana. *Writing and Madness* [*Literature/Philosophy/Psychoanalysis*]. Trans. Martha Noel Evans and Shoshana Felman. Ithaca: Cornell University Press, 1985.

Ferguson, Frances. "The Sublime of Edmund Burke, or the Bathos of Experience." *Glyph*, no. 8: 62–78. Baltimore: Johns Hopkins University Press, 1981.

Fogle, Richard H. *Hawthorne's Fiction: The Light and the Dark.* Norman: University of Oklahoma Press, 1964.

Foster, Dennis A. *Confession and Complicity in Narrative.* Cambridge: Cambridge University Press, 1987.

Foucault, Michel. *Madness and Civilization: A History of Insanity in the Age of Reason.* Trans. Richard Howard. 1965. Reprint. New York: Vintage, Random House, 1973.

Fowler, Alastair. *Kinds of Literature: An Introduction to the Theory of Genre and Modes.* Cambridge: Harvard University Press, 1982.

Freud, Sigmund. "The Uncanny." 1919. *Collected Papers*, 4. New York: Basic Books, 1959.

Friedman, Norman. *Form and Meaning in Fiction.* Athens, GA: University of Georgia Press, 1975.

Frye, Northrop. *Anatomy of Criticism: Four Essays.* 1957. Reprint. Princeton: Princeton University Press, 1971.

———. "Towards Defining an Age of Sensibility." In *Fables of Identity: Studies in Poetic Mythology*, 130–37. New York: Harcourt, 1963.

Gargano, James W. "'The Fall of the House of Usher': An Apocalyptic Vision." *University of Mississippi Studies in English* 3 (1982): 53–63.

Garrett, Peter K. "Double Plots and Dialogical Form in Victorian Fiction." *Nineteenth-Century Fiction* 32 (1977): 1–17.

Gilbert, Sandra M., and Susan Gubar. *The Madwoman in the Attic: The Woman Writer and the Nineteenth-Century Literary Imagination.* New Haven: Yale University Press, 1979.

Gillis, Christina Marsden. *The Paradox of Privacy: Epistolary Form in* Clarissa. Gainesville: University Presses of Florida, 1984.

Goetz, William R. *Henry James and the Darkest Abyss of Romance.* Baton Rouge: Louisiana State University Press, 1986.

Good, Graham. "Notes on the Novella." *Novel* 10 (1977): 197–211.

Griffin, Andrew. "Fire and Ice in *Frankenstein.*" In Levine and Knoepflmacher 49–73.

Grudin, Peter D. "*Wuthering Heights:* The Question of Unquiet Slumbers." *Studies in the Novel* 6 (1974): 389–407.

Hafly, James. "The Villain in *Wuthering Heights.*" *Nineteenth-Century Fiction* 13 (1958): 199–215.

Haggerty, George E. "Literature and Homosexuality in the Late Eighteenth Century: Walpole, Beckford, and Lewis." *Studies in the Novel* 18 (1986): 341–52.

Hartley, David. *Observations on Man.* 2 vols. 1749.

Hawthorne, Nathaniel. *The Centenary Edition of the Works of Nathaniel Hawthorne.* Ed. William Chavaret et al. 16 vols. to date. Columbus: Ohio State University Press, 1962–.

Hindle, Maurice. Introduction. In *Frankenstein*, by Mary Shelley, 7–42. New York: Penguin, 1985.

Hirsch, David H. "Poe's 'Metzengerstein' as a Tale of the Subconscious." *University of Mississippi Studies in English* 3 (1982): 40–52.

Hodges, Devon. "*Frankenstein* and the Feminine Subversion of the Novel." *Tulsa Studies in Women's Literature* 1 (1982): 155–64.

Holland, Norman N. *The Dynamics of Literary Response.* New York: Oxford University Press, 1968.

Holland, Norman N., and Leona F. Sherman. "Gothic Possibilities." *New Literary History* 8 (1977): 279–94.

Homans, Margaret. "Repression and Sublimation of Nature in *Wuthering Heights.*" *PMLA* 93 (1978): 9–19.

Howells, Coral Ann. *Love, Mystery, and Misery: Feeling in Gothic Fiction.* London: Athlone Press, 1978.

Hume, Robert D. "Gothic versus Romantic: A Revaluation of the Gothic Novel." *PMLA* 84 (1969): 282–90.

Iser, Wolfgang. *The Act of Reading: A Theory of Aesthetic Response.* Baltimore: Johns Hopkins University Press, 1980.

———. *The Implied Reader: Patterns of Communication in Prose Fiction from Bunyan to Beckett.* 1974. Baltimore: Johns Hopkins University Press, 1978.

Jacobs, Robert D. *Poe: Journalist and Critic.* Baton Rouge: Louisiana State University Press, 1969.

Jakobson, Roman. "Two Aspects of Language and Two Types of Aphasic Disturbances." In *Fundamentals of Language.* Ed. Jakobson and Morris Halle, 69–96. *Janua Linguarum.* Series Minor 1, 1956. 2d ed. The Hague: Mouton, 1971.

James, Henry. *The Art of the Novel: Critical Prefaces.* Ed. Richard P. Blackmur. New York: Scribner's, 1934.

———. *Hawthorne.* 1879. Reprint. New York: Macmillan, 1966.

———. *Henry James: Letters.* Ed. Leon Edel. 4 vols. Cambridge, MA: Belknap-Harvard, 1974–84.

———. *Henry James: Stories of the Supernatural.* Ed. Leon Edel. New York: Taplinger, 1970.

———. *The Notebooks of Henry James.* Ed. F. O. Matthiessen and Kenneth B. Murdock. 1947. New York: Galaxy-Oxford, 1961.

———. *The Turn of the Screw.* 1898. Ed. Robert Kimbrough. New York: Norton, 1966.

James, William. *The Principles of Psychology.* 1890. 2 vols. New York: Dover, 1950.

Jauss, Hans Robert. *Toward an Aesthetic of Reception.* Trans. Timothy Bahti. Theory and History of Literature, no. 2. Minneapolis: University of Minnesota Press, 1982.

Johnson, Barbara. "My Monster/My Self." *Diacritics* 12 (1982): 2–10.

Joseph, M. K. Introduction. In *Frankenstein, or The Modern Prometheus*, by Mary Shelley, v–xiii. 1969. Reprint, World's Classics. New York: Oxford University Press, 1980.

Kahane, Claire. "The Gothic Mirror." In *The (M)other Tongue: Essays in Feminist Psychoanalytic Interpretation,* ed. Shirley Nelson Garner, Claire Kahane, and Madelon Sprengnether, 334–51. Ithaca and London: Cornell University Press, 1985.

Kaston, Carren. *Imagination and Desire in the Novels of Henry James.* New Brunswick, NJ: Rutgers University Press, 1984.

Kendall, L. E., Jr. "The Vampirism Motif in 'The Fall of the House of Usher.'" *College English* 24 (1963): 450–53.

Kettle, Arnold. *An Introduction to the English Novel.* 1951. New York: Harper, 1968.

Kiely, Robert. *The Romantic Novel in England.* Cambridge: Harvard University Press, 1972.

Knoepflmacher, U. C. *Laughter and Despair: Readings in Ten Novels of the Victorian Era.* Berkeley: University of California Press, 1971.

Kristeva, Julia. *Powers of Horror: An Essay on Abjection.* Trans. Leon S. Roudiez. New York: Columbia University Press, 1982.

Lawrence, D. H. "Edgar Allan Poe." In *Selected Literary Criticism,* ed. Anthony Beal, 330–46. New York: Viking, 1966.

Leavis, Q. D. "A Fresh Approach to *Wuthering Heights.*" In *Lectures in America,* ed. F. R. and Q. D. Leavis, 85–138. New York: Pantheon, 1969.

Leitch, Thomas M. *What Stories Are: Narrative Theory and Interpretation.* University Park, PA: The Pennsylvania State University Press, 1986.

Lesser, Simon O. *Fiction and the Unconscious.* Boston: Beacon Press, 1957.

Levin, David. "Shadows of Doubt: Specter Evidence in Hawthorne's 'Young Goodman Brown.'" *American Literature* 34 (1962): 344–52.

Levine, George. "*Frankenstein* and the Tradition of Realism." *Novel* 7 (1973): 14–30.

Levine, George, and U. C. Knoepflmacher, eds. *The Endurance of Frankenstein: Essays on Mary Shelley's Novel.* Berkeley: University of California Press, 1979.

Levine, Stuart. *Edgar Poe: Seer and Craftsman.* Deland, FL: Everett/Edwards, 1972.

Lewis, Matthew G. *The Monk.* 1796. Ed. Louis F. Peck. 1952. New York: Evergreen, Grove Press, 1959.

Lewis, R. W. B. "Hawthorne and James: The Matter of the Heart." In *Trials of the World: Essays in American Literature and Humanistic Tradition,* 77–96. New Haven: Yale University Press, 1965.

Lévy, Maurice. *Le Roman "Gothique" Anglais 1764–1824.* Publications de la Faculté des Lettres et Sciences Humaines de Toulouse, Série A, Tome 9. Paris: Gallimard, 1968.

Lohafer, Susan. *Coming to Terms with the Short Story.* Baton Rouge: Louisiana State University Press, 1983.

Lukács, Georg. *The Theory of the Novel.* 1920. Trans. Anna Bostock. Cambridge, MA: MIT Press, 1971.

Macovski, Michael S. "*Wuthering Heights* and the Rhetoric of Interpretation." *ELH* 54 (1987): 363–84.

Male, Roy. *Hawthorne's Tragic Vision.* Austin: University of Texas Press, 1957.

Marder, Robert F. "From Tale to Short Story: The Emergence of a New Genre in the 1850s." *American Literature* 46 (1974): 153–69.

Martin, Terence. "The Method of Hawthorne's Tales." In *Hawthorne Centenary Essays,* ed. Roy Harvey Pearce, 7–30. Athens, OH: Ohio State University Press, 1964.

Mathison, John K. "Nelly Dean and the Power of *Wuthering Heights.*" In *Wuthering Heights,* by Emily Brontë, 333–53. Ed. William Sale, Jr. Norton Critical Edition. New York: Norton, 1972.

Maturin, Charles Robert. *Melmoth the Wanderer, A Tale.* 1820. Ed. Douglas Grant. 1968. London: Oxford University Press, 1972.

May, Charles E. "The Nature of Knowledge in Short Fiction." *Studies in Short Fiction* 21 (1984): 327–338.

McCarthy, Terence. "The Incompetent Narrator of *Wuthering Heights.*" *Modern Language Quarterly* 42 (1981): 48–64.

McElroy, John Harmon. "The Mysteries at Bly." *Arizona Quarterly* 37 (1981): 214–36.

Miller, J. Hillis. "Three Problems of Fictional Form: First-Person Narration in *David Copperfield* and *Huckleberry Finn.*" In *Experience in the Novel,* ed. Roy Harvey Pearce, 21–48. New York: Columbia University Press, 1968.

———. "*Wuthering Heights* and the Ellipses of Interpretation." *Notre Dame English Journal* 12 (1980): 85–100. Reprint. *Fiction and Repetition: Seven English Novels.* Cambridge, MA: Harvard University Press, 1982.

Moers, Ellen. "Female Gothic." In *Literary Women: The Great Writers,* 90–110. 1976. New York: Oxford University Press, 1985.

Monk, Samuel Holt. *The Sublime: A Study of Critical Theories in Eighteenth-Century England.* 1936. Rev. ed. Ann Arbor: University of Michigan Press, 1960.

Mottram, Eric. "Power and Law in Hawthorne's Fictions." In *Nathaniel Hawthorne: New Critical Essays,* ed. A. Robert Lee, 187–228. London: Vision, 1982.

Musselwhite, David. "*Wuthering Heights:* The Unacceptable Text." In *Literature, Sociology, and the Sociology of Literature,* ed. Francis Barker et al., 154–60. Proceedings of the Conference held at the University of Essex, July 1976. Colchester: University of Essex Press, 1977.

Napier, Elizabeth. *The Failure of Gothic: Problems of Disjunction in an Eighteenth-century Literary Form.* Oxford: Clarendon-Oxford, 1987.

Newman, Beth. "Narratives of Seduction and the Seductions of Narrative: The Frame Structure of *Frankenstein.*" *ELH* 53 (1986): 141–63.

O'Connor, Frank. *The Lonely Voice: A Study of the Short Story.* 1963. New York: Harper, 1985.

Paulson, Ronald. "Gothic Fiction and the French Revolution." *ELH* 48 (1981): 532–54.

Peck, Louis F. *A Life of Matthew G. Lewis.* Cambridge, MA: Harvard University Press, 1961.

Poe, Edgar Allan. *Collected Works of Edgar Allan Poe.* Ed. Thomas Ollive Mabbott. 3 vols. to date. Cambridge, MA: Harvard University Press, 1969–.

———. *The Complete Works of Edgar Allan Poe.* Ed. James A. Harrison. 17 vols. 1902. New York: AMS, 1965.

Poirier, Richard. "Visionary to Voyeur: Hawthorne to James." In *A World Elsewhere, the Place of Style in American Literature,* 93–143. New York: Oxford University Press, 1966.

Praz, Mario. *The Romantic Agony.* Trans. Angus Davidson. London: Oxford University Press, 1933.

Przybylowicz, Donna. *Desire and Repression: The Dialectic of Self and Other in the Late Works of Henry James.* University, AL: University of Alabama Press, 1986.

Punter, David. *The Literature of Terror: A History of Gothic Fictions from 1765 to the Present Day.* London: Longman, 1980.

Radcliffe, Ann. *The Italian, or the Confessional of the Black Penitents.* 1797. Ed. Frederick Garber. London: Oxford University Press, 1968.

———. *The Mysteries of Udolpho.* 1794. Ed. Bonamy Dobrée and Frederick Garber. London: Oxford University Press, 1970.

Rader, Ralph W. "The Coherent Incoherence of *Wuthering Heights.*" Paper presented at MLA Convention, Los Angeles, 28 December 1982.

———. "Defoe, Richardson, Joyce and the Concept of Form in the Novel." *Autobiography, Biography, and the Novel.* Los Angeles: William Andrews Clark Memorial Library, 1973.

Reeve, Clara. *The Old English Baron: A Gothic Story.* 1778. Ed. James Trainer. New York: Oxford University Press, 1967.

Reid, Ian. *The Short Story.* London: Methuen, 1977.

Restuccia, Frances L. "Female Gothic Writing: 'Under Cover to Alice.'" *Genre* 18 (1986): 245–66.

Ringe, Donald A. *American Gothic: Imagination and Reason in Nineteenth-Century Fiction.* Lexington, KY: University Press of Kentucky, 1982.

Sacks, Sheldon. *Fiction and the Shape of Belief.* Berkeley: University of California Press, 1964.

Saliba, David R. *A Psychology of Fear: The Nightmare Formula of Edgar Allan Poe.* Boston: University Press of America, 1980.

Saxena, M. C. "Edgar Allan Poe and His Theory of the Short Story." *Treveni* 45 (1976): 61–69.

Schleifer, Ronald. "The Trap of the Imagination: The Gothic Tradition, Fiction, and 'The Turn of the Screw.'" *Criticism* 22 (1980): 297–319.

Scholes, Robert, and Robert Kellogg. *The Nature of Narrative.* New York: Oxford University Press, 1966.

Scott, Peter Dale. "Vital Artifice: Mary, Percy, and the Psychological Integrity of *Frankenstein.*" In Levine and Knoepflmacher 172–202.

Sedgwick, Eve Kosofsky. *Between Men: English Literature and Male Homosocial Desire.* New York: Columbia University Press, 1985.

———. "The Character in the Veil: Imagery of the Surface in the Gothic Novel." *PMLA* 96 (1981): 255–70.

———. *The Coherence of Gothic Convention.* 1980. New York: Methuen, 1986.

Sheldon, Pamela Jacobs. "Jamesian Gothicism: The Haunted Castle of the Mind." *Studies in the Literary Imagination* 7 (1974): 121–34.

Shelley, Mary. *Frankenstein, or The Modern Prometheus.* 1818. Reprint. with "Introduction," 1831. Ed. M. K. Joseph. 1969. World's Classics. New York: Oxford University Press, 1980.

———. *The Letters of Mary Wollstonecraft Shelley.* Ed. Betty T. Bennett. 3 vols. Baltimore: Johns Hopkins University Press, 1980–88.

———. *Mary Shelley's Journal.* Ed. Frederick L. Jones. Norman: University of Oklahoma Press, 1947.

Shelley, Percy Bysshe. *The Complete Works of Percy Bysshe Shelley.* Ed. Roger Ingpen and Walter E. Peck. 10 vols. New York: Scribner, 1926–30.

Sheppard, E. A. *Henry James and* The Turn of the Screw. Oxford: Oxford University Press, 1974.

Shorer, Mark. "Fiction and the Matrix of Analogy." *Kenyon Review* 11 (1949): 539–60.

Sklovsky, Viktor. *Theorie der Prosa.* Frankfurt, 1966.

Sontag, Susan. *Against Interpretation and Other Essays.* New York: Farrar, Straus & Giroux, 1966.

Spacks, Patricia Meyer. *The Insistence of Horror: Aspects of the Supernatural in Eighteenth-Century Poetry.* Cambridge, MA: Harvard University Press, 1962.

Spark, Muriel. *Child of Light: A Reassessment of Mary Wollstonecraft Shelley.* Hadleigh, Essex: Tower Bridge, 1951.

Spivak, Gayatri Chakravorty. "Three Women's Texts and a Critique of Imperialism." *Critical Inquiry* 12 (1985): 243–61.

Sternberg, Meir. "The World From the Addressee's Viewpoint: Reception as Represen-
tation, Dialogue as Monologue." *Style* 20 (1986): 295–318.
Summers, Montague. *The Gothic Quest: A History of the Gothic Novel.* London: Fortune,
1938.
Tate, Allen. "Our Cousin, Mr. Poe." In *Poe, A Collection of Critical Essays,* ed. Robert
Regan, 38–50. Englewood Cliffs, NJ: Prentice Hall, 1967.
Thompson, G. R. *Poe's Fiction: Romantic Irony in the Gothic Tales.* Madison: University
of Wisconsin Press, 1973.
Todorov, Tzvetan. *The Fantastic: A Structural Approach to a Literary Genre.* Trans. Rich-
ard Howard. Cleveland: Case Western Reserve University Press, 1973.
———. "The Structural Analysis of Literature: The Tales of Henry James." In *Structur-
alism: An Introduction,* ed. David Roby, 73–103. Wolfson College Lectures, 1972.
Oxford: Clarendon-Oxford, 1973.
Trickett, Rachell. "*Wuthering Heights:* The Story of a Haunting." *Brontë Society Trans-
actions* 16 (1975): 338–47.
Vaid, Krishna B. *Technique in the Tales of Henry James.* Cambridge, MA: Harvard Uni-
versity Press, 1964.
Van Ghent, Dorothy. *The English Novel: Form and Function.* 1953. New York: Harper,
1967.
Varma, Devendra P. *The Gothic Flame: Being a History of the Gothic Novel in England:
Its Origins, Efflorescence, Disintegration and Residuary Influences.* London: A. Bar-
ker, 1957.
Veeder, William. *Mary Shelley and Frankenstein: The Fate of Androgyny.* Chicago: Uni-
versity of Chicago Press, 1986.
Voloshin, Beverly R. "Explanation in 'The Fall of the House of Usher.'" *Studies in Short
Fiction* 23 (1986): 419–28.
Walpole, Horace. *The Castle of Otranto: A Gothic Story.* Ed. W. S. Lewis and Joseph W.
Reed, Jr. 1964. World's Classics. New York: Oxford University Press, 1982.
———. *Yale Edition of Horace Walpole's Correspondence.* Ed. W. S. Lewis et al. 48 vols.
New Haven: Yale University Press, 1937–83.
Watt, Ian. *The Rise of the Novel: Studies in Defoe, Richardson, and Fielding.* Berkeley:
University of California Press, 1957.
Weiskel, Thomas. *The Romantic Sublime: Studies in the Structure and Psychology of
Transcendence.* Baltimore: Johns Hopkins University Press, 1976.
Wilbur, Richard. "The House of Poe." In *The Recognition of Edgar Allan Poe,* ed. Eric
W. Carlson, 254–77. Ann Arbor: University of Michigan Press, 1966.
Willen, Gerald. *A Casebook on Henry James's "The Turn of the Screw."* 2d ed. New York:
Crowell, 1969.
Wilt, Judith. *Ghosts of the Gothic: Austen, Eliot, & Lawrence.* Princeton: Princeton Uni-
versity Press, 1980.
Winsor, Dorothy Ann. "The Continuity of the Gothic: The Gothic Novels of Charlotte
Brontë, Emily Brontë, and Iris Murdoch." Dissertation: Wayne State University,
1979.
Wittgenstein, Ludwig. *Tractatus Logico-Philosophicus.* 1933. London: Routledge & Ke-
gan Paul, 1955.
Woolf, Virginia. "Phases of Fiction." In *Granite and Rainbow,* 93–145. London: Ho-
garth, 1958.
Yeazell, Ruth Bernard. *Language and Knowledge in the Late Novels of Henry James.*
Chicago: University of Chicago Press, 1976.

Index